WILD
FAITH

Also by Talia Lavin

Culture Warlords

WILD FAITH

HOW THE CHRISTIAN RIGHT IS TAKING OVER AMERICA

TALIA LAVIN

LEGACY
LIT

New York   Boston

Legacy Lit

Hachette Book Group

1290 Avenue of the Americas

New York, NY 10104

LegacyLitBooks.com

@LegacyLitBooks

First Edition: October 2024

Legacy Lit is an imprint of Grand Central Publishing. The Legacy Lit name and logo are registered trademarks of Hachette Book Group, Inc.

The publisher is not responsible for websites (or their content) that are not owned by the publisher.

The Hachette Speakers Bureau provides a wide range of authors for speaking events. To find out more, go to hachettespeakersbureau.com or email HachetteSpeakers@hbgusa.com.

Legacy Lit books may be purchased in bulk for business, educational, or promotional use. For information, please contact your local bookseller or the Hachette Book Group Special Markets Department at special.markets@hbgusa.com.

Unless otherwise indicated, Scriptures are taken from the King James Version. In public domain.

Scriptures noted NIV are taken from the Holy Bible, New International Version®, NIV®. Copyright © 1973, 1978, 1984, 2011 by Biblica, Inc.™ Used by permission of Zondervan. All rights reserved worldwide. www.zondervan.com The "NIV" and "New International Version" are trademarks registered in the United States Patent and Trademark Office by Biblica, Inc.™

Scriptures noted NLT are taken from the *Holy Bible*, New Living Translation, copyright ©1996, 2004, 2015 by Tyndale House Foundation. Used by permission of Tyndale House Publishers, Carol Stream, Illinois 60188. All rights reserved.

Library of Congress Cataloging-in-Publication Data

Names: Lavin, Tal, author.

Title: Wild faith : how the Christian right is taking over America / Talia Lavin.

Description: First edition. | New York : Legacy Lit, 2024.

Identifiers: LCCN 2024012036 | ISBN 9780306829192 (hardcover) | ISBN 9780306829215 (ebook)

Subjects: LCSH: Religious right—United States—History—21st century. | Christian conservatism—United States—History—21st century. | Christianity and politics—United States—History—21st century. | Right and left (Political science)—United States—History—21st century.

Classification: LCC BR526 .L388 2024 | DDC 320.55—dc23/eng/20240517

LC record available at https://lccn.loc.gov/2024012036

ISBNs: 9780306829192 (hardcover), 9780306829215 (ebook)

Printed in the United States of America

LSC-C

Printing 1, 2024

To my family, who always keep a place for me

To Alex, my rock and my shield

*To those who entrusted me with the darkest moments of their pasts,
in the hope of a brighter future*

And sin, young man, is when you treat people as things. Including yourself. That's what sin is.

—Terry Pratchett

In every age it has been the tyrant who has wrapped himself in the cloak of patriotism or religion or both.

—Eugene V. Debs

Surely the past is a monstrous harvest, a bitter reaping, And wounds enough are everywhere.
—Let us not stain ourselves with blood.
This is the word a woman speaks, if any man will deign to hear it.

—Aeschylus, *Agamemnon*

CONTENTS

WILD
FAITH

INTRODUCTION

The United States is and has always been a Christian nation—not necessarily in the sense of a theocracy but in the sense that Christianity permeates every aspect of public life and undergirds the basic assumptions of what private life should look like for everyday people. This includes those brought up casually in the church or who attend only once or twice a year. It even includes those who never went to church at all but had the image implanted in their heads of the God they didn't believe in: a big beard in the sky, a handsome and ill-fated son inclined to carpentry, lots of blood and thorns involved. Most of them probably have grandparents who believe and have eaten chocolate eggs for Easter, because chocolate eggs are very easy to believe in, even if you don't really believe in a god rising from the grave.

You could call this hegemony if you like; that's the term of art used by academics—the way a religion and its basic beliefs about sin and forgiveness overlay a whole country. It determines federal holidays and is a model for what decency should be. It's like background music, the kind that bores into your mind for the first few minutes in an elevator with its insistent pleasant drone or that you notice for the first few minutes after strolling into a CVS but that eventually fades, by its own ubiquity, into something you don't notice unless it stops.

If you are not a Christian in the United States—not merely someone born into a Christian family who stopped practicing nor even a determined atheist—but *not a Christian*, that is, a Jew, for example, like me, the author of this book, you do not have the ability to ignore the music. You find yourself standing in a little pool of silence, listening to it but not part of it. You know all about Christmas, and you'll never get a present. You recognize, in your bones, that the insistent subconscious music of Christianity is what guides the steps of everyone around you, even if they're not aware of it. Everybody else is dancing to a tune you aren't, so you'd better move quickly to avoid getting your feet stepped on.

You also, having grown up with that extra sense of hearing the music that everyone else doesn't, notice when there's a change in its tenor. You notice when the pleasant sound of Muzak metamorphoses, when there's a saw-blade whine to the notes, a more insistent drumming. You recognize, deep in your adrenal glands, when the music of hegemony becomes the music of conquest: the beat, in fact, of an army on the march.

The Christian Right is a force in American politics and has been for decades: half a century, to be precise, during which it has steadily gained in power. It started in schoolrooms, continued in courtrooms, and perseveres with the aid of people who are perfectly willing to call in bomb threats to hospitals and attempt to overturn elections. It features self-proclaimed prophets with a distinct interest in politics, newly minted apostles with very definite ideas about spiritual battle and its earthly components, and pastors eager to usher in the end of the world.

Its adherents have hymns and devotionals and speak in tongues on occasion, and the showiest of them are known to march through cities blowing ram's horns in an effort to topple, as Joshua once did, the wicked cities of the world. They have their own insular world, their own media apparatus. They have legislators who give fire-and-brimstone speeches from the badly carpeted rooms where laws are made. They have lawyers, too. And in case the lawyers fail, there is always the promise of congregations that might coalesce into mobs or arsonists whose burning, holy zeal coalesces into the tiny pinpoint of a Molotov cocktail.

They have all these things, working in tandem to create the rhythm of war music, the kind that shakes the ground under your feet. That kind of pressure—one of wild faith—seeks outlets wherever it can. In recent years the war music has reached a crescendo, and it is still building. All around you there are laws unfolding: laws about schools, laws about teachers, laws about wombs, laws about doctors, laws about abortifacients, laws governing the gender of children. There are also laws governing the way history is taught in this country, lest anything come between growing minds and the grand story of a land chosen by God to be the fertile ground for his very own battle between good and evil.

It's a big, strange story, full of dark little rooms where small men decide the fate of millions, and cavernous spotlit rooms on whose stages appear big men with waxen faces that only look good on television. It's a story of power developed in private and power proclaimed from the pulpit. It's a story of faith, money, demons, the end of the world, and all the tiny tragedies accumulating before that fated time of tribulation. It's the story of the unique evil the righteous can do, and it is happening all around you.

Everyone knows that to wage a just and righteous war, you have to strike down the men who think of themselves as warriors and who, in a patriarchy, feel duty bound to stand and fight. But everyone who has an inch of cunning knows that the best way to *win* a war—particularly a war for the soul of a country, rather than its mere earthly trappings—is to capture the women and children.

This book is about spiritual warfare: about the tens of millions of evangelical American Christians who believe that demons make war every day with the better angels of the human spirit. But it is also the story of women and children: women whose bodies are no longer their own property under the laws made by godly men. And children who face, in the homes of certain evangelicals, pain harder than iron.

This is the story of those children, told by them in dozens and hundreds of interviews to a Jew and brought to you in the hope that it might make people like you sit up and pay attention. It might make you listen to the music of war unfolding all around you, the sound of the final trumpets in the war to end all wars, the sound of an incidentally and demographically Christian nation becoming a Christian nation by law by force.

There are many faithful people in this country who kiss the cross or take Communion and love their neighbor and keep up with old friends and listen to a nice sermon or two. This is not a book about those people. It's about the other kind. The ones who won't stop until they've conquered the earthly realm and secured it for the host of Heaven, the ones who believe in a white and righteous world and whose worldly allies include a twice-divorced and multiply indicted former president who is even now being written into contemporary prophecies that ring with the timbre of divine authority; the ones who want women put into their place and children to be seen and not heard. This is the story of an army forged in church pews and around kitchen tables—an army that several decades ago awoke to its own power and has continued to acquire it ever since.

If you are reading this book, you are an enemy combatant in a war of the spirit that began before your birth and is being waged every day by determined, ordinary people you wouldn't look twice at if they passed you in the street. It doesn't matter that you didn't start this war, or that you might not believe in its basic premises. All around you is the white-hot music of belief, the rigid goose steps getting closer, of those whose movements are guided by its beat. It is coming for you, the rough music of God's justice, sweeping down from the high mountains, and down across the plains; into the tallest buildings, and the halls of power in particular. Only by knowing what makes up the notes—only by taking the time to notice and to recognize, as hard as that is to do, that the people on the march truly take it all literally—can you prevail. Read this book, and learn the melody of war. Only then can you take up whatever instrument you must and begin a countermarch of your own, the strange and beautiful cacophony of free will.

PART I

THIS IS HOW YOU WIN THE SPIRIT WAR

CHAPTER 1

DEVILS IN THE DINING ROOM

In 2022, an obscure representative from Louisiana named Mike Johnson posted to Facebook, voicing his deep concern about an upcoming FX show, an animated black comedy that featured Satan, voiced by Danny DeVito, as a main character. "Be sober, be vigilant; because your adversary the Devil prowls around like a roaring lion, seeking whom he may devour," Johnson wrote about the cartoon. This struggle, he said later on his podcast, was "serious, eternal business."[1]

The following year, in October 2023, Johnson was elected Speaker of the House, second in the line of succession to the presidency of the United States. His belief in demons was undiminished. From the upper echelons of government to the masses of the faithful, belief in the Devil and his minions has shaped American faith—and politics—for decades.

You may have heard the phrase *Satanic Panic*, a term for a culture war campaign rooted in demon-tinged hysteria, waged by Christian parents and law enforcement officers who were convinced that the most banal interactions were influenced by Lucifer himself. The Satanic Panic is generally judged to have peaked in the 1980s, with a slew of cases and convictions leveled against day care providers in particular, accusing them of associating with the Devil to corrupt children. Among the most famous was the McMartin case, in which a family who ran a preschool in Manhattan Beach, California, was accused in 1983 of allegedly sexually abusing hundreds of children and subjecting them to bizarre torments: building secret orgy tunnels under the school, flying in the air with them, sacrificing animals to Satan, and consorting with witches. (The case dragged on for an unprecedented seven years, and though charges were eventually dropped against all seven defendants—four members of the McMartin family and three preschool teachers—they had endured a lurid ordeal that is to date one of the longest and most expensive series of trials in US legal history.) All over the country, cases that dealt with "satanic ritual abuse," as it was called at the time by purported experts, led to very real jail sentences in very real prisons, sometimes for decades. The American public generally considers the Satanic Panic, insofar as it's considered at all, like a very drunk night—a moment of excess, soon forgotten; the whole thing has a haze of the unreal about it. But the truth about the Satanic Panic is that it never really ended.

One thing it became, though, is a little bit of a joke: sometimes, looking into the horrors of the past over a decades-long gap, humor rises up like a big pink mist, obscuring the real shape of things. It was always a little bit funny—that housewives, TV hosts, and worried working parents began to see demons in every day care. It seems, frankly, nuts how many people believed that perfectly mundane child care workers, men and women they'd seen every day for years, had suddenly developed an unquenchable thirst for the blood of goats and babies and even the ability to fly.

That's the thing about zealotry: its excesses often seem ridiculous and can be pointed out as such. But to the people who believe—really believe, to the bone—it is deadly serious. And if you're not paying attention, if you're sniggering at the absurdity of the details and thinking that all this is beneath the attention of the logical mind, well, the death in question might just be your own, whether a slow death by cruel policy or the hot, fast death meted out by the militant faithful.

The same motivations that led to the Satanic Panic are alive and well in the United States, and continue to influence our nation's politics, punditry, and policy. To understand the seriousness of what once was—and what still is—the font of belief and malice that drives the country's Christian Right, just look over your shoulder a few decades to the story of one couple and their unhappy fate.

It was an arid desert winter day on January 15, 1992, two years after the end of the McMartin trials, when a couple on the run was apprehended by Las Vegas police. They had been indicted by a grand jury in Texas months earlier and had fled to Nevada, where they'd cut and dyed their hair and obtained false identity papers, the *Austin American-Statesman* reported at the time. Their car was still listed in a national offenders' registry, however, and the cops had chased them through the winding streets to a cheap motel. Later, Fran Keller, then forty-four, of Austin, would claim that a cop had forced her to stand naked while being questioned. It was the midpoint of a long and terrible year for Fran and Dan Keller, a surreal gauntlet of humiliation that would last for decades to come.[2]

The previous August, the Kellers, proprietors of a small day care in the Oak Hill area of Austin, had become ensnared in a nationwide moral panic that pitted child care workers against parents and children. Day care owners across the United States were put on trial, from Massachusetts to South Carolina, from Tennessee to Florida to New York City. The Kellers—middle-aged professionals with no prior convictions—were no exception.

It all started when a three-year-old who attended the Kellers' day care, who had exhibited behavioral problems prior to enrolling, alleged that she had been sexually abused by them. By the end of the summer of 1991, two other children began alleging abuse. Prompted by psychologists, the children's allegations ranged from the grotesque to the bizarre. Parents with children in the day care connected with groups that purported to have uncovered a vast national network of satanic child abusers, including the Travis County Society for Investigation, Treatment, and Prevention of Ritual and Cult Abuse. According to a 1994 review of the case by *Texas Monthly* journalist Gary Cartwright, that organization alleged that the CIA had arranged a nationwide system of ritual torture "by which devil-worshipping perpetrators programmed and controlled victims, ultimately turning them into Manchurian Candidate–style robots."[3]

The idea of "satanic ritual abuse," a term that appeared in court documents and overheated church flyers alike during the period, came from a potent admixture of psychology and religious zeal that made its way into the national mainstream. One of the earliest boosters of the idea of an underground network of satanic child abusers was a psychiatrist whose bestseller, in 1980, sparked both a shift in psychological methods and a population-wide witch hunt.

Michelle Remembers, cowritten by a Canadian psychiatrist, Lawrence Pazder, and his patient and eventual wife, Michelle Smith, was a chronicle of supposed memories unearthed during long sessions between the doctor and his patient. Though she had blocked it throughout her life, Smith, as the book revealed, had been abused at the age of five by a ring of Satan worshippers who had tortured her, sexually abused her, and made her participate in bloody rites. They had summoned Satan himself to hurt the little girl. The physical scars, she said, had been lifted from her body, and the memories sealed away by the Virgin Mary herself, who had told her that the knowledge of her torment would return at "a special time"—in the therapeutic context of a doctor unveiling her long-repressed memories. Recovered-memory therapy, the practice of drawing out purportedly blocked-out recollections of early trauma, had just begun to gain purchase in psychological practice; the way *Michelle Remembers* rocketed to the top of the bestseller list gave it a heady boost. In the process, the book's sensational narrative catapulted the notion of rings of cult worshippers abusing children in the name of Satan into the popular imagination. Aided by the "M.D." displayed prominently after Pazder's name on the book cover, satanic ritual abuse entered the American imagination under the imprimatur of science, lent legitimacy by Pazder's credentials and the way a profession steeped in Sigmund Freud's theories embraced the idea of unlocking the hidden reasons for patients' pain and dysfunction. Though the practice has since been discredited, the notion of "recovering" repressed memories—and their potential outbreak in multiple personalities, a diagnosis that has since also been largely discredited—was the cutting edge of psychological research in the 1980s and early 1990s.[4]

Not just medical but law enforcement authorities embraced the notion of ritual abuse; the psychiatrist Colin Ross, for example, claimed in a book published by the University of Toronto Press to have "encountered more than 300 patients with memories of alleged Satanic Ritual Abuse"—and his work was cited by the Department of Justice. In 1995, while working as the associate clinical professor of psychiatry at the Southwestern Medical Center in Dallas, Ross published *Satanic Ritual Abuse: Principles of Treatment*, a book chronicling patients' encounters with Satan and clinical treatment recommendations.[5] He claims to have served as an expert witness in more than fifty court cases, including that of Billy Joe Harris, dubbed the "Twilight Rapist" by authorities for a series of sexual assaults on elderly women ranging in age from sixty-five to ninety-one. Ross's testimony that Harris was suffering from multiple personality disorder was key to the defense's strategy—excluded by the courts as fundamentally unreliable "junk science."[6] By 2008, Ross began claiming to have the ability to release energy beams from his eyeballs.[7] Nevertheless, he was one of several figures who interwove a wild theory of satanic ritual abuse, psychological practice, and legal authority into the juggernaut that became the Satanic Panic.

In the Keller case, psychologists and parents influenced by these theories continued to question the children[8]—and the toddlers produced increasingly violent and implausible allegations. The process stretched out for months, during which psychologists and parents interrogated the children with lurid leading questions, causing the children to become increasingly fearful. In addition to repeated child molestations, the Kellers were accused of taking the children to a nearby cemetery to dig up graves; baptizing an infant in blood; giving the children blood-laced Kool-Aid to drink; forcing the children to kill people and skin animals as sacrifices to Satan; putting horse manure into a child's asthma nebulizer; burying the children alive; dressing them in satanic regalia; and breaking the wings of doves because they were the symbol of Christianity. "The little children are talking, and they are telling tales of being buried alive with animals, painting pictures with bones dipped in blood, being shot and resurrected, digging up a body in a cemetery and nailing it together, having giant germs implanted in their bodies and making pornographic movies at gunpoint," the *Austin American-Statesman* reported breathlessly in 1992.[9] The day care, it seemed, was a working brothel that trafficked the children, who were sedated with drugs injected into their anuses and between their toes. During the investigation, the sheriff's department conducted land and air searches of nearby cemeteries, searching for evidence of ritual murder or burials. Nothing of relevance was found. One child accused the Kellers of cutting the finger off a gorilla in a nearby park. In fact, the park had neither a zoo nor a free-roaming Texan gorilla.

"One thing I noticed about the day care panic was very strange magical thinking among people who seemed like normal working people," Debbie Nathan, one of the most clear-eyed contemporaneous reporters on the panic in the 1980s, told me in an interview. The book she coauthored with lawyer Michael Snedeker in 1995, *Satan's Silence*, offered a searingly skeptical view of the infamous McMartin preschool trial, even as ritual abuse cases continued to unfold around the nation. Nathan recounted an experience in which a father with a child at McMartin resolutely denied alibi evidence for a defendant accused of child abuse. The father had told Nathan, "He could have been in two places at once because he is a Satanist, and Satanists have that ability."[10]

The day care panic was driven by a transpartisan spectrum of individuals: overzealous prosecutors seeking to advance their careers by appearing tough on crime against children; psychologists convinced that they had found a new key to the human psyche; and feminists and victims' rights advocates who seemed, finally, to have reached a moment in which sexual abuse was taken seriously. Meanwhile, the Christian Right, predisposed to see Satan's work in the world in general and particularly in public child care, which allowed women to work outside their homes, was glad to fan the flames. In *We Believe the Children: A Moral Panic in the 1980s*, Richard

Beck explained that the rising influence of evangelical Christians, then at a new zenith of political power under the presidency of Ronald Reagan, had helped push the narrative and make it politically viable. "Fifteen years of grassroots organizing had turned evangelical organizations like Focus on the Family and Moral Majority into some of the most powerful political groups in the country and mobilized conservative Christians of many denominations around right-wing causes," he wrote. "The threat of satanic cults had been a consuming preoccupation among evangelicals since the early 1970s."[11]

In this sociopolitical context, the moral panic over supposed legions of satanically abused children spread over the entire fabric of society. Conservative Christian America feared an imminent moral collapse, driven by feminism's sinister deracination of the nuclear family. Christian parents concerned about preserving their children from satanic influences destroyed books and CDs during public events.[12] More chillingly, the moral panic was ultimately both undergirded and enabled by those elected to power: prosecutors across the country filed charges stemming from the panic, with future US attorney general Janet Reno playing a large role in a high-profile Florida ritual abuse prosecution.[13] Several states proposed laws against "diabolic cults" and ritual abuse; such laws were actually passed in Idaho, Illinois, and California.[14] It was gospel belief in the media and among ordinary citizens that rings of sex abusers were everywhere.

Back in Texas, the Kellers were studying other cases in which day care providers had been accused of sexually and ritually abusing children. They knew about the mounting accusations against them, the impossibly violent crimes of which they were accused. The statistics were grim. After a grand jury indicted them in 1991, they fled to Las Vegas. By the time their trial began in November 1992, the ludicrous nature of the allegations mattered little. They had run, and therefore they were guilty—of child molestation on a colossal scale in the service of Satan.

The couple was ultimately sentenced to forty-eight years in prison for aggravated sexual assault of a child. After extensive appeals, they were at last released in 2015 after the sole physical evidence in the case, the testimony of an ER doctor who alleged that a three-year-old girl's hymen showed signs of rupture, was debunked in a cover story for the *Austin Chronicle*. (The doctor who initially examined the girl, Michael Mouw, admitted at the trial that he had not had the specialized knowledge to conduct a pediatric sexual abuse examination in 1991, and that he had subsequently seen images that indicated that the girl's hymen was consistent with "normal variants" of hymens. "I wouldn't touch that [case] with a 10-foot pole now," he told the *Austin Chronicle* in 2013, citing a "rush to judgment" that had been prevalent at the time.)[15]

By the time they got out, Fran was sixty-three, Dan seventy-two; they had spent two decades behind bars. In 2017, Travis County district attorney Margaret Moore declared the couple "actually innocent," and the state of Texas agreed to pay the Kellers $3.4 million in compensation for their wrongful convictions. They were among hundreds of day care workers accused of lurid and fantastic crimes in league with the Devil and among dozens who spent years or decades in prison. The allegations of satanic ritual abuse leveled against the Kellers were part of a national maelstrom fueled by Christian zealotry and aided by credulous pundits, such as Geraldo Rivera, who made an infamous, breathless two-hour NBC prime-time special in 1998 entitled *Devil Worship: Exposing Satan's Underground*. "A nationwide network of satanic criminals exists," he intoned gravely to an audience of millions. "This is not a Halloween fable. This is a real-life horror story."

In the books, articles, and studies exploring the phenomenon of the Satanic Panic, scholars and journalists have tried to pinpoint the origins of the storm. The recovered-memory trend that swept psychology on the success of authors such as Ross and Pazder led to wild accusations in a kind of clinical folie à deux. Feminist scholars have argued that the fact that day cares were the primary targets of the sexual abuse panic was due to a nationwide backlash against the feminist movements of the 1970s and '80s, which saw more and more women working outside the home—and thus needing professional care for their young children. Others point to

Americans' perennial fascination with cults and an innate national culture of conspiracy theory. At the heart of the Satanic Panic and why it went so wide and deep, from backcountry Texas to the Justice Department, is the wild Manichaean brand of religiosity that casts every part of life in the public sphere as part of a titanic struggle between good and evil. It is a style of religious thought that is deeply embedded in the American psyche and to this day echoes through the beliefs of tens of millions of American Christians, particularly evangelicals.

Around 14 percent of the US population, nearly 50 million people, identify themselves as white evangelical Protestants.[16] "Though [white evangelicals] make up just 14% of Americans overall, they remain the largest single religious group among Republican voters with the power to sway party priorities," noted reporter Becky Sullivan on NPR's *Morning Edition*.[17] The politics of evangelicals are overwhelmingly conservative. Though a minority, they punch far above their weight politically, with reliable votes, full coffers, and lockstep political ideology, pulling the nation ever further toward a straight, white theocracy. Around 80 percent of white evangelicals voted for Donald Trump in the 2016 election, rising to 84 percent in 2020;[18] the same population overwhelmingly holds right-wing beliefs, including panic over the shrinking white population of the United States.[19] Sixty-eight percent do not believe the United States has the responsibility to admit any refugees at all, and over half express concern over the prospect of living in a non-white-majority country.[20] Evangelical faith is inextricably linked with right-wing politics, thanks to a decades-long, focused movement to preach politics from the pulpit. The efforts of this determined minority have irrevocably changed the face of American culture in ways that are only accelerating. While evangelical beliefs exist along a spectrum, the most extreme voices are often the loudest, and a cohort of zealots who believe they are divinely sanctioned to make the United States a de jure Christian nation have turned our politics into a kind of cursed ground where demons cavort, awaiting a purification by fire.

Even after the height of the Satanic Panic, when the Devil danced in headlines from coast to coast in the 1980s and '90s, evangelical authors continued to fan the flames of fear about demons. Demonological literature was distributed by the mammoth evangelical company Christian Book Distributors and sold by Lifeway Christian Resources, a nationwide chain run by the Southern Baptist Convention that had 170 stores across the country at its peak.[21] Some of the books were practical guides to dispelling demons; others richly imagined novels that populated American cities with Hell's minions. The most successful—and influential—of these was Frank E. Peretti's *This Present Darkness*, a 1986 novel that laid out, in supermarket-thriller prose, a battle between angels and demons for the soul of an American town. In the book, a stalwart fundamentalist minister does battle with the hidden influence of demonic forces that have taken control of a local psychology professor, a liberal pastor, the chief of police, and elected officials. A profoundly literal viewpoint on spiritual warfare, the novel also reflects Christian Right anxieties in the 1980s: the prevalence of more liberal views of Christianity, higher education, losing control of one's children, and the ungodly attitudes of some secular authorities. It resonated with its evangelical audience as much as Stephen King or Tom Clancy ever did with the general public. The book topped Christian bestseller lists for 150 consecutive weeks after its release and sold more than 2 million copies over subsequent decades.[22] While some pastors and Christian authorities groused about its hyperliteral interpretations—at one point, demons disable the car horn of the pastor's wife, while an angel tells her to release her parking brake[23]—it was a brisk, thrilling encounter with spiritual warfare that made far more of a mark than a weekly sermon or a theologian's quibbles. "Holy moly, the way people I knew took that book seriously—and lived their lives accordingly," one former evangelical told me.

Peretti's worldview became commonplace among evangelicals in the intervening decades: if bad things, things counter to fundamentalist theology, happen in the world outside, or if sexual temptations or the desire to engage with secular culture beset evangelicals from within, there is a ready answer: demons surround each of the faithful, seeking to lure them from the blazing path of truth.

———

WHEN YOU CLOSE YOUR EYES, WHAT DO YOU IMAGINE LIVES IN THE DARK-ness beside you? There are so many things too small to see: microbes and molecules, protons and quarks, and faraway nebulae burning off beyond the horizon. But for many millions of Americans—51 percent of the country, according to one poll[24]—the darkness is populated by bigger, more frighten-ing things: demons and their consorts, feeding on hapless human beings, as one early American Pentecostal minister put it, "like ticks on cattle."[25] These parasitic forces exist to draw humanity into a long and terrifying battle—the eternal struggle of the godly engaged in spiritual warfare.

The dog days of July in Portland, Oregon, mean wildfire season, a time of conflagration that seems to get longer and hotter each year. In several cities throughout the state in 2023, fireworks had been banned on the Fourth of July for fear of sparking wildfires. But the crowd of several thousand that gathered in Portland's Pioneer Courthouse Square on July 13, 2023, for a "Jesus March" weren't afraid: they were on fire for the Lord and marching in a display of militant Christian faith meant to "establish the kingdom of God on Earth."

That Jesus March wasn't the first, though Portland was a symbolic des-tination. United Revival, an evangelical group created in 2018, had orga-nized several such marches in 2023, each in cities stereotyped as cauldrons of sin: San Francisco, Los Angeles, Seattle. Since the dawn of the Trump years, Portland had been infamous in right-wing media for being the site of repeated clashes between far-right marchers and left-wing counter-protesters, a trend that accelerated into nightly violence during the racial justice protests of summer 2020. Now the Jesus Marchers—members of some two hundred churches brought together by United Revival—flew Christian flags, raised crosses, and marched in ranks in matching Jesus T-shirts. Opposing them were knots of countermarchers holding up banners supporting trans rights. The Jesus Marchers blew ram's horns, biblical symbols of a call to battle.

"Portland, Oregon, can be saved," the marchers chanted. Some marchers were carrying bear mace; others, Christian nationalist flags and T-shirts for right-wing causes; a contingent was present from the Three Percenters, a national armed militia group.[26] Preachers held forth on the need to "preserve traditional marriage." The marchers were there, they said, to cleanse the darkness that had descended on Portland, "to pray and prophesy light into that darkness."[27]

United Revival makes it abundantly clear just what sort of darkness it believes itself to be fighting. In its mission statement, it stresses its belief in an "eternal punishment for the unsaved"—and adds, "The Christian life is filled with trials, tests, and warfare against a spiritual enemy."[28] The Jesus Marchers were there, with banners raised, to save the people of Portland from the maw of Hell. It was a spiritual war, and they were on its front lines.

The Satanic Panic never receded from the evangelical mind, which only became more focused on demons in the intervening years, thanks to the influence of authors such as Frank Peretti and his legion of imitators. "Demonic forces want to lure us into their deceptions of power and supernatural activities," Tonilee Adamson and Bobbye Brooks wrote in a 2015 guide to understanding spiritual warfare. "We have a tendency to act like a two-year-old child who closes her eyes and places a blanket over her head, really believing that no one can see her because she cannot see them. Just because we cannot see the spiritual realm does not mean it is not there."[29]

All over the country, believers cast Satan as their principal foe, with his dark minions, incarnate and ethereal, constantly arrayed in force—and these Christians cast their lives in martial metaphors to oppose him.

Those who beseech God on behalf of the sick and other causes describe themselves as "prayer warriors"; during the peak of the covid-19 pandemic, evangelical memes encouraged believers to abandon the fleeting earthly protection of masks and vaccines and "suit up with the whole armor of God," a reference to Ephesians. The combat may be invisible, but it is no less real for that. Tens of millions of Americans view this discarnate clash and its fleshly parallel as a bitter struggle for the soul of a country in peril—and their foes as in league with actual demons, sulfurous, reeking, and mortally dangerous.

If mainstream credulity sparked the Satanic Panic in the 1980s and '90s, the contemporary attitude of popular media toward such beliefs is one of genteelly amused condescension, largely dismissive of the movement's contemporary analogues. Look, if you will, for a feature in a mainstream newspaper that addresses just how widespread the bloody and apocalyptic right-wing faith of the evangelical Right truly is—much less one that addresses its impact; you will be a long time searching. Among a commentariat hermetically sealed in secular bubbles educated at a handful of elite institutions, there is a persistent skepticism that these people believe what they say they do and a running streak of apologia seeking to bridge the gap between the mild-mannered rhetoric of Jesus and the most ferocious of his followers. Above all, there is an unwillingness to look the Devil in the eye and understand that for tens of millions of Americans, politics and spiritual warfare are one and the same. Whether it's cynicism, laziness, or both, this milquetoast commentary—or simple omission of the plain fact that a theocratic movement is growing in the United States— has misled much of the public into dismissing these beliefs as the fantasies of a tiny slice of fired-up congregants rather than a large, powerful movement aiming—and often succeeding—at shaping the public sphere of the United States in its own image.

Yet despite this profound lack of informed commentary, Americans' relationship with the Devil stretches back centuries, and that sinuous and winding track leads directly to the present. The American view of Satan is both all-pervading and deeply literal minded. The enemy warned of from megachurch pulpits has precisely the shrewd and inexhaustible aims written about by John Milton in *Paradise Lost* in 1667:

> *To do ought good never will be our task,*
> *But ever to do ill our sole delight,*

As being the contrary to his high will
Whom we resist. If then his Providence
Out of our evil seek to bring forth good,
Our labour must be to pervert that end,
And out of good still to find means of evil.[30]

In his overview of our nation's relationship with the Devil, *Satan in America: The Devil We Know*, the historian W. Scott Poole grounds an admixture of pop culture, theology, and politics in one founding principle: to those who believe fervently in a spiritual war, "America is the Unfallen Angel, secure in its innocence, but beset by thousands of dark foes." This faith in a fundamental innocence can be used to paper over the violence of nationalism, and to cast social discord or opposition in the sinister light of the occult. "America has been in love with the dark at almost every stage of its history, eager to view its enemies as satanic," Poole wrote. "Powerful social groups have used this image of evil to explain their enemies to them and to legitimize acts of violence against those they have constructed as demonic."[31]

Puritan colonists saw the Devil in Salem's matrons; Thomas Jefferson's political opponents depicted him as obeying Satan's desires to sow atheism; landowners in the antebellum South cast enslaved people's rebellions as foul witchcraft. In the twentieth century, Christian fundamentalists saw Mephistophelian influence in the works of labor unions, Jews, social democrats, Catholics, and, later, heavy-metal music and Dungeons & Dragons.[32] Supposed candidates for the title of Antichrist, meanwhile, have ranged from Franklin D. Roosevelt to Barack Obama to George Soros to Joe Biden.[33]

In the latter half of the twentieth century, Satan saw a major revival in popular culture, with the Devil at the forefront of American cinemas and libraries. In 1967, the Jewish author Ira Levin wrote a horror classic, *Rosemary's Baby*, which centers around an innocent woman coaxed by Satanists into a demonic birth; the book sold 4 million copies and was adapted into an Oscar-winning film the next year. Three years later, following up on Levin's success, William Peter Blatty created a sensation with his violent depiction of demons in his novel *The Exorcist*. The film adaptation of *The Exorcist*, released in 1973, launched a real-life exorcism craze that had large numbers of Americans beseeching bemused priests to cure their spiritual ailments. From those strange seeds grew a garden of belief that entangled millions of people—and led to tragic consequences for children, parents, and day care workers. Later in life, Levin reflected that his success with *Rosemary's Baby* had led to a Satan craze that had sparked a doctrinal revival of demonology. "I feel guilty that 'Rosemary's Baby' led to 'The Exorcist,' 'The Omen.' A whole generation has been exposed, has more belief in Satan," he said in 2002. "I don't believe in Satan. And I feel that the strong fundamentalism we have would not be as strong if there hadn't been so many of these books."[34]

By 2020, the already strong tendency to see the Devil everywhere resurfaced in full bloom during a pandemic—a time of social, political, economic, racial, and domestic upheaval. Demonology's current manifestations rhyme with its recent past, as Christian parents bombard school boards to remove harmful books and cancel events with gay performers to "save the children" from Satan's influence. In its national senescence, America is replaying its greatest hits in ragged crescendo: a renewed Red Scare sweeping through schools, encouraging parents to report subversive materials just as their parents reported satanic day care workers; a pathological rummaging through the cupboard of Western fixations, seeking objects of blame; and a religious Great Awakening of the most odious sort, with millions of people inculcated into wild and intemperate faith.

The Christian Right, a movement of millions that mixes ardent zeal with hard-right social conservatism, has been on the march for decades. It is difficult to overstate the scope of its influence and its success in changing both cultural conversations and laws. In the 2020s, this manifests itself in the book bans spreading from state to state, outlawing schoolchildren being exposed to LGBTQ and racially diverse content. Consider, also, the increasingly difficult straits in which abortion providers and, by extension, pregnant women find themselves across the country; the ascendant movements opposing birth control, gay marriage, and even divorce that are beginning to influence policymakers; and so much more. These are the battlefronts of the spirit war. They are thoroughly rooted in the ideal of a Christian country that adheres to narrowly defined Christian moral values in order to triumph over the Devil. That the beliefs that give rise to this extraordinary determination are often wild or extravagant does not lessen their consequences or the seriousness with which they are held. To members of the Christian Right, Satan's hand is everywhere extended, and it is the duty of each of the faithful to fight in the street, the court, and the heart.

⁓

IN WASHINGTON, DC, IN 2021, A TIDE OF CHRISTIAN NATIONALIST HYSteria washed over the nation's capital. Thousands of protesters took to the city to challenge the purported tyranny of the United States' shambolic, piecemeal covid-19 response, a refrain echoed across the frozen water of the Reflecting Pool under the long marble gaze of Abraham Lincoln. "This is a war on religion, this is a war on the children," rapped the MAGA hip-hop duo Hi-Rez & Jimmy Levy in an antivaccine anthem called "This Is a War." "The devil he hides in ego and pride... / Fuck your medication... / I'll just keep on praying / For your salvation."[35]

Throughout the day, Christian nationalist imagery, from crosses to entreaties to get "vaccinated in the blood of Jesus," was a notable presence among rallygoers. Injunctions to buck worldly authorities—and medicine—in favor of God's, along with a flood of profit-motivated pseudoscience, lent the event an unmistakably fundamentalist overtone. Nearly a quarter-million dollars had been raised for the proceedings on the far-right Christian fundraising site GiveSendGo.[36] Amanda Moore, a freelance journalist covering far-right movements who attended the rally, described seeing signs depicting Dr. Anthony Fauci, the public face of the nation's covid-19 response, as a demon; others encouraged all those in the capital that day to "obey Christ, reject tyranny."[37] The Trump-hatted thousands appeared to believe, like many of their compatriots, that their physical presence at the rally was a corollary to the supernatural war being fought invisibly all around us, all the time.

This belief in the supernatural renders a population ripe for belief in conspiracy theories. If you are looking for the Devil in your dining room, you're likely to find him; and the harder you look, the more you'll see his movements everywhere, until the whole world looks like a witches' sabbath conducted under the shadow of a dark and hideous hand.

The term *apophenia* was first coined in 1958 by the German military psychiatrist Klaus Conrad to describe the "abnormal connectedness between seemingly unrelated meanings" that he observed in his young patients, soldiers he studied showing early signs of schizophrenia. The term was first used in English in 2001 in an academic book about poltergeists and hauntings. As the Swiss psychologist Peter Brugger told Slate in 2014, outside of descriptions of schizophrenia, apophenia is "the tendency to be *overwhelmed* by meaningful coincidences."[38] It's a motivator for gamblers who see patterns in their wins and losses—and stake ever-higher amounts on their false perceptions; it's behind Bible-code theological fads and the enduringness of Dan Brown's novels. And it's a kind of manic, messianic apophenia that drives evangelical demonology—a tendency that has become increasingly strong and increasingly visible in recent years.

Among the most famous of the spirit warriors of the GOP is Paula White-Cain, Donald Trump's most prominent religious adviser, who demanded, in a thunderous January 2020 sermon, that "in the name of Jesus, we command all satanic pregnancies to miscarry right now. We declare that anything that has been conceived in satanic wombs, that it'll miscarry. It will not be able to carry forth any plan of destruction, any plan of harm."[39]

Satanic wombs notwithstanding, Cain's pronouncements came from a contemporary demonology movement that has been ascendant in certain sectors of American evangelical Christianity for decades. In 2000, Doris Wagner, the wife of the enormously influential prophet-preacher C. Peter

Wagner, published a book called *How to Cast Out Demons: A Guide to the Basics*. She and her husband, in their roles as heads of Global Harvest Ministries, became integral parts of a movement that influenced millions of Christians to examine the world in starkly spiritual terms—as one scholar put it, their self-assigned task was mapping the "fearful geography" of the spirit world and transposing it over the earthly realm. Wagner explained, "Hostility toward teaching morals through such simple things as the Ten Commandments in schoolrooms, heavy-metal music encouraging sinful thoughts and behavior, and the agenda of the homosexual community" contribute to "demonic activity in great abundance."[40]

As a result, she asserted, there has been an attendant surge in enthusiasm for exorcising demons—even if certain "misunderstandings" have led to the rituals having a death toll. "I have heard of several deaths because of mistreatment when demons were manifesting, such as holding a person down and placing pressure on an artery until a heart attack ensued. Another couple tried to bludgeon a demon out of their son with a cement block and he died of injuries," she wrote. "Casting out demons has gained a bad reputation in some circles because of misunderstanding and abuse." In lieu of such crudities, Wagner said, she has opted for "long and arduous" deliverance sessions, which involve prayer, invocation of the name of Jesus, and a lengthy questionnaire that features blood pacts, curses, and Masonic regalia, issued beforehand in order to determine the nature of the demonic influence.[41]*

Perhaps the most infamous case of abusive exorcism is that of Jane Whaley, the leader of the Word of Faith Fellowship, a congregation based in Spindale, North Carolina. The church was founded in 1979 by Whaley, a former math teacher. Over the ensuing decades, the church developed branches in a number of counties and countries, swelling to a membership

---

* Among the questions posed by Wagner to would-be exorcees: "Were you a breast-fed baby?" "To your knowledge, has any close family member been a Freemason, Oddfellow, Rainbow Girl, Mormon, Eastern Star, Shriner, Daughter of the Nile, Job's Daughter, Elk or De Molay?" And: "Is there any Masonic regalia or memorabilia in your possession?" "Have you had any advanced education?" "Have you ever made a pact with the devil? Was it a blood pact?" "To your knowledge, has any curse been placed on you or your family?"

of nearly three thousand people. Despite the geographic sprawl of the church, its central leader, Whaley, distinguished herself among fundamentalist Christians with what was alleged in court documents to be a pervasive, brutal regimen of control whose central method was violent exorcism. In a 2017 Associated Press investigation, legions of former church members confided to reporters that routine casting-out sessions of demons included the infliction of physical violence, such as punching, kicking, and slamming congregants into walls—including very young children.[42] Toddlers were told that they harbored Satan; congregants deemed to have broken from the church's strict rules (which included prohibitions against reading newspapers and shaving beards) were routinely imprisoned in a windowless storage room, alone in moldy darkness for long periods of time. Children in the church's associated schools were encouraged to beat classmates they perceived as having committed infractions that might have been caused by demons. Whaley was convicted of assault in 2004 after a member described a "blasting" session in which congregants would gather around the supposedly possessed sinner and scream and shout at him or her for hours, often in concert with physical violence; in 2014, five members of the church were indicted for kidnapping and assault after a former congregant, Matthew Fenner, testified that they had imprisoned and beaten him to the point where he thought he might die in order to exorcise the "homosexual demons" from him. So real were the demons in the minds of Whaley and her loyal spiritual soldiers that physical pain became a conduit for a cleansing of the soul—regardless of the damage done along the way.[43]

It's easy to dismiss Paula White-Cain's satanic pregnancies, Jane Whaley's prolific beatings, and Doris Wagner's blood pacts as the wild beliefs of fanatics—or it would be, if their brand of charismatic, brash, God-touched worship didn't hold such a fierce grip on the core and most active base of the Republican Party. Views that perceive demonic activity in the actions of people and nations are by no means fringe: they are squarely in the Republican mainstream. In his very first speech as Donald Trump's CIA director, Mike Pompeo, who would go on to become secretary of state, pronounced Julian Assange a "demon";[44] popular preachers and Christian commentators have told their flocks that critics of Trump are "possessed by demons."[45] "The demonic left will stop at nothing to defend its religious ritual of sacrificing babies to the god of self," read a 2022 article on the mainstream-right website the Federalist, castigating abortion rights protesters.[46] It's hard to exorcise the politics from evangelical demonology. As journalist Katherine Stewart pointed out, C. Peter Wagner and his theological cohort introduced into American spiritual vernacular the idea of "territorial spirits": demons who occupy places and institutions "strategically," such as abortion clinics, the LGBT community, and the Democratic Party. These malevolent forces don't simply advocate for things that believers oppose; they are evil personified and need to be cleansed.[47] The politics of spiritual warfare is always cast in a pitch of frantic urgency, with millions of mortal souls at stake. The equation of Democrat and demon, to a group of people who very much believe in demons and the necessity of casting them out, draws politics and faith together to a very dangerous precipice.

Reactionary ideology and fervent belief in demons have long gone hand in hand in American culture. As Poole put it, Christian conservatism, opposing social change as embodied in the civil rights and feminist movements, felt an increasing need to see "the devil embodied in its cultural opponents."[48] One response to the rapid social change derived from the protest movements of the 1960s was a renewed fundamentalism among the millions of Americans who identified as evangelical Protestants. It was a form of faith that took the Devil literally, spurring an exorcism mania, a renewed interest in prophecy, and an embrace of impending apocalypse. They felt that their world had been destabilized by civil rights, feminism, gay rights, and antiwar student protests; as will be elaborated on more fully later in this book, the Christian Right rose as a reactionary counterbalance to progressive social change and peopled America with demons in the process.

This large, passionate reactionary cadre would later catapult *Pigs in the Parlor*, an elaborate taxonomy of hundreds of ways demons can infest a single human spirit, onto bestseller lists from the 1970s and onward. The publisher's sales copy boasts that the book has 1.5 million copies in print and has been translated into more than a dozen languages.[49] As of this writing, it is number two in the "Pentecostal and Charismatic Christianity" category of books on Amazon and number seventeen in "Christian Spiritual Warfare." Spiritual, moral, and social anxiety, for some, are more easily processed through demonology, which both externalizes the threat and increases the stakes of any given conflict.

The battle between God and Satan is, as ever, mirrored in the human world, spilling out onto the National Mall and carried out in legions of voting booths. On November 6, 2020, in Clark County, Nevada, a crowd of Trump supporters gathered outside the county election administration office, kneeling in prayer, swaying and lifting their hands in an incantation for victory. One Trump supporter braced herself against the glass front of the office as if against Jerusalem's Wailing Wall, keening in prayer.[50]

The doctrine of spiritual warfare is widespread among numerous evangelical denominations and has a particular influence on the authoritarian politics of the extreme Right. Republican congressmen, gubernatorial candidates, senators, judges, and presidential candidates alike routinely appeal to crowds by citing a worldview in which the LGBTQ "agenda" and the desires of liberal unbelievers are driven by demons. Moreover, leading Republican figures are intimately familiar with the peculiar terminology of spiritual warfare. In a 2022 speech at the right-wing evangelical Hillsdale College, then presidential candidate and Florida governor Ron DeSantis quoted a key verse from Ephesians that is central to the doctrine: "Put on the full armor of God. Stand firm against the left's schemes. You will face flaming arrows, but if you have the shield of faith, you will overcome them," he told the Christian audience; as Katherine Stewart noted, he deftly substituted "the left" where the Bible says "the Devil."[51]

For those in battle with dark forces, Christian spirit warriors advise a specific set of spiritual armor. The "whole armour of God," which Christians are encouraged to don before thwarting the Devil in Ephesians 6:11–18, consists of six specific items. To suit up against the Devil, you

must obtain this wardrobe: the belt of truth, the breastplate of righteousness, the sandals of the gospel of peace, the shield of faith (to "quench all
the fiery darts of the wicked"), the helmet of salvation, and the sword of
the Spirit. Those clad in the holy fabric and hammered metal of the mandated six heavenly garments may survive unscathed.[52]

The armor of God is necessary because demons are omnipresent. The
ongoing Satanic Panic is now so commonplace and so widespread that it
has swayed elections even in state races. As Brandy Zadrozny, an extremism reporter with NBC, noted, David Leavitt, a politician in Provo, Utah,
lost his reelection as prosecutor in part because of widespread, false internet rumors that he and his wife led a "ritual sex abuse cult."

The rumors had been started, Zadrozny reported, by a YouTuber
named Nicholas Rossi, who had faked his own death in 2020 and fled to
Scotland to avoid rape charges in Utah, a prosecution pursued by Leavitt.
In 2022, while fighting extradition from Scotland for the alleged rape
and claiming to be an Irish orphan named Arthur Knight, Rossi obtained
and posted a 151-page document from a dismissed case against a therapist
that, according to NBC, "included gory allegations of sexual abuse and
mass murder from the 1980s and '90s perpetrated not just by the therapist, but by more than a dozen other members of the Provo community,
including David Leavitt and his wife." The unsubstantiated, previously
dismissed allegations were part of a brand-new 2022 investigation into
"ritualistic child sexual abuse and child sex trafficking that occurred in
Utah County, Juab County, and Sanpete County during the time between
1990 and 2010," which had just been announced by Utah County sheriff
Mike Smith, who had backed Leavitt's opponent. Smith denied leaking
the documents to Rossi, but once the information was available online,
a network of conspiracy theorists on mainstream and right-wing social
media sites took it and ran with every grisly, unproven detail. Leavitt's
wife, an assistant professor at BYU, was barraged with emails calling for
her firing, alleging that she was involved with satanic ritual abuse, was a
demon herself, and was part of a ring of sexual abusers holding children
captive in pizza parlors (the pizza parlor accusation being part of a broader,

weirder conspiracy theory). That the rumors had been started by an individual whose notoriety derived from a rape accusation, an international escape, and an impersonation of a disabled Irish orphan mattered little in the brackish ecology of conspiracy theorists and those willing to portray themselves as true Christian protectors of the innocent. Leavitt said he was unlikely to ever run for office again after a press conference in which he was forced, by the peculiar alchemy of moral panic that lent weight to the absurd allegations, to deny that he or his wife had ever murdered or cannibalized children for Satan; the cost, he said, was too high.[53] In 2024, Utah became the first state in decades to propose a bill to specifically bar "ritual abuse" of a child; House Bill 196, which has not yet passed at the time of this writing, would impose felony charges on any adult who forces a child to ingest human bones or witness the sacrifice of an animal—classic Satanic Panic tropes recurring unadulterated fifty years after the initial accusations of ritual abuse in the United States.[54]

While politics is a principal sphere of battling the Devil, it is by no means the only one the ultraconservative, prophecy-inclined evangelical world is focused on. In fact, there are seven areas—the "Seven Mountains of Societal Influence"—which were laid out by Bill Bright, the founder of the far-right Christian youth organization Campus Crusade; and Loren Cunningham, the similarly inclined founder of Youth with a Mission, in 1975. The thesis is loosely derived from a cryptic passage in Revelation (perhaps the most beloved book of the Bible among fundamentalists): "And the angel carried me away in the Spirit into a wilderness, where I saw a woman sitting on a scarlet beast that was covered with blasphemous names and had seven heads and ten horns...And here is the mind which hath wisdom. The seven heads are seven mountains, on which the woman sitteth." From this scanty textual basis, Bright and Cunningham engaged in a bit of creative exegesis and came up with the Seven Mountain Mandate, or "7M" to its most loyal adherents.[55]

Further popularized by the publication of *Invading Babylon: The 7 Mountain Mandate*, by the megachurch leader Bill Johnson and the self-proclaimed prophet Lance Wallnau, in 2013, the Seven Mountain

Mandate demands that believers "take the seven mountains of culture for Christ's Kingdom." The seven mountains are as follows: government, family, education, religion, media, arts and entertainment, and business. Total dominion over these spheres is key to winning the spiritual war against Satan. Johnson and Wallnau make clear that obtaining absolute Christian control of secular pursuits, such as politics and journalism, is a duty required of those faithful who would wage war against Satan: "The shocking truth is that each mountain is a spiritual mountain! The Devil's skill in leading us to think differently has resulted in the spiritual invasion of foreign deities into every area once held by followers of Christ...If the Church leaves a vacuum by failing to occupy these high places with the teaching of the Kingdom, the enemy will seek to disciple the nations by building strongholds of deception that are guarded and advanced through those decision makers who rise to the top of the seven mountains of culture." This theory gives an intense spiritual gravity to every minute squabble in the culture wars: it becomes much more urgent to get your claims heard and to win if you believe you are saving every piece of the wretched world and rendering it precious in God's sight.[56]

"People who subscribe to this idea understand the whole of human history as a consequence of the cosmic battle of Satan against God," explained the scholar Elizabeth McAlister in a 2016 article. "The movement is political in that its intercessors imagine they are part of an elite group of God's agents, participating in a massive social transformation of the world into the Kingdom of God."[57]

The world of the Christian Right is largely insular, shunning worldly influence. It has its own schools and universities, its own movies, its own microcelebrities, its own methods of parenting and marriage, its own trends. It exists as part of the United States yet holds itself separate, because holiness demands separation from the profane.

Slowly and then quickly, like a climber who's glimpsed the peak, the Christian Right is working to ascend its seven mountains. Its members believe that they are obeying the mandate of Heaven by turning the United States into a Christian nation—a theocracy that brooks no opposition and has no room for those of other faiths or none at all. The United States has always been a land overpopulated with prophets, and this unsettled decade has led to a new wave of self-proclaimed redeemers ready to reveal the blazing path toward righteousness—and use, in a favorite evangelical phrase, "the sword of the Lord" to cut down any in their path.

Outside the perfervid world of demonology and its believers, down at the bottom of the seven mountains, where most of us live, it's a challenge to determine precisely how to contend with a political landscape in which a large proportion of one side believes that its opponents are literally in league with the Devil. In the face of such conviction, it's difficult not to shrink away or to try to combat it on its own terms—*I'm not in league with the Devil*, or *There's no such thing as the Devil*—but this is more or less a futile exercise. It's better to get a firm foothold on the brimstone and heave ourselves out of Hell. But in order to escape a struggle we never chose, we must take into account the rhetoric on the Christian Right and who is providing it—and take stock of their theology as the existential threat to a pluralistic democracy it truly is.

CHAPTER 2

FILTHY LUCRE

Beyond our zealous faith, the other great American preoccupation—
the one we're most famous for, the one that makes our streets proverbially paved with gold and less proverbially paved with strip malls—is
money.

It would be a great mistake to think that money and faith live in separate realms. Faith can be the biggest cash cow of them all. It can be a
golden calf, if you believe hard enough. It can even be a man with dyed
golden hair, a man whose carefully crafted public image—drawn for him
for decades by credulous reporters even as it was undermined by determined and cynical ones—painted him as the very image, the embodiment, of wealth and success.

All over the world of the right wing, there are plenty of vendors at conservative conferences and GOP campaign stops and on a vast, shabby network of websites that offer concrete and physical sustenance—a gaudy
panoply of things to eat, wear, and inject in order to supercharge the body.
"Glyconutrients, or neutraceuticals—health supplements that promise
almost miraculous results—are constantly being pitched to conservatives
by voices they trust," wrote *Washington Post* reporter David Weigel in a
2015 piece on former GOP presidential candidate and subsequent Trump
administration secretary of housing and urban development Ben Carson's

supplement-promotion side hustle that by now feels almost quaint.[1] It's nearly a decade later, and things have progressed to antivaxxers treating their covid symptoms with bleach enemas and selling USB keys with stickers on them claiming to be "quantum holographic shields" against 5G radiation. The health scam, disaster prep, and right-wing paranoia worlds overlap so neatly that the Venn diagram resembles a stack of pancakes. And all of them operate on faith. And cash. Faith, cash, and confusing return policies.

Nothing exemplifies this ethos better than Natural News, a natural-health "news" site turned supplement-sales empire whose traffic is in the millions of page views per month. The site is a mix of New Age medical woo and wild-eyed Christian fundamentalism that might seem, at first, incongruous. But each realm asks the same thing of its constituents: belief. And that is present in abundance. The site's unwieldy headlines include "Comet Impacts, Pre-Adamic Civilization, Lost Worlds and the Luciferian WAR Against Humanity";[2] and "The America We Grew Up In Is Already Gone—What Remains Is Some Sick, Perverted Leftist Version of the Twilight Zone Where People Now Identify as Cats and Dogs."[3] It's a turbid mix of hokum, alien surveillance, Christianity, right-wing ideology, and banner ads, and you can buy black cumin seed oil, colloidal silver nasal spray, and Surthrival Immortality Quest Chaga Mushroom Extract ($64 for 50 milliliters) on the site, too, once you've finished learning how to prep for the Luciferian war.

Just as crystal healing might seem like a bad fit with Bible-thumping Christianity, the landscape of right-wing grift is a positive orgy of unlikely bedfellows and thrives on the juxtapositions and overlaps of seemingly distinct realms of belief. For a long time pundits puzzled at the way the evangelical Right seemed drawn to Donald Trump over candidates with more well-burnished Christian credentials. Ted Cruz, for example, who also ran for president in 2016, had the smug confidence of a man who had spent all of his time in public office pushing for a brutal, hard-minded vision of Christian nationalism and expected his due reward. Despite that, he was cast off like chaff and wound up groveling to a man who had publicly insulted his wife and accused his father of being an accomplice to John F. Kennedy's assassination.

Donald Trump is an apparent liar and cheat, and even compared to his peers in the shifty world of real estate, insofar as it can be proven, he is probably a thief. He is a multiply alleged adulterer with a track record of rather unimaginative sexual immorality that ought to make a preacher blush, as well as an alleged rapist. He is anything but a holy man. His religious gestures have always seemed perfunctory, stilted, and phony—bumbling through Bible quotes, grimacing when prophets laid hands on him. But above all things, he is and will forever be a con man. He is a salesman selling you himself, larger than life, his florid complexion a reflection of your own red anger. He sells you an image of a man draped in wealth and cloaked in martyrdom, a man of infinite power who will wield it against your enemies. All he requires from you in return is belief. The image of a wealthy and righteous savior is consistent with the "prosperity gospel," a strain of Christian belief that tautologically posits that wealth comes to the righteous, and therefore makes a virtue out of wealth. From Trump's spiritual mentor Norman Vincent Peale to contemporary preachers like Creflo Dollar and Kenneth Copeland, this gospel has fueled a cascade of grift and private jets since the 1950s.

Throughout Trump's campaigns he promised the Christian Right in particular whatever they wanted—abortion banned, immigrants restricted—and made them believe he could do it. And do it with style. Not fire-and-brimstone style, not pulpit thundering, although the atmosphere at his rallies gets pretty windy and pretty full of denunciations. Rather, his charisma owes more to the Borscht Belt than the Bible Belt—all those wisecracks, those rambling asides, the bouffant hairdo, the absurd gestures. He offered, too, a sense of his own omnipresence. He has always had the urge, common to emperors and gods alike, to stamp his name on everything: towers and planes, steaks and water bottles, a university that folded like cardboard in the wind at the least sign of scrutiny, T-shirts, hats, mailing lists, and legions of believers. The object has always been quantity rather than quality, and over time the quantity has grown to the millions.

What he asked his audiences to do was trust him. And to believe. And they were so good, so very good, at doing that already, especially when the voice was telling them what they really wanted to hear, deep down.

"White Evangelicals have come to view themselves as a besieged minority, and Donald Trump, for all his faults, has committed to a common desire to take America back to its days of greatness in the 1950s," wrote the columnist Ed Kilgore in *New York* magazine in 2019, accurately predicting that white evangelical support for Trump would be overwhelming in the 2020 election.[4] What he sold them—what he's always sold everyone—is a dream: the dream that he was omnipotent and rich, even when he was broke, and could give you what your heart most desired for the cost of unwavering devotion. A recurring donation, after all, bears not a little resemblance to a tithe. He made a penumbra built of their fervency, becoming what used to be called, in very old religions, a fetish: an object designed to be a focus of belief, its wellspring and its center. He exploited his followers' hatred and their desire to wrench the world backward to a time when they were on top. He fed their conviction that they were being persecuted in terrible ways, and he wielded it, burnished it, and turned it into a fearsome weapon. His greatest skill, forged in the crucible of the big, loud New York tabloid circuit, was to seem larger than life—as prophets do. And he offered them all they wanted at the low, low price of every virtue they'd told the world they had. "Trust me," he said, and "Believe in me," he said underneath that and addressed the National Prayer Breakfast and shook the hands of pastors, and captured them utterly.

What he had, suddenly, was an iron-hard belief in him beyond a con man's wildest dreams: he had a flock to herd and guide and lead. And to sell things to—hats and flags and T-shirts and even NFTs—as tribal marks that they were his. By 2024, he was even selling $59.99 patriotic Bibles, shilling them throughout a trial in which he was accused of paying hush money to a sex worker to cover up an affair. And his followers bought them and hung them and wore them where everyone could see them. And he grew even larger. In the paintings by the American folk artist Jon McNaughton, a sort of right-wing, cut-price Jacques-Louis David for the Thomas Kinkade set, Trump always has a celestial glow around him and sometimes literal angel's wings, as he does things such as heroically run across a football field or teach a man to fish or take the place of Washington crossing the Delaware in the prow of a rowboat. You can buy T-shirts of Trump's 2023 mug shot from Fulton County Jail with such slogans as "Thug Life," "Never Surrender," and even—tellingly—"American Martyr."[5] A man who died for your sins can't say much, but a man who's been indicted for his own can say as much as he feels he needs to. And much of what he needs very badly to do is to recapture that alchemical fizz of belief, hatred for the other, and desire to rule to transmute himself from an angry indictee back into a president. And, of course, help a lot of other people make a lot of money along the way.

In a crowded contemporary information landscape, the way credulousness, cash, and cynicism can commingle is nowhere better evinced than the right-wing conspiracist movement QAnon, a collection of people obsessed with Satan and his children. Far from collapsing after the Trump presidency's end, the conspiracy theory–cum–cult has gone on to metastasize, fed by a reservoir of antivaccine sentiment and covid-era paranoia. While conspiracy theories have reached bigger and more widespread audiences in the social media era, the covid-19 pandemic was a watershed moment for a large minority of Americans, causing a fundamental breakdown of trust in government, mainstream media, and scientific consensus, as numerous social surveys have found.[6] As belief in conspiracy theories has risen and the Right has increasingly developed its own independent and often unhinged media sphere, the chasm between realities has been a fertile breeding ground for believers and those willing to take advantage of their belief.

QAnon attained its chief prominence during Donald Trump's first term, and though it has largely dissipated into a broader, more sprawling conspiracy movement, its embers are everywhere, smoldering under heated beliefs in conspiracy throughout the nation.

Sociologists and journalists have struggled to categorize the conspiracy movement and its followers. Is it a political movement? A new religion?

A cult? It has elements of all these things. There is a basic set of beliefs, namely that Donald J. Trump, both during and after his presidency, is waging a holy war against a secret cabal of pedophiles whose members include prominent Democrats such as Hillary Clinton and her advisers. There are accompanying behaviors and rituals: the YouTube videos about the world of QAnon; the frantic decoding of "Q drops," tersely worded message board posts, which now number more than four thousand. Some adherents even claim to have extracted secret messages encoded by the clock hands in the backgrounds of posted photos. There is a prophet, Q; and a godlike figure, Trump. Its central slogan offers the impression of a crusade, a long march: "Where we go one, we go all."

But historians offer another thesis for the purpose QAnon and its descendants serve. The "nocturnal ritual fantasy," a term coined by the historian Norman Cohn in his landmark study of European witch trials, *Europe's Inner Demons*, is a recurring trope in Western history, and it is often a politically useful one. Deployed by the Romans against the early Christians, by Christians against Jews, by Christians against witches, by Catholics against "heretics," it is a malleable set of accusations that posit that a social out-group is engaged in perverse, ritualistic behaviors that target innocents—and that the out-group and all its enablers must be crushed. The blood sacrifice of children, the despoiling of crops and live-stock, and the calling of malevolent spirits under the cover of night are all common themes.[7]

QAnon began in October 2017 in the fetid corners of the anonymous online message board 4chan. It consisted, at first, of cryptic messages by a mysterious individual who purported to have "Q Clearance"—a designation by the Department of Energy that enables its holder to access top secret information.

Over the past seven years, Q has migrated to 8kun, an even shadier anonymous site, and the conspiracy has grown vast and jungly, migrating away from its origins as the believers in one specific, cryptic prophet. The loose movement has allowed for a range of other conspiratorial beliefs to drift in, from the existence of a lizard Illuminati to a government cover-up of alien landings. While the initial movement, beset by disappointments and internal schisms, has faded, its basic beliefs—a global cabal based on child predation, the "deep state" whose malignant influence colors every imaginable governmental policy, the role of Trump as savior and more—have suffused American conspiracy thought and been absorbed into its bloodstream. There have been six-figure fundraisers to combat purported election fraud, uncover secret government malfeasance, or elect fringe candidates to office—always finding willing audiences ready to uncover the terrible truth by the power of cash and faith.

Disseminating the lore of Q can be a lucrative business. On the video-streaming site Twitch, a number of the site's top-earning channels purvey conspiracy content, including a woman named Terpsichore Maras-Lindeman (streaming under the name "ToreSays"), who earned a cool six figures for her QAnon content[8] when she began pushing election fraud conspiracy theories in 2019.[9] The year before, she'd been fined $25,000 by a North Dakota judge for claiming she was going to put on a Christmas concert for the homeless—it was "canceled"—only to spend the cash raised at Target and McDonald's and on waxing treatments. That didn't make a dent in her earnings—or her reach, which ranged into the tens of thousands of viewers before she was finally banned by the service in 2022.

QAnon and its descendant movements are also, at their core, suffused with evangelical Christian beliefs. The anonymous communiqués known as "Q drops" frequently use verses from the New Testament to emphasize their cryptic messages, which inevitably warn Q believers of a conspiracy reaching to the highest levels of government. They are then parsed by thousands of eager conspiracists, who go on to disseminate this purported knowledge in blogs, social media posts, YouTube videos, and email chains—carrying the word of God seeded in a figure they hold in near-divine reverence. In 2023, videos on far-right sites such as the YouTube alternative Rumble carried Christ directly into the heart of conspiracy theories: "The Hammer of Judgement, Demon Aliens, Volcanos and Hell ♥ Forecast by Jesus Christ ♥"; "Jesus says…Civil war is coming and it will be bloody…Pray for Donald Trump."

This kind of salvo, connecting public events, demons, and prophetic power, is something millions of American evangelicals find comfortingly familiar. It mirrors their childhood information diets, in which ministers cooked up apocalyptic predictions from Bible verses and spiritual warfare doctrine placed a demon on every shoulder. As the journalist and ex-evangelical Sam Thielman put it in 2020, many evangelicals grew up with a mindset that "takes metaphorical passages in the Bible and tries to decode them into both individual prophecies that refer directly to current events, as well as a larger meta-prophecy ending in the Rapture of believers to heaven, the coming of the Antichrist, and the battle of Armageddon."[10] No wonder they've taken so well to digital-era conspiracy theories: they were raised seeing signs and wonders, coded miracles, and tribulations. They just took it to social media and found a plethora of new souls to convert.

It's not just Facebook posts spreading the overheated gospel of the great child-snatching epidemic; in the summer of 2023, an unlikely indie hit movie called *Sound of Freedom*, subsidized by some six thousand right-wing donors contributing $501 each and distributed by the overtly Christian Angel Studios, utilized a well-known Q-adjacent film star, Jim Caviezel, to spread the word. *Sound of Freedom* earned an unusual $250 million worldwide—nearly unheard of for an indie flick—"largely on the strength of a marketing campaign encouraging religious audiences to not only attend the movie but 'pay it forward' by buying tickets for other people," according to an investigation by Vice.[11]

Caviezel has star power for Christian audiences in his own right. He's most famous for his role as Jesus in Mel Gibson's 2004 *The Passion of the Christ*, a depiction of Jesus' death widely critiqued for anti-Semitism, which reflected the wild-eyed, hard-right Catholicism of its director.

Since his turn as the Messiah, Caviezel has undergone a steady, erratic, and very public radicalization, eventually becoming the square-jawed, blue-eyed mouthpiece of America's most inflamed conspiracists. So he was a natural choice to give QAnon's lurid fantasies of child abduction the Hollywood treatment. In the movie, he plays Tim Ballard, a former special agent for the Department of Homeland Security and subsequent founder of Operation Underground Railroad, an anti-child-trafficking organization that claims to have rescued the downtrodden and enslaved all around the world. Ballard is a real person, but the film, naturally, allocates him tightly written, faith-inflected catchphrases, most notably "God's children are not for sale." (Sweatshirts with that slogan, however, are for sale on Angel Studios' website for the low price of $44.99.) The film is a simple story about a Christian hero busting up a Colombian child-trafficking ring, rescuing children with the steady gaze and high-cheekboned machismo of a warrior whose heart is pure. In the film's trailer, "My Country 'Tis of Thee," sung in haunting chorus by a little girl, undergirds scenes in which Caviezel's eyes shift from blue to green, lit by inner torment, and his gentle Christian wife (Mira Sorvino) urges him to quit his government job to go rescue those kids. It premiered, of course, on July 4. Just a few weeks later, Donald Trump hosted a screening of the film at his Trump National Golf Club Bedminster in New Jersey.[12] The film's marketers knew precisely who they were aiming at.

But the ruddy-faced, muscle-bound Ballard left Operation Underground Railroad around the time of the film's premiere—and ahead of an avalanche of bad press that nearly equaled the groundswell of hero worship from the film's devoted audience. Ballard's depictions of OUR's operations had, it seemed to those who began to investigate him more thoroughly, long been riddled with exaggerations; he was, perhaps, prone to the kind of self-made mythmaking that can add up to something that smells like a lie. OUR has, for example, employed the services of a psychic in conducting a raid on the Dominican Republic–Haitian border; its highly touted overseas rescue missions sometimes allegedly involve high-dollar donors' and volunteers' participation after slapdash training and, according to Vice's sources and accounts from former volunteers, allegedly require little by way of prior surveillance, communication with local authorities, or extensive care for putatively rescued trafficking victims.[13] More damningly, one of OUR's chief success stories was a raid that rescued a young woman from smugglers. But according to Vice's investigation, the young woman in question, who had been coerced into sex work and raped repeatedly for years between the ages of fourteen and seventeen, had, in fact, rescued herself: she had fled the trafficking ring on her own and didn't look back until it came time to testify against her abusers in federal court. That didn't stop Ballard and OUR—whose relationship with the young woman identified in court documents as "Liliana" was never clarified—from claiming that they had rescued her, a flat untruth; or claiming that she was from Central America, not Mexico; or exploiting her story in a series of op-eds, press conferences, and congressional testimonies by Ballard as the emotional center of his argument for the building of a border wall between the United States and Mexico. (When these reports were made public, OUR released a statement calling Vice's reporting "inaccurate" and "agenda-driven.") As to the millions of dollars that pour in to OUR, precisely how they are spent and where remains opaque.

An investigation by *Rolling Stone* added further layers to the rotted allium of questionable behavior surrounding *Sound of Freedom*; according to the magazine, Angel Studios is part of a complex web of financial ventures by a Mormon family, the Harmons, whose mission to crowdfund right-wing and religious movies has something of a shell game quality. Angel Studios' financial shenanigans "may violate financial regulations, and could invite scrutiny from either the Securities and Exchange Commission or the Federal Trade Commission," *Rolling Stone* wrote, a claim denied by Angel Studios. One thing is certain: all those donations meant to be for tickets to *Sound of Freedom*—the "pay it forward" scheme that rocketed the movie to the top echelon of indie films—didn't necessarily make it into the hands of impoverished but virtuous theatergoers ready for enlightenment. The fine print, on a separate Q&A page, revealed that Angel Studios was ready and willing to use any leftover cash from the $30 million it raised for "marketing," "credit card fees," and studio "overhead."[14] On the fundraiser page, baffled donors left question after question about when and how they would see financial returns on their investment. Some, however, were simply thrilled to be a part of a spectacle of untrammeled faith. "Whether it profits me financially it will profit me spiritually, investing in God, His Son Jesus and His Holy Spirit never leads to non-profit," commented Rose Marie Wolford, a donor, on the film's crowd-funding page in 2023.

Once the film made it to theaters, a curious phenomenon began to accompany the screenings: videos cropped up on TikTok, YouTube, Twitter, and Instagram claiming that the film had been beset by mysterious issues—and they smelled like suppression. There had been a strange smell in an AMC theater showing the movie; a screening had been delayed by fifteen minutes; one movie theater had been too cold, another too hot; in another screening, the volume had been so low as to be nearly inaudible. To an audience of avid conspiracy theorists who thought of the film as their personal triumph, any inconvenience could not be coincidental. It was deliberate suppression of the film that confirmed all their priors, all the stories told in overheated online forums and low-fi, droning videos on YouTube. The fact that the film earned some $250 million was immaterial; it was being suppressed by the enemies of truth, by the thieves of children. A strange smell in a theater where you are seeing *The Little Mermaid* is just too many spilled sodas or overexcited toddlers whose potty training is erratic. But if you're looking for a sign, if all you do is look for signs and omens, the smell of burned popcorn and filthy carpets becomes the smell of brimstone.[15]

In the febrile QAnon mindset spread by *Sound of Freedom* and a steady stream of online propaganda, child trafficking isn't just for sexual purposes. In an echo of the blood libel, one frequently cited theory among the QAnon community holds that global elites feel the need to procure so many children in order to harvest their blood. The children are sources of adrenochrome, a chemical whose derivative is sometimes used to stop hemorrhage and is readily available for purchase online. QAnon adherents posit that adrenochrome has potent hallucinatory effects (it doesn't) and is used by elites to ensure their immortality. Moreover, adrenochrome is "extracted from the pituitary glands of tortured children," in the words of one QAnon sage, in blood-drinking rituals dedicated to Satan.[16]

In the real world, Republican governors in Arkansas and a slew of other states have engaged in a steady campaign of rolling back child labor laws, despite the documented propensity for underage workers to be injured at much higher rates than their adult counterparts and despite any quaint notions that children shouldn't, for example, work for minimum wage at slaughterhouses. This doesn't seem to bother QAnon adherents or even register on their radar. If it's not hidden—if it's, in fact, signed into law by a grinning Sarah Huckabee Sanders surrounded by besuited children with the pale, scared faces of Victorian ghosts[17]—it might as well not exist. Children being hurt in public doesn't matter; the only important truths are secret.

Echoing this dichotomy, the Christian Right has set up a parallel, insular universe of homeschool curricula and legal defense groups that fundraise off fear—fear of gays, fear of trans people, fear of the Marxist dictatorships of social studies teachers in small-town America—and use the funds to enrich the coffers of churches that oftentimes are busy concealing sex abuse scandals of their own. It's easier, really, to believe in a cabal of satanic pedophiles running the government than to worry that your kid's youth pastor might be a predator. At the end of the day, what the sprawling right-wing economy sells is fear and the means to assuage it.

The idea of a secret cabal engaged in ritual is an important one to QAnon adherents, according to Julian Feeld, a cohost of the *QAnon Anonymous* podcast and a careful observer of the phenomenon. "Adrenochrome extraction and child trafficking, cannibalism and pedophilia are all part of an ancient cult, in their eyes, of elites consuming this blood for long life," he told me. "Ritual is central to their beliefs." He described attending a QAnon rally at which one speaker postulated that Hollywood Boulevard, as a whole, serves as an "adrenochrome shrine" and that the red carpet rolled out at industry events symbolizes the blood of sacrificed children.

All of this has precedents in the nocturnal ritual fantasy. "The basic idea is that a persistent delusion exists in European cultures that shadowy, conspiratorial groups gather together in secret to plot the overthrow of society," Dr. Michael Barbezat, a medieval and early modern historian and research fellow at Australian Catholic University, told me in an interview.

"As part of their plotting, the conspirators supposedly ritually abuse, murder, and consume innocent children."

The nocturnal ritual fantasy becomes dangerous when it is adopted by those with political power. "Historically, violent persecutions happen when accounts of satanic child abuse cults get taken up by political leaders," Barbezat noted. "Things happen when those with power become interested in the kinds of ideas these marginal thinkers are promoting or weaponize them. Often leaders have ulterior motives in their interest in these ideas."

The burning of witches, Jews, and heretics may feel long past; the stakes pulled up, the bones long crumbled into ash. But as the language of the mainstream Right continually ramps up into existential territory—with a popular Fox News host braying before the 2020 election that a Joe Biden win would mean that Trump supporters would literally be murdered, with "blood everywhere";[18] Trump's campaign rhetoric becoming ever more violent, decrying immigrants as "poisoning the blood of our country" and predicting a "bloodbath" if he fails to be elected in 2024[19]—it's difficult to overlook the utility of a movement that already casts the world in stark, Manichaean terms. Since the 2020 election and the insurrection that succeeded it, that language—and accompanying actions—has only become more heated, and the utility of the fringe only more pronounced, as yet another tangled election stretches its kraken limbs over the country.

The question that underlies the nocturnal ritual fantasy is: Who benefits? In the case of QAnon, which depicts the Republican presidential nominee as a god-emperor locked in perpetual battle against unimaginable evils, the answer is simple. It is easier to imagine violent predation by political opponents—and perhaps unleash vengeance against them—when you already believe that they consort with demons and drink the blood of children for amusement. Imagine enough blood, and you may be inclined to go spill some; or if not inclined to spill blood, to donate as much money as you can to ensure good triumphs. Victory over the Devil is worth more than anything, and it requires full coffers.

Much like the alt-right before it, which faded into obscurity as its white supremacist ideals hit the Republican mainstream and were comfortably absorbed into it, QAnon may be something of a victim of its own success. The researcher Alex Kaplan at Media Matters for America kept track of no fewer than 107 candidates for Congress in the 2020 election who "have endorsed or given credence to the conspiracy theory or promoted QAnon content."[20] Most of them lost on the federal level, although QAnon endorsers were elected to local, state, and municipal offices around the country in droves, taking advantage of low turnout. In 2022, even more candidates who openly endorsed QAnon ideas about blood, hellfire, and the New World Order—supercharged by the conspiratorial fever that gripped the nation during the covid-19 pandemic—ran for national office, mostly without success.[21] But as a *New York Times* report on the 2022 elections put it, QAnon's ideas had transcended their origin; even if open embrace of conspiracy was too gauche for voters, some elements of QAnon had become party orthodoxy, particularly when it came to the belief that the 2020 presidential election was illegitimate. "On the campaign trail, Republican candidates avoid talking about the idea that a cabal of pedophiles is preying on children, a core tenet of QAnon. But they embrace false claims that liberals 'groom' children with progressive sex education. When criticizing covid-19 restrictions, many Republicans riff on QAnon's belief that a 'deep state' of bureaucrats and politicians wants to control Americans," *Times* reporter Stuart Thompson wrote. "The most prominent talking point with echoes of QAnon, though, is the false claim that the 2020 presidential election was stolen from Mr. Trump. The movement pushed that idea long before any votes were cast, and before Mr. Trump catapulted the claim to the mainstream."[22]

The "deep state," a term for malevolent, secret officials buried deep within governmental infrastructure that has been popularized by QAnon, had interfered, injustice had been done in secret, and the election of Joe Biden was fraudulent. Entire seething ecosystems of conspiratorial belief sprang up around state vote counts and individual election officials, driven by an apophenic determination to turn the mass of banal details that make up an election in a democracy of hundreds of millions of people into a pattern of wrongdoing. QAnon's iconography and its more outlandish claims are recherché enough to shrug off, but its core—the idea that a wrong has been done in secret and can be rectified only by Donald Trump and his believers—has only grown.

In the four years since Trump went down swinging, belief that the 2020 election was stolen has jumped from the conspiracy fringe to the Republican mainstream like a blaze over a firebreak and found plenty of fuel. In the 2022 election, candidates who openly professed QAnon-style beliefs were few, but those who were, in the parlance of pundits, "election deniers," were legion. In the 2024 elections, with Donald Trump himself at the helm, still more are bound to follow the line that isn't quite the Republican official creed but hovers just underneath, animating the crowd.

The true power of QAnon has always been in the massive scale of its zealous constituency—along with those who might sympathize, fellow-travel, or simply find, in the warm embrace of fellow conspiracists, a substitute for fellowship and community rare enough in a postpandemic, isolated, digitally fractured society. Even if the movement has become so big and chaotic that it may no longer profitably be called QAnon—the movement having eaten itself and gone on to devour others in the bargain—it's a mindset, one of determined, blazing belief that the world has gone wrong in very specific and very hidden ways that only a true "researcher" knows; it's believing in 5G radiation causing plagues, in powerful people drinking child blood, in the evils of vaccines, in the necessity of having an arsenal and homestead of your very own for the inevitable moment when everything goes to hell. And of course, it's about paying out handsome sums to the purveyors of safety: the apocalypse meal kits, the shelter salesmen, the ambient fug of merchandise whose sales hook is terror. It's knowing that when Hell comes to visit you'll be ready, even if you're armed only with foreknowledge. It's knowing who your enemies are and that there are an awful lot of them. Against the broader backdrop of the movement's mass appeal, QAnon's truly terrifying potential is still untapped—namely, what its followers might be induced to do, or do on their own, in order to act against the ultimate and shocking evil they are perennially discovering and rediscovering.

"I think of it as a civilization eating its own vomit," Barbezat told me. "These kinds of accusations make excellent weapons for those trying to remake the world."

The accusations are spreading, hastened by a digital world tailor made to spread lurid disinformation far more swiftly and widely than truth can travel. Facebook posts about human trafficking, the locus of a broader, socially acceptable moral panic, one that feeds steadily into QAnon's darker intimations, are shared far and wide, with no vetting of their improbable statistics. In June 2020, a viral claim that New York's Central Park was host to some thirty-five thousand malnourished, caged children kept in underground tunnels spread over Facebook. The source of the claim was a man named Timothy Holmseth, who purports to be affiliated with the nonexistent "Pentagon Pedophile Task Force." Holmseth claimed to be an integral part of the Trump administration, with no apparent supporting evidence. "There is ONE MAN between Timothy Holmseth and President Trump," reads Holmseth's bio on his website—which also features donation links on PayPal, Zelle, and the far-right Christian fundraising site GiveSendGo.[23]

All over social media, QAnon followers prayed for the mole children. They wrote them poetry. They were convinced that the mole children were being treated in Central Park's coronavirus field hospital or spirited away to the military hospital ship USNS *Comfort*. No one with authority would admit that they had known about the mole children, but the QAnon followers knew. The mole children had been rescued by the forces of good. The fight was ongoing, and they were part of it. They had become an online army for the spirit war, a struggle that preceded the development of QAnon but that nonetheless welcomed the flood of new recruits; the dour, paranoiac mood was perfect fodder for a doctrine that cast its acolytes as part of a perpetual and titanic spiritual struggle.

"We are facing greater spiritual battles today than ever before," wrote Benny Hinn of the eponymous—and cash-flush—Benny Hinn Ministries that year. "There has been a release of demonic activity on earth during the past few months—unseen in world history. And it should be no surprise that we will undoubtedly witness an even greater release of darkness over the coming months." Donations to Hinn's antidemonic forces have a suggested minimum of $25, but you can donate $300 with one click.[24]

Trump himself has coyly and not so coyly cozied up to a movement that conveniently views him as a supernatural savior figure with the power to hide codes in clocks and rescue trafficked children—and even more conveniently, potentially show up as a supportive mob. He has certainly leaned into the Red Scare elements that underlie much of American right-wing conservative paranoia, while crudely sowing skepticism about the integrity of the American justice system and the country's elections. After being indicted on charges of felony racketeering and conspiracy to defraud the United States in Fulton County, Georgia, in August 2023, Trump sent out a missive to the millions of people on his mailing list, positioning himself as a beleaguered champion prepared to do battle with the godless Commie hordes. It read, in part:

Our once free Republic where citizens were presumed innocent until proven guilty is gone.

In its place is a Marxist Third World dictatorship led by an incompetent yet crooked tyrant who tries to place your fate in the hands of vengeful and corrupt prosecutors.

Communism has finally reached America's shores...

I WILL **NEVER SURRENDER** our country to these radical tyrants who seek to destroy it.

"CONTRIBUTE $250 >>," read one of the large red donation buttons beneath the text.

Trump's was the mug shot heard around the world, and in concert with his words it was designed to force his supporters into action.

Adherents to QAnon and analogous movements are perfervid Trump supporters by necessity, as Trump's valiant battle against ultimate evil

forms the spine from which the many limbs of the conspiracy grow. While
the initial flock were largely Republican and right leaning, during the frenetic early years of the covid-19 pandemic, there was a wave of new émi-
grés into the Q landscape. New Age moms and influencers with previously
vaguer politics have migrated from crystals and wellness to taking down
a world-straddling cabal of demonic pedophiles. Sound healers, crystal
enthusiasts, and Reiki practitioners began, suddenly, to post about "saving
the children," the New World Order, the Devil, and Donald Trump, a
phenomenon so pronounced that in 2020, a collection of yoga teachers
and leaders in the yoga community joined together to make an Instagram
statement against the penetration of violent conspiracy theorists into the
wellness influencer space, protesting that "Qanon does NOT represent
the true values of the wellness community."[25] Antivaccination beliefs and
consequent conspiracy theories about a hypothetical covid-19 vaccine provided a gateway to QAnon in many of these cases: the twin conspiracies
merged seamlessly into the broad, sprawling whole. In the years since, the
motley group of travelers down the rabbit hole of conspiracy has grown—
and become both more radicalized and more isolated from the outside
world.

The enveloping umbrella of self-declared "truth seekers," as conspiracists often identify themselves, is broad enough to shelter a great variety of beliefs, from alien landings to a flat earth to the power of prayer
to liberate captive child slaves. Its power comes from its vagueness, the
sense that any secret knowledge, any willingness to "research the truth"
(doing "research" means trawling the conspiracy swamps of the internet),
is enough for entry into a club of those who know that only what is hidden is true and the simplest of explanations are the most suspicious.

In this parallel universe, pedophiles are everywhere: in the highest echelons of government and business, in Hollywood, ensconced in foster care
homes and gas station parking lots. The number of children kidnapped and
abused by the cabal, in the statistics that cram the garish graphics passed
around on social media, typically measure in the hundreds of thousands
per annum, orders of magnitude higher than law enforcement statistics

bear out. One popular figure posits that 916 children go missing per hour in the United States, a total of just over 8 million per year—or around 10 percent of the entire child population of the United States. You might think that if one in ten children in the United States were kidnapped each year, you might have heard of it. If so, according to QAnon adherents, you are naive about how much the government hushes it up. And if the government were hushing it up, paying blood prices to all those grieving parents, one would perhaps wonder where such an impregnable interagency initiative might come from, since this kind of watertight bureaucracy has never existed in any other area of the US and indeed perhaps any other national government; even the Stasi and the KGB left traces, the ghosts of Black Marias sailing up Moscow streets like sharks.

Among the many issues with QAnon's obsession with children is the fact that sex trafficking doesn't operate by the playbook they imagine. In the QAnon conception, child abduction happens when malevolent strangers, possessed by lust and/or the Devil, pluck innocent girls and boys from the clutches of their parents in grocery store parking lots and use them for nefarious purposes. In this worldview, every stranger is a potential threat, every public outing a potential stage for tragedy. It's a mindset that makes you advocate for concealed carry; it makes you clutch your kids with an iron grip; and it makes you look askance at anything remotely resembling a threat, such as a van parking too close to your car, someone with a dodgy-looking tattoo, or anyone speaking to you in public at all. If all this sounds familiar, it's because moral panics never really die, they only hibernate. The QAnon mindset is really a warmed-over variant of the "Stranger Danger" moral panic that first made public spaces a fraught world of moral hazard in the 1980s, a misguided public awareness campaign that made parents look frenetically outward for those who would harm their kids.

The trouble is that according to sex trafficking survivors[26] and their advocates, the vast majority of human trafficking simply doesn't work that way. Most people who are coerced or forced into sex trafficking are victimized within their own milieu: by boyfriends, parents, relatives, older acquaintances. Sex trafficking and child sexual abuse can strike within picket-fenced suburban homes and at the glowing white children of the conspiratorial imagination, but they are far more likely to affect people from impoverished backgrounds, those who suffer abuse at home, those whose vulnerability is built in from birth. They don't have to look like someone kidnapped by a stranger from a parking lot; in fact, they almost never do.

Still, the absence of a plague of missing children doesn't bother the believers. You could bounce pennies off their faith—or get them to spend quite a lot of dollars to fight it, if you are so inclined.

National statistics and nonprofit organizations that actually deal with human trafficking and aid its victims are not much use in a fight against someone who persistently believes that the only truths are the ones that are hidden and thus immune to fact-checking. Drawn by the lure of the truth that is hidden tantalizingly out of reach, seemingly normal suburban women spread Facebook memes and TikToks about securing their cars against abduction, about the elaborate military-style precautions they take to prevent their children from being kidnapped—a cinematic variety of fear that significantly alters their day-to-day lives, based on years of continually spreading conspiracy theories. So the wild overestimation of child abductions continues and runs around the world so fast that the truth gives up and goes back to bed.

As the apotheosis of this conspiratorial sprawl, Trump's politics are a raft of promises, most often of vengeance and so riddled with conspiracy that they can often be used as the launch point for subgrifts among his acolytes. Take his famous border wall, for example; a grift that grew off its unlaid stones like a parasitic vine was one of the most illustrative tales of the Trump presidency and its associated money-hungry leeches. The scam started with GoFundMe, a good place to raise a few bucks. "We Build the Wall" was a crowdfunded effort to fulfill Donald Trump's signature campaign promise. ("We're going to do a wall; we're going to have a big, fat beautiful door on the wall; we're going to have people come in, but they're going to come in legally.") Helmed by human yeast infection and slovenly right-wing ideologue Steve Bannon, the Colorado businessman Timothy

Shea, and the charismatic triple amputee Brian Kolfage, among others, it raised more than $25 million in 2028 for a big, fat, beautiful publicly funded monument to racism. Figures such as Tim Ballard, the former CEO of OUR; and Matt Hagee, whose Christian bona fides were flawless, were bellowing for the wall. "Borders are a blessing...We serve a God of order, not chaos," wrote Hagee in a sermon on his ministry's website, entitled "The Blessing of a Border." That aegis of authority, the knowledge that the border wall was a symbol of necessary order in a world growing ever more chaotic, helped the groundswell of support—and money, by digital transfer and checks in spidery elderly writing sent to a PO box and deposited very quickly—find its home.

The advisory board was populated with a murderer's row of MAGA-world's showiest detritus, habitués of right-wing conference stages, whose gaudiness of affect is surmounted only by their acrid ideology: Erik Prince, the rich-kid mercenary king of Blackwater;[27] the militantly anti-immigrant Kansas attorney general Kris Kobach; former Milwaukee sheriff David Clarke, under whose supervision jail inmates died at three times the national average[28] and who walks about with a Muammar Gaddhafi–style wall of medals pinned to his chest; and more flotsam from the shoals of misery. Needless to say, Prince, Kobach, Clarke, Kolfage, and Bannon all define themselves as faithful Christians as an essential part of their public image.

They built just under five miles of wall so rickety that a "series of gashes" appeared in the structure; and, according to ProPublica, the stretch of bollards that constituted the only physical manifestation of We Build the Wall was in danger of toppling into the Rio Grande.[29]

Where did the money go? How much wall can $25 million really build? The answer to that is still unclear, although bizarre side endeavors—such as spreading rumors that a butterfly sanctuary was being used for human trafficking after said sanctuary objected to the wall—probably didn't help the cause.

Also not helpful? The hundreds of thousands of dollars siphoned into the pockets of just a few guys, who became the subjects of a criminal case.

Kolfage, whose prior endeavors included harvesting emails via inflammatory fake news articles[30] and calling Barack Obama a "halfbreed" on Facebook, initially told his Instagram followers that he'd been indicted for being a "major threat to the globalist agenda to have mass migration into the U.S." In April 2023, he was sentenced to four years in prison for "defrauding hundreds of thousands of donors" and taking $350,000 for his own personal use, despite having publicly pledged not to take "a penny" from the efforts to build the wall.

Andrew Badolato, a ham-faced Florida finance guy who once allegedly ratted a Mafia loan shark out to the FBI,[31] likewise pleaded guilty and was sentenced to three years in prison.[32]

Steve Bannon, whose arrest dramatically took place on a Chinese billionaire's luxury yacht off the coast of Connecticut, was pardoned by Donald Trump in the last few hours of his presidency. Presidential pardons cover only the federal judiciary, however; Bannon still faces New York State charges over We Build the Wall—and, as of this writing, will be tried for allegedly defrauding donors of $15 million. The reason this case feels so novel is because of the elite impunity running rampant across the country's upper economic echelons. The felons and accused felons in question weren't extraordinary except in terms of the publicity they generated. This sort of scam along smaller lines is practically omnipresent in a bullish culture of bootstraps and self-salesmanship, and tribalism based around fear and loathing offers an excellent jump start to any con.

The signature, fizzing mix of strong emotions that constitute Trumpism may originate from its figurehead, but unlike prosperity, it has a tendency to trickle down. The world of MAGA is a chaotic assortment of individuals who work day and night to capture that fizz, even to bottle it.

There's a Trump-themed Red Bull–esque beverage called Winning Energy, whose shabby aura is the quintessence of the MAGA aesthetic. Its website's home page has the vibe of a Klan meeting with a cash bar, a seedy lounge singer covering "Deutschland über Alles," gilt that comes off on your fingers, a $999 deal on a late-night infomercial with the volume cranked all the way up. The can says its ingredients are liberal tears, but the label adds glucuronalactone and pantothenic acid. Very thin women in bikinis hold up the beverage in promo photos; it's endorsed by an evangelical rapper and a graying male YouTuber whose videos include "Basic Bitches 101." Winning Energy promises to help you kick "Sleepy Joe" syndrome, and it comes in a sugar-free edition. Its founder is Timothy Shea, who is currently in prison for the We Build the Wall grift.

Are Kolfage, Bannon, and Shea true believers? Do they really spend their lives dreaming about infrastructure-based ways to terrorize migrants, or is it all just for the money? Did they betray their principles by their theft, and does it matter if those principles were worth betraying? Does the fact that the thousands of donors didn't see this coming indicate a much broader culture of right-wing grift? Of prominent hate figures—not just the pure fraudsters but also the demagogues and politicians such as Donald Trump; the UK professional racist Stephen Yaxley-Lennon, aka Tommy Robinson; and the snake-oil tycoon Alex Jones—the question is often asked: Do they sincerely believe all this shit—or are they just trying to make a buck?

The answer is yes. These two motivations coexist more naturally than you'd think and are often tough to tease apart. The desire to gull cash out of a public with shared sadistic inclinations pervades the right-wing activist sphere. Peeking into MAGAworld reveals a kind of carny quality: everything feels cheap and thinly drawn, the collective touchstones (the loathing of immigrants, vengefulness, Christian patriotism, a generalized miasma of racism) are gestured to in perfunctory ways, the products and people are filmed lightly with sweat. It's America, and everybody has to hustle to make a living.

Inevitably, in the daily sordid grind of capitalism, the choices we make soil us. But some routes to a dollar are more befouling than others. We all sell something—our time, our bodies, our words—but it's the choice to sell hatred and its associated products that really coats the soul in spray tan. This is, of course, not a new phenomenon—the second iteration of the KKK was arguably a robe-sales MLM—it just has Instagram now, it's coming to you live, and the saturation level is 100 percent.

The contemporary right-wing hustle is all full-color cartoons rendered unwittingly grotesque, like those on Winning Energy's bottles. As fitting as it seems that MAGAworld wants to sell you a cup of tears, the company's caffeine-infused kitsch hardly reaches the penny-ante stage of Trumpy hucksterism. In July 2023, Shea was sentenced to sixty-three months in prison for conspiracy to commit wire fraud and money laundering. (In a kind of grifter ouroboros, the *New York Times* reported that tens of thousands of dollars were routed from the We Build the Wall cash pool to Winning Energy, most of which was used to purchase around fifty thousand cans of the drink.)[33]

Tracing the outlines of Christian Right grifts is easy enough. One relatively obscure publication—*Not the Bee*, the sister, more serious news site associated with the right-wing Christian humor publication the *Babylon Bee*—offers plenty in its newsletters. The headlines of the paid advertisements the publication sends out to its subscribers are a stark and evocative demonstration of all the ways fear, faith, and empathy can be ruthlessly channeled for monetary gain. None of these companies have been convicted of any crime, to my knowledge; preying on fear is not illegal, nor is providing false comfort for it. The machinations of the right-wing cash machine operate within the laws of man and the laws of nature, tapping into primal fear for cash.

A sampling of emails sent throughout 2023: "Beware the Digital Dollar: Unveiling Its Terrifying Realities!" reads an advertisement from Allegiance Gold, LLC.

"Your gift will save preborn babies," reads one ad for Focus on the Family. "In the coming weeks, thousands of confused, fearful women will face the most terrifying decision imaginable: whether to choose life for their unborn baby. That's why Focus on the Family is working hard to reach them with 'proof of life'—the truth about the precious life that grows within them. Right now, just $60 can save the life of a preborn baby!"

Another: "These ministries are being targeted for their faith," from the Alliance Defending Freedom, a far-right national Christian legislative organization. "Ministries are being attacked because they seek to live out the Gospel and refuse to compromise their faith and God-given mission…The requests for legal help keep pouring in. We need the help of friends like you to stand against this growing hostility toward religious liberty."

Another: "Our country is crumbling before our very eyes. While you can't fix it on your own, **you can prepare for what's coming**. But if you put it off any longer, it will be too late. My Patriot Supply has helped *millions* of families prepare for emergencies. Yours is no exception. Whether you're a seasoned survivalist or *just* starting your journey, their 3-Month Emergency Food Kit is a crucial building block for your preparedness stockpile." (Incidentally, the kit is $600 and offers several buckets of shelf-stable, horrifying-looking slop.)

And on and on: appeals to the conscience, to the heart, to God, and always a gurgling wellspring of fear that leads straight to the wallet. The means of an apparent scam are just as important as its ends, and the viability of a $25 million campaign to keep Mexicans at bay or to funnel funds into stopping Democrats from drinking children's blood is dependent on the broader well of hatred submersed in the public id. Siphoning from that basin of vitriol is an art suited to every kind of seeming scammer: prophets and purveyors of potions and supplements and weight loss gizmos, the born-again and the beatified and the beautiful, conspiracists of every stripe, all the base and wretched of the earth.

It's so close that you can literally reach out and touch it. There is an entire right-wing economy that works selling nationalism-branded, fear-tinged products that serve as both tribal emblems and defiant blows against a world controlled by "woke," venomous, liberal cabals. This ranges from soap—Right Wing Naturals offers nine "masculine" scents "approved by patriots"—to razors from Jeremy's in "socialism-resistant" bags, "so you don't have to cut away your values every time you shave your face." You can obtain Black Rifle Coffee's AK-47 espresso roast for $15.99 for twelve ounces, complete with a skull and a flag on its packaging in case anyone doubts your anti–gun control stance early in the morning. When Bud Light had a trans influencer promote its beer, setting off a right-wing fracas, a tanned, muscular right winger named Seth Weathers stepped up and offered a transphobia-friendly buzz, selling Conservative Dad's ULTRA RIGHT 100% Woke-Free Beer ("America's been drinking beer from a company that doesn't even know which restroom to use"). You can buy America First cheese and blueberries from Patriot Foods and batteries from Interstate Batteries—"our Purpose (to glorify God)"—whose "community partners" include a women's clinic rife with misinformation about abortion. You can buy "pro-life, pro-family, pro-constitution" protein bars from MuscleUp. And so on—each branded with anger, opposition, defiance, and just enough nimble web design to seem reliable. It's a staggering "parallel economy," as Kathryn Joyce put it in a New Republic article,[34] one built on a desire for quick cash as much as a sense of being righteously aggrieved. Perhaps the two are inextricable.

As I type this, somewhere in America someone is clicking on a cash-for-gold link buried in a listserv email they received because they once donated to Mike Huckabee; and that person may be a senior or an impoverished person or a ruddy-faced boat owner of the American gentry or may be in on the scheme. There is nothing in this country not driven by money in some form or fashion, and hate is a perpetual-motion machine of profit. There's a great gaudy armature of mammon built around it, rickety enough to topple into the Rio Grande, slick as liberals' tears. As Rick Perlstein put it in a seminal 2012 piece on the right-wing direct-mail sales phenomenon that has come to embody and consume conservative ideology in the United States, "It's not really useful, or possible, to specify a break point where the money game ends and the ideological one begins. They are two facets of the same coin—where the con selling 23-cent miracle cures for heart disease inches inexorably into the one selling minuscule marginal tax rates as the miracle cure for the nation itself. The proof is in the pitches—the come-ons in which the ideological and the transactional share the exact same vocabulary, moral claims, and cast of heroes and villains."[35]

Sometimes enough willing, fervid people can change the world. Sometimes the reason for stirring up genocidal sentiment lies at the bottom of an empty pocket. Both can be true at the same time. Either way, the bollards stand lonely on the border, the hate laws keep rolling out of legislatures, the boot presses at the throat, the brutes cash out. As surely as the turning of one year and the dawning of a new one, a sucker's born every day; meat loves salt, and grift loves hate.

There are two material pieces to a con, the con man and the mark, and the puzzle is figuring out how they fit together. The dance of deception requires two partners at least; without its supporting blocks, a pyramid scheme would crumble; a siren song dies in the throat when there's no one there to hear it. They say you can never fool an honest man, but honesty can mean an honest faith that a demagogue has a direct line to God, that Christ desires a white-led America, that God chooses strange instruments and one of them is Donald Trump. Perhaps it's easier to fool an honest man, after all, as long as his honest zeal is strong enough to strike sparks from.

For obvious reasons, most accounts of deception focus on the scammers, from the excitement of watching someone get away with bad things to the inherent thrill of deceit. Think of that little masterpiece *Catch Me If You Can*, with Leonardo DiCaprio eeling his way through a glamorized version of the con man Frank Abagnale Jr.'s, life story: witnessing a man painstakingly fabricate credential after credential, fake his way through the most august of professions on cojones alone creates a thrumming little spike in one's adrenaline, even from the safety of a movie theater seat. Less inspiring than the slick figure in the rented uniform, perhaps, is the sucker who takes the bait: some schmo hoping for a quick buck, a little love, or a cure for whatever ails him. Faith is just as crucial a component of the swindle as anything else, the cruel coda to the story of Pandora's box. What we hope for can hurt us as badly as anything else.

"Cons thrive in times of transition and fast change, when new things are happening and the old ways of looking at the world no longer suffice," wrote Maria Konnikova in *The Confidence Game*, which examines the psychology and history of con artistry. "That's why they thrive during revolutions, wars and political upheavals...There's nothing a con artist likes better than exploiting the sense of unease we feel when it appears the world as we know it is about to change."[36]

Thus arose the proliferation of scams around the gold rush in 1848, the relentless westward expansion of the United States, the various transformations of the Industrial Revolution. One of the biggest financial rackets in the nation's history involved Crédit Mobilier of America, a sham corporation established to help build the transcontinental railroad a century and a half ago. Transition begets unease, unease begets a desire for certainty, and the more frenetic that desire, the more even the appearance of suavity and confidence wins unearned trust and creates ill-gotten gains. Religion is a balm in times of transition, too; it is tribulation that begets gods and prophets, and all that faith streams toward some figure of authority who feels inclined to cup it in his spray-tanned hands.

What makes contemporary right-wing con jobs such stellar examples of this axiom is that the politics they exploit are the direct result of a fear of change. Conservatives as a whole skew older and whiter than the population at large, and so they tend to consider themselves the people who have the most to lose from societal shifts. In the evangelical Christian community, this fear is enhanced by a communitywide persecution complex: an indoctrination from birth to believe that the Christian Right is perpetually under siege by a nefarious secular culture that is out to deprive them of their religious freedom, one that hates Christians on principle with as much senseless malice as the lions in the Colosseum that were set on the Christians of old.

This position offers an inherent vulnerability to fearmongering about the future. It's particularly oriented around an overt hostility to new generations' threatening mores, from interracial relationships to subversion of gender norms to a tendency toward socialism. In an age in which the dog whistle has largely been abandoned in favor of the bullhorn, there is a great deal of money to be made in the scapegoating industry and still more in the arena of the alleged great fight for the soul of Western civilization.

This vulnerability also forms the spine of the robust beast of conservative grievance, a superstructure that is perfectly happy to fan fears of antiwhite racism, baselessly accuse gay and trans schoolteachers and children's book authors of pedophilia, and make a bundle while doing so. This is a multimillion-dollar industry, and it isn't an overt grift per se, just a series of newsletters, publications, and odious social media gurus such as Chaya Raichik (better known as Libs of TikTok) who go around making the lives of that day's selected targets for ire (teachers and journalists, usually) miserable, danger-filled, or both. Of course, all of this is just the long, cheap penumbra of the great grift, the one that goes to the very top: the one that seeks power and money and sees them as synonyms, and uses fear and faith as marketing copy to attain its goals.

It's always easier to focus on the con man than the mark. But to ignore the mark, the people from whom flow the endless font of willing belief and ready cash, is to ignore a shiver rippling across the nation's flesh. It's the restless ire of those who ceaselessly, insatiably hunger to justify their bigotry and their fear; those who want above all else to be soothed by a sense of righteousness. They believe themselves to be persecuted and are willing to pay to manufacture evidence of that persecution. They believe themselves to be seated at the right hand of God or at any rate somewhere in his general beneficent vicinity. They are legion and have deep pockets, and industries have sprung up around them, from the Florida Keys to Southern California and in myriad less sunny places in between. They are as inevitable as the progress of a railroad; they march through like steel tracks, scarring the landscape as they go.

How you feel about all this depends in part on your definition of grift: Are overtly fraudulent claims required, or do vibes-based grievances suffice as a premise for fundraising? Do sham products have to be rustled up, Ponzi schemed, castles built on clouds, or is the mere fundamental misrepresentation of reality enough to qualify as a scam? If the former, the American Right is riddled with enough supplements that turn you blue or claim to make your brain function at wizard level to more than do the job. If the latter, well...there seems to be no bottom at all.

The commonality in all this is fear: the sensation of it, the stoking of it, the rage it generates. Like any strong emotion, fear creates an opening. To interrogate the mark, we have to track backward from the con. The person who seeks mushroom powder to secure immortality, the person preparing for a war against the Devil, the person who damns his country as full of delusional dog people is a fearful one and a rageful one. It's someone who fits Konnikova's definition of a mark perfectly: filled to the skin with unease at change and ready to drown all skepticism in the assurances of others.

Fear isn't sexy; it doesn't make copy as juicy as scams. But it is a motive force as strong as lust, as ubiquitous as hunger. It also transmutes easily into anger in an emotional alchemy that hides vulnerability beneath a carapace of rage. The marks of right-wing cons will empty their bank accounts to the last penny in an effort to try to make the earth stand still—and this is true, on vastly differing scales, of small-dollar and billionaire donors alike. Still, the world doesn't stand still; it never has. Even the prophet Joshua got the sun to pause in the sky for only a day and only once.

Religious faith can be a balm to the soul, a healer of the heart, a way to push back at the ever-present knowledge of mortality. It can also be a door through which con men slip if they speak the right language of belief, of war, of the unholiness of social change. And terror is a gap so wide that even the clumsiest of grifters can stroll right through it, carrying a hatful of promises, a sack of black seeds to plant in the fear-lush heart.

CHAPTER 3

PROPHETS IN THE PARLOR

Writing about the American Right without Christianity is like rendering the *Mona Lisa* without her eyes or creating a cup without a bottom. Christian viewpoints and principles, and the structures and social impetus of religion, are that central to it.

Yet religion in America has always been an unwieldy thing, full of fire and blood, driven by divine inspiration, by revelation that has often enough shifted the course of world events. This has been true since the very beginning of this country and even before.

Many of the settlers who arrived here in the 1600s were fleeing the religious turmoil of the English Civil War; some were Puritans, others were members of various millenarian sects. The blood-soaked soil of these colonies has, from their earliest days, been fertile ground for faith, the wilder the better. So many fruits were pillaged from the New World—tomatoes, avocados, pineapples—while other, stranger fruit took root here that have left their mark upon the world. Mormonism, Scientology, and Seventh-day Adventism all started here, alongside much smaller groups. For some movements, such as the Branch Davidians or the People's Temple—cults that wound up massacred by the US government or engaged in mass suicide, respectively—the wounds they inflict become visible only when tragedy erupts.

But even within the mainstream of American evangelical Christianity, with its tens of millions of adherents, a feral and barely constrained violence with the ardor of prophecy seems perennially on the verge of breaking through. A vivid example is an event series called FlashPoint Live, run by a charismatic Christian group that includes wealthy, well-coiffed, famous televangelists such as Kenneth Copeland as well as Christian Right celebrity speakers such as Mike Lindell, a Trump adviser and the CEO of the company MyPillow. Since 2021, huge crowds at FlashPoint Live events have adopted a chilling credo called the "Watchman Decree," which asserts, in part, "We are God's ambassadors and spokespeople over the earth...because of our covenant with God, we are equipped and delegated by Him to destroy every attempted advance of the enemy. We have been given the legal power from heaven and now exercise our authority."[1]

The basis of why Christianity holds such power and why the faithful do the things they do in the name of God has its roots in a very human hunger—one that transcends this country and even this millennium. It's a desire that goes back to the mists of prehistory, the Upper Paleolithic age. The hunger to believe, to understand the world, is built into our blood, and it has a power of its own. It is the drive to seek—and to be led.

One issue that divides faithful Christians is a theological matter that may at first seem abstruse: whether Christ will return *before* the prophesied "Millennium," a thousand-year Golden Age of Christian rule on Earth—the doctrine of premillennialism—or afterward, the doctrine of postmillennialism. The theologian Loraine Boettner explained postmillennialism as follows: "The kingdom of God is now being extended in the world through the preaching of the gospel and the saving work of the Holy Spirit in the hearts of individuals, that the world eventually is to be Christianized and that the return of Christ is to occur at the close of a long period of righteousness and peace commonly called the millennium."[2] Postmillennial eschatology dictates that Christians must establish Jesus' kingdom on Earth through continual spiritual intervention and "Christianizing" of the world in order to attain the bliss of the Second Coming. It is this belief that powers the Christian nationalists of America, who believe that they are, in spreading and mandating Christian doctrine, acting as the agents of God's return. Their reading of the Lord's Prayer is literal: when they say "Thy will be done on Earth as it is in Heaven," they mean that they are the ones elected to carry it out.

As in other social movements, an extreme fringe prepared to enact violence works in concert with a much broader mainstream, working toward policy change at the local and national levels. Driven as they are by a supernatural zeal, this effort has been tremendously successful—and its effects are felt, whether we know it consciously or not, in every fraught arena of our nation's public life. Eschatology is a potent lens, one that imbues every action with end-of-the-world urgency. The fundamentalist contingent of evangelicals believe that Scripture is inerrant, each word perfected by God, and engage in a continual application of these texts to current events—a model that serves as an engine of ascendant theocracy.

When Donald Trump came to power, many evangelicals, including members of his own cabinet, which consisted in large part of members of the Christian Right, saw in him an echo of a figure presaged in biblical prophecy, the reincarnation of a monarch who had lived more than two millennia before. As foretold in the prophecies of Isaiah, that figure was Cyrus the Great, the emperor of Persia, who in the year 538 BC granted the return of exiled Jews to their homeland of Israel and enabled the building of the Second Temple. Cyrus was, in the words of the *Christian Courier*, "a pagan in sentiment and practice, yet...an unconscious tool in the hands of the Lord."[3]

Seeing in Donald Trump a return of Cyrus, the heathen who would become God's instrument, was a popular view among evangelicals leading up to and after Donald Trump's 2016 election. In the countdown to the 2016 presidential election, when a tape was released revealing a series of lewd comments Trump had made during the filming of the TV show *Access Hollywood*, including his now-infamous assertion that he could "grab [women] by the pussy," evangelical leaders doubled down on the comparison. In 2017, the prophet Lance Wallnau told the Christian

Broadcasting Network that God had visited him and explicitly made the analogy, citing Isaiah 45:1, which references Cyrus as the Lord's "anointed." "I heard the Lord say, 'Donald Trump is a wrecking ball to the spirit of political correctness,'" Wallnau told the TV station. "After I met him I heard the Lord say, 'Isaiah 45 will be the 45th president.' I go check it out; Isaiah 45 is Cyrus."[4] Cyrus was an agent of the restoration of God's kingdom; so, too, would Trump be, and evangelicals voted for him twice in great numbers.

The view that Trump had been chosen by God as an imperfect instrument, a vessel of prophetic fulfillment, continued throughout his first term and beyond. In November 2019, the fervent evangelical Rick Perry, a former governor of Texas and then secretary of energy in charge of the nation's nuclear arsenal, explained on the morning show *Fox & Friends* that he believed Donald Trump to be chosen by God. "I actually gave the president a little one-pager on those Old Testament kings about a month ago and I shared it with him," he said. "I said, 'Mr. President, I know there are people that say you said you were the chosen one' and I said, 'You were'...If you're a believing Christian, you understand God's plan for the people who rule and judge over us on this planet in our government." Pete Hegseth, a host, concurred, adding, "Followers of the president hear the attacks in the media about who he is and his background and they dismiss it, and say, God has used imperfect people forever, because we're all imperfect, but what he has withstood is really unlike what any other mortal could withstand."[5]

It's a crowd Trump has willingly played to, particularly in the case of Christian Zionists (a group discussed at greater length in the next chapter). In fact, his decision in 2017 to move the US Embassy from Tel Aviv to Jerusalem was received with rapturous gladness by his evangelical supporters as the fulfillment of biblical prophecy. Michael Evans, a leading Christian Zionist and the founder of the Jerusalem Prayer Team, which claims to have led 30 million evangelicals to participate in prayers for Israel, found it not just to be thrilling—but also prophetic. "As somebody who has wanted and prayed and hoped for this for more than forty years, I see us in the middle of prophecy right now," he told the Christian Broadcasting Network. "Finally we have a leader with moral clarity who will do the right thing and the righteous thing. And by the way, he's told us over and over only two forces put me in the Presidency, God and the Evangelicals."[6]

Understanding American politics through the lens of prophecy didn't begin with Donald Trump, nor did the prophetic spirit begin here in the twenty-first century. Trump's theologically inspired champions have many historical analogues whose roots are deep in America's strange, God-soaked soil. This is a country that gives rise to prophets like mushrooms in the wet, that abounds with revivals and awakenings.

Prophecy in all its many moods—from dark foreboding to outright incitement to bloodshed—has been part of the American landscape since its very beginnings. In the Bible, the prophets have distinctly different characters, legible in their predictions: Ezekiel's hallucinogenic mania, Jeremiah's dour scoldings, the salvation Joel offers through earnest prayer. All of them claimed to speak with God's voice, and that unites them; many others have followed in the path they trod.

America's profound spiritual susceptibility is epitomized in its Great Awakenings, four successive waves of religious fervor that have swept the country in the three successive centuries since the 1700s, leading to explosions of itinerant preaching, church membership, and prophecy. The first, in the 1730s, gave rise to a man whose militant preaching led his followers to take up arms for slaughter—Reverend John Elder, the "Fighting Parson," whose Presbyterian militia perpetuated the 1763 Conestoga Massacre against unarmed and helpless Susquehannock Native Americans.

The history of this country is speckled with prophets from Joseph Smith, the founder of Mormonism, to the unfortunate William Miller. Miller's prediction that the Second Coming would occur by October 22, 1844, was so widespread that its failure became known as the "Great Disappointment." Joseph Smith started a movement that became one of the world's fastest-growing religions, blazing a bloody trail from New York to Utah and sowing dreams of extraplanetary afterlives. In 1877, the theologian and prophet Nelson Barbour published a book entitled *Three Worlds, or the Harvest of this World*, which purported to prove, through a "grand system" of "perfect organization," that biblical prophecy could be mapped onto the entirety of human history and prove that Christ was about to come back. The movement that Barbour's work undergirded became known as the Bible Student movement, dedicated to spreading the word of the imminent return of Christ—and subsequently, after numerous schisms over failed prophetic predictions, gave rise to the Jehovah's Witnesses movement, which has survived and thrived well into the twenty-first century.

And those are just the examples from upstate New York. Prophets and their flocks have sprung up from Maine to Los Angeles, from Tennessee to Oregon—including in their number pseudoscientist utopians such as the prophet Cyrus Teed, who led a cult from Moravia, New York, down to Florida on the strength of the belief that he had been visited by God in the form of a voluptuous woman who had revealed to him the earth was hollow and that his followers would be immortal if they refrained from sexual congress. On Teed's death in 1908, his followers believed that he would be imminently resurrected and refused to bury him for five days; in 1921, his tomb was washed out to sea by a hurricane. In the spirit of prophecy, he had renamed himself "Koresh," the Hebrew form of "Cyrus."[7]

Teed is one of many prophets in America's past and present—prophets who wring the divine from politics, gurus who lead their cults to their deaths, social media grifters spinning hashtags they gild with the breath of the divine. It's a daring claim, to speak to and for God. But once it is made and is paired with a silver tongue or a skilled pen, it wakes a seemingly boundless hunger in those who read and listen: the need for God, the need for immortality, and the need for a life beyond the bounds of the body.

Evangelical Christianity in America has always been defined by ecstatic belief—from the speaking in tongues of Pentecostal sects to the testimony and music of megachurches. There are soaring denunciations from the pulpit; the exorcism of demons; rites of testimony and of witness. Within the broad aegis of evangelicalism, there are myriad divisions, one of which is the acceptance—or not—of contemporary prophecy; mainstream denominations, such as Methodists, Presbyterians, and Baptists, believe that the era of prophecy ended after the writing of the New Testament. Millions of American Christians, however, are members of nondenominational, charismatic, or Pentecostal sects, wherein latter-day prophecy and miraculous healing are commonplace events. The sector that claims the mantle of prophet and even of apostle—a kind of higher-order church elder who claims "spiritual authority" over churches and congregations—is growing ever more powerful within the ranks of the faithful.

Even as mainstream American Christianity shrinks, with church attendance dropping year after year, the prophetic movement within the evangelical church is growing. Charismatic Christianity, the font from which the modern prophets spring, is similar to Pentecostal worship, and by some measures, it is the fastest-growing religion in the world. According to an online database, Atlas of Pentecostalism, developed with the aid of the Pulitzer Center and Columbia Journalism School, one-quarter of the world's 2 billion Christians now identify as Pentecostal, which differs from other Christian denominations in its fulsome embrace of prophets, apostles, and ecstatic public rebirths in Christ. "Every day, 35,000 people are born again through baptism with the Holy Spirit," write the project's authors.[8] To be born again, in Christian parlance, is a moment of public conversion to Christianity that entails a kind of rebirth in the Holy Spirit, an awakening from spiritual death; those who count themselves as born again are among the most zealous in the faith. Although Pentecostalism and the charismatic movement more broadly have no central governing authority, approximately seven hundred church networks worldwide are affiliated with the movement, and that number is steadily growing.

From the wellspring of the charismatic and Pentecostal movements has grown a more directed and explicitly political project that aims to combine politics and Christendom under the mantle of prophetic inspiration. The New Apostolic Reformation, or NAR, aims to establish a new branch of Christianity that makes contemporary prophets and apostles central to the faith. NAR also explicitly aims to establish a kingdom of Christ on Earth, gaining as much temporal power as possible. The term emerged out of a 1996 conference of five hundred evangelical leaders in Pasadena, California. It was coined by a white-bearded theologian, C. Peter Wagner, who publicly espoused a vision of all-encompassing spiritual warfare. In 2011, he told NPR's Terry Gross that the tsunami that had engulfed Japan and threatened it with nuclear disaster had arisen because Japan's emperor had had sexual congress with a demonic sun goddess.[9] Prophets, ministers, and evangelists who support NAR's principles, along with those of similar movements, have embedded themselves deeply within the Republican Party.

NAR voices came to the forefront during Donald Trump's first campaign for president. They got louder during his presidency and remain a raucous chorus of divine prediction at the edges of the MAGA movement. They include figures such as Sean Feucht, the long-haired Christian rocker who has earned millions with a combination of Christian music, public stunts, and militant, blood-tinged prophecy. He rose to fame during the nation's scattered covid-19 lockdowns, holding enormous prayer-and-worship concerts in cities across the United States that had limited the size of public gatherings in order to prevent the spread of disease; those affairs are chronicled in a 2022 documentary produced by Feucht entitled *Superspreader*.[10] After the collapse of *Roe v. Wade*, Feucht tweeted to his hundred thousand followers, "When the devil's sacrifice is no longer protected by our Supreme Court watch how his people rage."[11] He suggested that vengeance on the "Philistines" was the appropriate reaction to abortion rights protesters.[12] Like those of other charismatic prophets, Feucht's prophecies are not calls to penitence, as the jeremiads of the Old Testament were; they are reflections on current events, a form of divinely inspired and politically convenient narrative. On May 5, 2023, in a "prayer action" with his congregation, Feucht gathered a crowd to pray against a trans-inclusive Pride flag painted on a crosswalk in Wisconsin, averring that the "blood of Jesus" would cancel out the "flag of perversion."[13] He set up a ministry in a million-dollar row house on Capitol Hill and dubbed it Camp Elah, after the place where David slew Goliath. He has since used it for numerous prayer events, inviting public officials to take part in ecstatic gatherings with explicitly political goals, such as praying over IDF soldiers visiting the Capitol during the Israel-Hamas war. "Our prayer is for *Camp Elah* to be a launching point for the next generation of Davids; men and women who fearlessly slay giants in the land," he wrote. "God has opened an incredible door on Capitol Hill—*Camp Elah* is just a smooth stone's throw from the U.S. Capitol and the Supreme Court, and we are EXCITED to see how He uses this place to take back territory for His kingdom."[14]

Another figure, the self-proclaimed apostle and prophet Dutch Sheets, has spent the past few decades advocating for the destruction of any border between church and state. He plans to propel into being—through prophecy, political advocacy, and prayer—a Christian nation that tolerates no other faiths or faithlessness. Sheets is the coauthor of the Watchman Decree and countless other devotionals and books; he crisscrosses the country to share his message that "the greatest harvest of souls in history is about to begin."[15]

Sheets and Feucht are both zealots and showmen, a combination that goes together perfectly in the country of tent revivals and fire-and-brimstone megachurch sermons. Bigotry and style go together as neatly as tar and feathers. They are also among a scattered but committed legion of far-right Christian prophets who have sought to bridge the gap between a boundless knowledge of the divine and the attainment of earthly power. Writing in the *New Republic*, Elle Hardy, the author of *Beyond Belief: How Pentecostal Christianity Is Taking Over the World*, declared NAR "Christian dominionism for the twenty-first century"—a decentralized movement based on the dual principles of apostolic revelation and political ruthlessness.[16]

If all prophets were solely doomsayers, however, they might not attract as big an audience as they do. Some offer custom-tailored bromides and assurances of the imminent wondrous fates of their followers. Others, fewer in number, claim to have the divinely bequeathed power to heal.

Their métier is often rhythmic, mesmeric chanting, interspersed with "speaking in tongues," the Pentecostal practice of breaking out into a staccato of nonsensical syllables, gripped beyond the bounds of normal language by the Spirit of the Lord. It is easy to find examples of charismatic evangelical prophecy; they abound on YouTube, as well as on Christian sites and ministries' websites. In a video in which the prophet Cindy Jacobs gives her predictions for 2022, one is struck not only by the horoscopelike generalities of her predictions ("Good things will come for you"; "The Lord says teamwork is dreamwork") but by how similarly the prophet acts to any other preacher in the world of ecstatic Christian worship. She breathes on her congregants, and they fall back as if knocked over by a divine wind. She speaks in tongues, lays her hands on people in benediction, and pants out her predictions in a Texas drawl, her sequined shirt glittering in the megachurch spotlights.[17]

Following in the footsteps of other prophets, the modern charismatic prophets claim their authority directly from God. You can see it on the faces of Cindy Jacobs's congregants—a hunger for the divine, a yearning beyond the needs of the body. "They've combined multi-level marketing, Pentecostal signs and wonders, and post-millennial optimism to connect directly with millions of spiritual customers," Bob Smietana wrote of the charismatics on the *Christianity Today* website.[18] There is a certain QVC-ish hucksterism to Jacobs's prophecies: "The Lord just wants you to know that He is going to give you solutions," she wrote in June 2022. "There are solutions coming for you."[19]

Despite her seemingly benign prognostications, Jacobs's influence is leveled directly toward political ends. After *Roe v. Wade* was overturned, she wrote, "I prophesied twenty years ago that one day a memorial to the holocaust of the unborn children would be built on the National Mall in Washington, D.C., and that will happen!"[20] In 2016, several influential members of MorningStar Ministries, a charismatic organization that lists her as one of its speakers, prophesied that Donald Trump would win the presidency; Lance Wallnau, a prominent exemplar of NAR principles, published a book entitled *God's Chaos Candidate* in which he called

Trump a "rugged wilderness voice" who would save America from its "fourth crucible" of violent turmoil.[21]

By 2020, the prophets were no longer content to prognosticate; they began to march. The "Jericho Marches" of 2020—in which participants rallied against the certification of the presidential election results, which proved Trump had lost—were organized by prophets such as Jill Noble. Noble's apostolic visions pit the Christian faithful against the evils of the world. "We are in the days that the early church longed to see," she wrote in a Facebook post on July 11, 2022. "There is a remnant of Believers who refuse to align with the Babylonian system. This company of passionate whole-hearted lovers of God will be small in number and will demonstrate supernatural power."[22] To topple the evils of Babylon, believers must act to countermand them. It is an aggressive, militarized form of prayer; as the scholar Elizabeth McAlister put it, "The Christians who engage in this high-level warfare are on a mission to transform territories, institutions, nations, and the land itself."[23]

The Jericho Marchers were also present on January 6, 2021, at the Capitol Building in force, blowing their ram's horns, hoping to echo the book of Joshua: "It shall come to pass, that when they make a long blast with the ram's horn, and when ye hear the sound of the trumpet, all the people shall shout with a great shout; and the wall of the city shall fall down flat." In the book of Joshua, the wall of Jericho did fall. "And they utterly destroyed all that was in the city, both man and woman, young and old, and ox, and sheep, and ass, with the edge of the sword."[24]

The Jericho Marchers may have been prominent on January 6, but they are far from alone in their marriage of politics and prophecy. Their explicit desire to reshape the United States in a narrow Christian image is not unique. In order to understand the viewpoint of a contemporary political prophet, I spoke to Pastor Steve Hall of Greeley, Colorado, the founder of Calling the 7000. On his website, he declares that "God took me to the past to save the present and future…just as God called Elijah to deliver and restore Israel from the tyranny of King Ahab and Jezebel."[25] Hall is a member of the Black Robe Regiment, a singularly sinister-sounding entity that purports to be inspired by the pastors who took the rebels' side in the American Revolution. The regiment, according to its website, is a Christian nationalist network of churchmen and laypeople who acknowledge their "biblical responsibility to stand up for our Lord and Savior and to protect the freedoms and liberties granted to a moral people in the divinely inspired US Constitution." It's an unabashed combination of religion, nationalism, and militancy—and one that a variety of conservative pastors have claimed affiliation with.[26]

Hall told me that his first prophetic moment had come at the age of eight, when he experienced a rapturous communion with the Holy Spirit while watching a revival led by the charismatic televangelist Oral Roberts. Decades later, after a rededication of his life to Jesus and a political awakening, he had experienced the Holy Spirit speaking through him, telling him that America needed to be restored to its biblical origins or the country would not survive. "It's like the Holy Ghost—the Holy Spirit just quietly in a gentlemanly tone giving me the words to say," he told me. "It's a gift that God has given me and has trusted me with to not abuse it. And do I prophesy over people? Yes, I do. Do I do it willy-nilly? No, I don't. Can I do it right on the spot, well, maybe, but I can't do it in and of myself; it's driven by the Holy Spirit, it's not by my heart or by my mind."

The "7000" referred to in the name of Hall's ministry comes from 1 Kings 19:18 in the aftermath of the Prophet Elijah's mass slaughter of the prophets of Baal: "Yet I have left me seven thousand in Israel, all the knees which have not bowed unto Baal, and every mouth which hath not kissed him."

Hall's website includes a rambling denunciation of President Lyndon B. Johnson, fulsomely echoed in our conversation, for introducing legislation, while he was a senator, that prohibited churches from engaging in political activity while remaining tax exempt; a full-throated embrace of the Seven Mountains Theory; and a ferocious commitment to Christian nationalism.

On the phone, Hall told me that he believes that while the nation's founding documents are not Holy Scripture, they were divinely inspired and "God-breathed," a Christian foundation of truth that America has turned away from, by "kowtowing" to "other religions."

When I asked Hall to provide an example of the "truths" America has turned away from, he offered three examples: one, the existence of social safety net programs (which should, he said, be left to church and society and are "not the government's place to deal with"); two, a reflection on the Fox News–fed paranoia that "grade schools are being flooded with pornography"; and three, the fact that sometimes trans women are accepted as women. "We are literally in public schools programming kids with the thing that it's okay to make a pronoun up," he said. God told him that sinners, like gay people, need to be instructed "in love" that their way of life is evil, he said, and incidentally, the separation of church and state is an "absolute lie." According to the intimate voice of the Holy Spirit that guides Hall's actions, the nation must be redeemed by a return to the New Testament: "When we do not adhere to those biblical truths, this nation will not survive."

Hall's mantra, "Reclaim, rebuild, and restore," isn't just a singular flight of fancy. The mantra is a signal of Christian Reconstructionism, an extremist subset of Calvinism that has had a huge influence on the Christian Right. Christian Reconstructionists—or "Rebuilders," as they often call themselves—advocate for a system of government called *theonomy*. Theonomy is a hypothetical system in which biblical law, particularly the judicial penalties of the Old Testament, including the stoning of adulterers and rebellious sons, is the formal basis of the laws of the United States. While Hall and others like him advocate for a New Testament viewpoint that incorporates the potential for forgiveness, other Christian Reconstructionists interpret a biblical judicial system as requiring the death penalty for homosexuality, witchcraft, adultery, and blasphemy. Among the ideology's most famous advocates was the preacher and theologian R. J. Rushdoony, who is credited with inspiring the modern Christian homeschooling movement.

Another prominent student of Christian Reconstructionism was Bill Gothard, whose Institute in Basic Life Principles provided the curricula for tens of thousands of homeschooled Christian children for decades. More telegenic leaders, such as Pat Robertson and Jerry Falwell, also lent their support to the movement; Robertson's florid and frequent predictions that asteroids would strike the wicked fall directly into the tradition of prophecy and punishment. The geographical center of Christian Reconstructionism, according to Professor Crawford Gribben, the author of *Survival and Resistance in Evangelical America: Christian Reconstruction in the Pacific Northwest*, is in Idaho, Montana, Wyoming, and the eastern portions of Washington and Oregon—a region the faithful call the "American redoubt."[27]

Churches in Idaho and throughout the Pacific Northwest advocate a fully Christianized United States, one that does away with what Rushdoony called the "heresy of democracy" and religious pluralism. National groups such as the Black Robe Regiment, the Wall Builders, and the Biblical Voter movement seek to marry a florid American patriotism with a biblical eye-for-an-eye approach. One frequent target is the Johnson Amendment, Hall's signature obsession, which prohibits political activity by churches. Other fixations include the purported "moral collapse" of American society due to its tolerance of feminism, sexual immorality, and secularism.

The Black Robe Regiment asks its members to sign the Gideon's 300 Pledge, which states, "The Church as Light of the World and Salt of the Earth (Matt. 5:13–16) is Sole Curator (trustee, steward) of the Civil Society and Guardian of the Blessings of Liberty" against "temporal governance in the hands of the children of disobedience."[28] The pledge's name is, of course, biblical: in Judges 7, God selects three hundred soldiers among tens of thousands to help the prophet Gideon battle the Midianites. Despite being overwhelmingly outnumbered, the three hundred, with Gideon's supernatural help, destroy the Midianites and carry the heads of their chieftains away as battle prizes. The Gideon's 300 Pledge is similarly constructed in a spirit of battle, designed for pastors to sign, and, in doing so, acknowledge the supremacy of the Christian God over earthly authority. The pledge also requires pastors to encourage their flocks to vote in every election; this and similar convictions are the core of the Christian

Right's success over fifty years of dogged effort. At the heart of the movement is the will of the faithful to change the nature of earthly authority, and, to a startling degree, despite their relatively small numbers, they have succeeded.

In America, liberty and tyranny are words braided into foundational documents, concepts that have become sacred over centuries. In 1967, the sociologist Robert N. Bellah posited that America has its own "civil religion"—"a collection of beliefs, symbols, and rituals with respect to sacred things and institutionalized in a collectivity." The Pledge of Allegiance, the flag soaring above public buildings and the anthem echoing through sports stadiums, the Statue of Liberty, and the notion of the American dream are its constituent parts, inviting all those who come here to be a part of it.[29]

But in the hands of the Christian Right, civil religion and Christian faith have blended together into a seamless and militant whole, one with less welcome and more steel in its heart. The Gideon's 300 Pledge is an exemplar of that admixture, one that rings with the voice of dual authority: American nationalism and two millennia of Christian tradition. It's a deliberate blurring of the line between earthly authority and the responsibilities of religion, and a movement that mixes faith in Jesus with faith in a peculiarly American vision of "liberty."

The prophets, the Gideon's 300 Pledgers, and their allies have mingled faith with Republican politics inextricably in ways that continue to shift and to grow. Right-wing politics and prophecy continued to work in tandem following the January 6, 2021, insurrection. In 2022, Pennsylvania gubernatorial candidate Doug Mastriano campaigned alongside and took advice from a prophet named Julie Green among a fleet of other extremists. In wild-eyed videos with titles such as "Mass Arrests Signal Victory's Arrival" and "FLOOD of Truth Engulfs World" and on her similarly zealotry-sodden website, Green indulges in overtly political prophecies, mixing the language of Old Testament mysticism with contemporary right-wing conspiracy theories. Each video garners hundreds of thousands of views. The perspective she often writes and speaks from is that of God himself.

A sample from a post in August 2022 entitled "The Rise of My Trumpet Is About to Be Heard":

> For I, the Lord, this day want My children to continue to declare their victory and the enemies' defeat...
>
> ...If you are wondering, and some of you are, Benghazi will be exposed. Hillary will pay for that, and so will Obama, "the Biden," John Kerry, Eric Holder, and Susan Rice, among others. The truth is coming for you... Oh no, it is all being exposed along with the plot against all the former presidents who wouldn't bow to the One World Government. It's all happening, My children, so hold on and get ready for great changes around the world...
>
> A whale will be in the news for an unusual reason.[30]

In Green's cosmology, Donald Trump is an agent of Christ ("My children, he is listening and obeying Me and My Prophets concerning the perfect timing to move"),[31] while Nancy Pelosi drinks the blood of children for Satan. Green routinely travels the country for events, speaking to paying audiences such as the Quad Cities Prayer Breakfast in Bettendorf, Iowa; a "Patriots Arise" conference in Quarryville, Pennsylvania; and alongside former Trump national security advisor and current conspiracy crank Michael Flynn at a "Reawaken America" tour in Idaho—all held in September 2022 alone. Green is a prominent figure in Republican politics because her large flock of believers lends candidates spiritual cachet; it's a matter of faith by association, particularly in the case of determinedly earthbound politicians such as Donald Trump. Green's political prominence is a further sign of the blurring of the lines between Christian faith and Republican politics—one that for evangelicals signals the arrival of a Christian America that is a godly kingdom.

Looking into the eyes of those enthralled by a prophet, you can perceive a ravenous hunger for connection: the yearning for the touch of the hand or the breath from the mouth of a charismatic preacher to fill you with the wind of God; the hope that you are not alone in the universe; that you and the rest of the flock can create an island of sanctuary for yourselves and watch in comfort as the world succumbs to its ailments. It is the hunger to be among the elect, to be immortal, to be one with the divine, and to welcome the End Times. Medieval Christians often looked to the image of Fortune's Wheel, which symbolized the turning of fate that cast down the rich and uplifted the needy. But among modern Christians the hunger to turn Fortune's Wheel with one's own hands to one's own ends—the need to scorn the caprices of fate and lift up the prophet in his certainty and zeal—predominates.

The prophets of America combine prediction with action, whether to scour the country clean of all enemies and set Jesus at the country's helm or to create a paradise in a hollow earth. The hunger for the divine certainty they represent can lead hundreds of people on treks across the country, as Joseph Smith's followers did; or to engage in slaughter, as the followers of John Elder did. It can lead thousands of people into revolt or riot, millions into cruelties unfathomable to those untouched by gods or prophecies. It can lead you to believe that your political opponents drink the blood of children and that an election was fraudulent, and to blow a ram's horn in the street to shake the foundations of Washington, DC. It is the hope of the prophets and their followers to shake the walls of the wicked world down—and hasten Christ's return and the world's ending.

CHAPTER 4

THE AGONY AND THE ECSTASY

In October 2023, war broke out in Israel. Beginning with the slaughter of more than a thousand Israeli civilians by the terrorist group Hamas and continuing with bombardments, invasion, and starvation of the fenced-in Palestinian enclave of Gaza, the conflict was a devastating humanitarian crisis that drew the attention of the entire world.* For some American evangelicals, however, the slaughter was an occasion for celebration.

For a number of evangelical leaders who specialize in the prophetic, it was the beginning of the end of the world. "Does the ongoing bloodshed in Israel point to a potential fulfillment of Bible prophecy?" asked the evangelical Christian Post on October 10, 2023, three days after the initial massacre.[1] The evangelical pastor Greg Laurie, author of more than seventy Christian books and a former spiritual adviser to the Trump administration, had a ready answer. "Fasten your seat belt because…you're seeing Bible prophecy fulfilled in your lifetime in real-time before your very eyes," he said in a video posted to YouTube that week that racked up 1.4 million views.

Laurie is among the millions of evangelicals who view the modern state of Israel as "God's timepiece," whose demise will serve as the starting point

---

* Parts of this section were originally published in *Rolling Stone* magazine.

for the end of the world. It is these evangelicals who consider themselves Christian Zionists and whose unswerving support for Israel has a profound impact on Republican foreign policy. Its roots are in a stark vision of apocalypse that will culminate in the ecstatic Rapture of Christian believers, even as the rest of the world descends into misery. As thousands died in Israel and Gaza and the war cast the region into turmoil, some American evangelicals reacted with almost palpable glee.

"It is obvious that Israel's enemies do not recognize that God has given that land to the Jews and that the Jews must be in the land for the final End Time prophecies to be fulfilled," wrote Wayne J. Edwards, the pastor of Heritage Baptist Church in Perry, Georgia, as the death toll continued to rise. "Just think! God has allowed us to see the day when His prophetic clock started running again. We are the generation to see the final biblical prophecies come to pass. Rejoice! The King is coming!"[2]

It was a cheering on of the Apocalypse from the cheap seats, a heady sense that the end of the world had started in the field of corpses. The chorus of voices eagerly anticipating Christ's return from that violent beginning epitomized evangelicals' reliance on prophecy—not least in directing their views of US foreign policy and their unwavering support of military aid for Israel, the better to witness conflict on a global scale, the battle of Gog and Magog prophesied by Ezekiel.

In the previous chapter, I mentioned a theological split between pre- and postmillenarian believers—those who seek to establish a theocracy that will enable Christ to return and those who eagerly await the signs of the End Times, certain that the Second Coming will be preceded by a period of seven years of deadly turmoil, the Tribulation. Among Christians, those who see in contemporary conflict—and in the generations of signs and omens that preceded it—the beginning of the end of the world are generally premillenarians, although this does not mean that they are content to await the coming of the Messiah passively. They seek to hasten it, if not by establishing an outright theocracy in the United States, then by treating the world as an apocalyptic chessboard whose pawns they may manipulate to set up the triumph of their King.

"These are the folks who believe that there will be a millennium in the future, a golden age, where Christ reigns on Earth, [and] they believe that before Christ will return, there will be a tribulation where Christ defeats evil," explained the politics professor Elizabeth Oldmixon in a Vox interview, describing Christian Zionists. "There will be natural disasters and wars, and perhaps an Antichrist, as the Book of Revelation notes. Then at the end of that period, the people of the Mosaic covenant, including the Jews, will convert. Then after their conversion, the great millennium starts."[3]

Prophecy, as illustrated in the previous chapter, is a mainstay of American evangelical Christianity that has grown ever more prominent in recent years. But it is the ultimate prophecy that fuels that hunger for God among the flock—the irresistible return, again and again, to the end of the world and with it the ultimate vindication of Christian faith. To that end, devoted Christian Zionists have spent some $65 million in support of ongoing Israeli settlement within the disputed territory of the West Bank; volunteer "Christian farmhands" have devoted their labor to further shoring up the Jewish presence in the "biblical heartland"; and the faithful solicit dollars, hearts, and minds to make imminent the end of the world.

One particularly grotesque element of Christian Zionism is the fact that while its views on Jews are intensely utilitarian—they must own the land of Israel, then die en masse, as a trigger condition for Jesus' return— their views on Palestinians are even darker. Palestinians, being extraneous to the Apocalypse, are viewed as an obstacle to its coming. Evangelicals have accordingly made alliances with the most extremist elements of Israeli society, joining together in a mutual desire to expel or annihilate Palestinians from the "biblical heartland." The necessity of such an annihilation is a major part of why Christians are so militant about "standing with Israel": by eliminating Palestinians, Jews edge closer to the eschatological preconditions that will presage Christ's return. This has been borne out over decades, with evangelical advisers to George W. Bush causing that administration to slow-walk support for a nascent Palestinian state and the Trump administration's open support for ever more aggressive

Jewish settlement within Palestinian territory. The influx of ready evangelical cash has also led to a rightward drift among Israeli governments, culminating in a Benjamin Netanyahu administration led by open extremists such as Bezalel Smotrich and Itamar Ben-Gvir, who before entering high office gained notoriety in Israeli society for their genocidal statements about Palestinians. The influence of evangelicals from across the sea is a mixture of zealotry and money whose ultimate goal is to bring the Apocalypse into being by force of will and by the manipulation of geopolitics. It is a literal vision of a world-swallowing inferno, and those who are dedicated to hastening Christ's return are doing their best to fan the flames.

The most striking—and literal—endeavor in this vein is a joint project among eschatologically minded evangelical Christians in the United States and a fringe sect of Jewish zealots in Israel, who have sought since 1989 to breed a red heifer without blemish. As dictated in the purity rituals outlined in Numbers 19, the sacred cow's ashes are a precondition for the return of Jewish sacrifice in a rebuilt holy temple.

"A longing for the rapture and the return of Jesus on Earth is at the core of Evangelicalism," wrote Lawrence Wright in a 1998 *New Yorker* article about the red heifer initiative. "These prophecies require three great events before the Messiah can return: the nation of Israel must be restored; Jerusalem must be a Jewish city; and the Temple, the center of worship and sacrifice in the ancient Jewish world, which was last destroyed by the Romans in 70 A.D., must be rebuilt…In order for the Jews to rebuild the Temple and prepare the way for the return of the Messiah they must be purified with the ashes of a red heifer."[4]

For generations, a collection of Mississippi cattle breeders, led by a Pentecostal preacher named Clyde Lott, has sought to breed a red heifer without blemish in Israel, so its ashes may be scattered over the beginning of a new world. As recently as September 2022, five red calves were shipped by a Texan rancher and minister, Byron Stinson, to Ben Gurion Airport and met with great acclaim by members of a Jewish-evangelical partnership organization known as Boneh Israel (Building Israel).

Although the heifer and its ashes are a potent example of biblical literalism, the apocalyptically oriented strain in Christian thought has far more prominent and moneyed representatives. Perhaps the most famous of these is Pastor John Hagee, the founder of the enormously influential lobby Christians United for Israel (CUFI), an organization that claims 10 million members (significantly more than the approximately 8 million Jews who live in the United States). CUFI, founded in 2006, routinely runs missions, fundraisers, campaign initiatives, summits, marches, and "Stand with Israel" prayer meetings. Its influence is difficult to overstate; it is the foremost Christian Zionist organization in the country. Its calendar for November 2023 showed events in Washington, South Carolina, Utah, Maine, Illinois, and California—amassing in population centers from coast to coast.

Hagee also, as indicated in his public rhetoric, seems to personally despise Jews, a fact he has revealed in numerous sermons over the years. His interest in Israel and its population is purely utilitarian: Christian Zionists love Jews like a hungry man loves a chicken wing; it's an interest born out of need whose end is total consumption. Despite his fiscal and propagandist support of Israel, Hagee has rationalized the history of persecution of the Jews as divine punishment for their disobedience of Christ. He has stated that Adolf Hitler was a "half-breed" Jew and that the Antichrist will be a homosexual, deceiving Jew; he has also accused "Rothschild bankers" of controlling the US economy. In a late-'90s sermon, he famously remarked that God sent Adolf Hitler, a "hunter," to help Jews reach the promised land. (Hagee isn't the only prominent Christian pastor to embrace Christian Zionism while denigrating Jews: Robert Jeffress, an internationally famous televangelist, gave the prayer at the opening of America's new embassy in Jerusalem in 2018—while having maintained for decades that Judaism leads people "away from God...to an eternity of separation from God in Hell.")[5]

The same year he founded CUFI, Hagee wrote a book laying out his specific geopolitical thesis of the End Times titled *Jerusalem Countdown: A Warning to the World* (later adapted into a Christian thriller film in 2011).

In it, he predicted a vast and bloody war preceding Christ's return and the Rapture, in which Russia and Islamic nations descend on Israel and are slaughtered: "How many dead will there be? According to [Ezekiel 39] verses 11 and 12, the physical death is going to be so massive it will take every able-bodied man in Israel seven months to bury the dead," Hagee predicted. "The message is that God is in total control of what appears to be a hopeless situation for Israel. He has dragged these anti-Semitic nations to the nations of Israel to crush them so that the Jews of Israel as a whole will confess that He is the Lord."[6]

Despite—or perhaps because of—his blood-drenched rhetoric, Hagee is a prominent figure in the American evangelical landscape and in the Republican Party. He has appeared repeatedly with Donald Trump while courting other prominent right-wing political figures. Mike Pence, Nikki Haley, and Ron DeSantis all appeared beside Hagee at Christian events during the 2023 Republican primaries. (Haley, a former governor of South Carolina and Trump's ambassador to the United Nations, actually launched her presidential campaign at a rally where Hagee spoke.) Not incidentally, their opinions on the Israel-Hamas war have been bullish, and several GOP presidential candidates vowed to attack Iran militarily. "We need to go and take out their infrastructure," Haley said during a GOP primary debate.[7]

"As a believer in dispensationalism, Hagee embraces a very specific theodicy: the 1,000-year reign of Christ on earth. Those who share this theology see the establishment of the modern state of Israel as a key milestone," explained a writer at the conservative Brookings Institution in a rebuke of Hagee's extremism during the 2008 presidential campaign. "Future ones include the ingathering of the Jews within Israel…After that, things really get moving: Different sects have different sequences, but these often include a Rapture, when the dead whom God wishes to redeem are resurrected and the living who are chosen for salvation are brought to heaven; the Second Coming; and the Antichrist's annihilation in Armageddon. For some dispensationalists, the Jews will also have to die in the process."[8]

Hagee is very much in the last camp. In the Armageddon he so eagerly anticipates and seeks to bring closer through militant policies in the Middle East—advocating war with Iran after an Iranian missile barrage struck Israel in April 2024, for example—Israel will be covered with a "sea of blood."

Neither are his views isolated and unrepresentative of the evangelical community at large. In a poll conducted in 2017 by the Southern Baptist Convention–affiliated organization Lifeway Research, a staggering 80 percent of evangelicals agreed with the statement that the creation of the modern State of Israel was a "fulfillment of Bible prophecy that shows we are getting closer to the return of Jesus Christ."[9]

The prevalence of this mindset on the Christian Right is reflected in Hagee's personal popularity among Republicans. Should Joe Biden win the 2024 election, Hagee will have to content himself with his staggering influence over congressmembers and governors; should the contest fall to the GOP, the pastor and his bloody, apocalyptic extremism will have a direct line to the Oval Office once again—this time in the shadow of a protracted, agonizing conflict in the Middle East.

From red heifers to Middle East wars and beyond, Christian belief in the United States is undergirded by a yearning for the Millennium and Christ's return. The prophetic clock that is ticking ever closer to that date of triumph dictates the responses of millions of American Christians to world events both at home and abroad. During the peak of the covid-19 pandemic, to cite a recent and prominent example, Christian observers in the United States saw another dramatic prefiguring of the End Times— and based their responses to public health campaigns on a violent interpretation of the book of Revelation.

Back in November 2020, when Donald Trump was still president and covid-19 vaccines had yet to reach American arms, one TikTok user went viral for her belief that the shots would signal the end of the world. Taylor Rousseau, a platinum blond, blue-eyed devout Christian TikToker, turned up the moody, throbbing strains of James Arthur's Christian anthem "Train Wreck" and carried out a one-woman, forty-second theological melodrama. In a red hat and impeccable makeup, she plays a martyr who refuses a vaccine—complete with microchip—mandated by the murderous state authority. She's beaten to death (the blood is a ketchup-like substance, the mascara smeared) for that refusal, being teleported to the Pearly Gates, where God (in a very large font) declares, "Well Done, Good and Faithful Servant." The tag on the video, verbatim: "#pov you're required to take the mark of the beast (vaccine) or you die, but you know what Gods word says so you deny it ♥"

The video spread immediately because it was ferocious, messy, and wild, spawning legions of imitators and parodies. The vaccine wasn't yet an operative reality—we were still hovering in the cureless-plague era, a miasma of fear, restriction, and offscreen deaths in overcrowded ICUs—but already someone had slotted it into eschatology, predicting the Apocalypse in a time of cataclysm. There was already a plague, and locusts were despoiling whole countries. Time felt warped and strange and heavy. Maybe it really was the end of the world.

The concept of the "Mark of the Beast" is derived from a gnomic passage in the book of Revelation, the final book of the New Testament:

> And he causeth all, both small and great, rich and poor, free and bond, to receive a mark in their right hand, or in their foreheads:
> And that no man might buy or sell, save he that had the mark, or the name of the beast, or the number of his name. (13:16–17)

In Revelation, the Mark of the Beast distinguishes the faithful from the faithless; those who reject it, even on pain of death, will be among Christ's elect. While that idea clearly has a lot of staying power, it's been a very long time, since around AD 95, when John of Patmos most likely composed his ominous vision of evil dragons, blood-drinking whores, golden girdles, and cryptic numerology. The book has been a point of contention throughout Christian history—it was a late and controversial addition to the biblical canon; Martin Luther used it as a rhetorical weapon against the Vatican, which responded in kind. But despite its long, dramatic past, many American evangelicals have, for generations, considered Revelation to be a deeply contemporary and urgent vision.

The idea that the covid-19 vaccine was the fabled Mark of the Beast exploded with the arrival of widespread vaccine rollouts and mandates. Two TikTok hashtags, #MarkOfTheBeastIsTheCovid19Vaccine and #VaccineIsTheMarkOfTheBeast, reached some seven hundred thousand views in 2021 before being banned by the service. An RNC official in Florida declared that Michigan governor Gretchen Whitmer was acting as a servant of Satan, forcing her constituents to get the mark in the form of the vaccine. The rapper Kanye West echoed the claim, saying the vaccine was the "mark of the beast…They want to put chips inside of us, they want to do all kinds of things, to make it where we can't cross the gates of heaven," he told *Forbes* in July 2020.[10] The view has cycled through far-right internet spaces, particularly on Trumpist forums and white nationalist–friendly sites such as the heavily Christian and deeply racist Twitter clone Gab. Though it's difficult to poll for such an esoteric belief, public figures and publications across the country have felt a need to address it, consulting health care workers, pastors, or, in the *Oklahoman*'s case, a "Biblical prophecy expert" with intimate knowledge of the end of the world. The prophecy expert, Reverend Mark Hitchcock, the senior pastor of Faith Bible Church in Edmond, Oklahoma, and the author of the books *Corona Crisis: Plagues, Pandemics, and the Coming Apocalypse*; *The End: A Complete Overview of Bible Prophecy and the End of Days*; and *101 Answers to Questions About the Book of Revelation*, assured readers that the vaccine wasn't the Mark of the Beast.[11] "When people talk about taking the mark of the beast (Antichrist), they will literally be taking his mark or his name upon them. It will be a pledge of allegiance to him or a pledge of loyalty," he told the *Oklahoman* in January 2021. "No one is going to take the mark of the beast accidentally. They are going to be willfully, knowingly taking it."[12] Still, he said, given the "totalitarian aspects" of life under President Biden, he felt he understood why the faithful were seeking out prophecies about the end of the world.

Christian eschatology looms large in the American evangelical mind; according to a Pew Research Center poll from 2010, a full 41 percent of Americans expect Jesus Christ to return by 2050.[13] The historian Randall

Balmer called premillenarian dispensationalism a "theology of despair" because once it caught hold at the turn of the nineteenth century, evangelical Christians could look ahead to the Rapture and give up their previously held notion that the faithful should live better lives on an earth that would shortly be crisped to bits in the fire of Apocalypse.[14]

Crucially, the core of this belief system is the notion that all biblical prophecy is not only entirely literal, it is, to quote Tim LaHaye, a coauthor of the ultrapopular Left Behind series, "history written in advance."[15] Many scholars, by contrast, view Revelation as a thinly veiled critique of the Roman Empire, with the Mark of the Beast referring to likenesses of the emperor Nero on imperial coins, seals, and stamps. Supporting this thesis is the much touted scriptural companion to the Mark of the Beast—the Number of the Beast, 666, as laid out in Revelation 13:18: "Here is wisdom: Let him that hath understanding count the number of the beast, for it is the number of a man; and his number is Six hundred threescore and six."

The number 666 has been a gold mine for pattern seekers across time (at one point or another, the "man" in question has been theorized to be the prophet Muhammad, Kaiser Wilhelm, Adolf Hitler, and more). But the most commonly held opinion among scholars and theologians is that it indicates the emperor Nero, whose name and title in gematria, which assigns a numerical value to each Hebrew letter, add up to 666. John of Patmos, a witness to the brutality of the Roman war against the Jews in AD 66, would have had reason to point his wrath at the god-emperor of Rome—and equal reason, for fear of political reprisals, to bury that wrath under a layer of code.

Of course, if you buy that 666 means Nero, that means John of Patmos's prophecies refer to events of the first-century Roman world. That's antithetical to the stance of Christian futurists, who are on constant tenterhooks for the Apocalypse. Much of the premillenarian dispensationalist worldview hinges on elaborate extrapolations from individual verses across both testaments, with Daniel and 1 Thessalonians particularly favored, and atextual, multi-millennial gaps inserted at convenient points in prophecy. It's an obsession with the End Times that sees Armageddon everywhere, particularly in contemporary politics, which are perpetually teetering on the edge of a time of great persecution for Christians. The fear of persecution as laid out in prophecy and the belief that the faithful must secure Christ's return through their actions engender both fear and ecstasy in believers. For postmillennialists, this entails securing a kingdom of Christ on Earth; for premillennialists, it means a game of immanentizing the eschaton, drawing the Apocalypse closer and closer to the blissful End of Days.

The most popular vision of premillenarian End Times eschatology was embodied in Tim LaHaye and Jerry B. Jenkins's Left Behind series, a particular adaptation of Revelation that features rugged, wholesome American Christians (its protagonists are named Buck Williams and Rayford Steele) finding salvation amid the turmoil of Tribulation. Like Frank Peretti's *This Present Darkness*, the Left Behind books offered a populist, action-packed view of theology that burned its way into the evangelical mind with far more impact than a dry sermon or a Sunday school lesson ever could.[16] Since its release as a sixteen-book series of novels between 1995 and 2007, the series has sold more than sixty million copies. It's also been adapted into a best-selling graphic-novel series, a film starring the former *Growing Pains* actor and current Christian Right fanatic Kirk Cameron, and the eschatological proof text of a generation of young Christians.

As apocalyptic visions began to dominate the Christian cultural landscape, former evangelical writers such as Slate's Joshua Rivera have noted that an evangelical upbringing led them to a constant state of ecstatic tension about the likelihood of the End of Days. "It's hard to overstate how large the rapture loomed while I was growing up in the evangelical world. As a child, I was taught that I might live to see the end of the world," Rivera wrote in 2021. "I learned how to see it coming, too: How the nation of Israel was 'God's timepiece' hitting marks on a prophetic timeline, how the machinations of the Catholic Church and the United Nations would soon come to a head and form a one-world government, how God would be driven out of America's public square as people looked to other things for salvation."[17]

That was okay, though, because it meant that the end was near and the faithful would have a reward better than eternal life after death. They'd skip death entirely, "caught up...in the clouds" as 1 Thessalonians 4:17 puts it, before the earth was allowed to rot in Tribulation; the faithful would observe those horrors in comfort, in the bosom of Christ. The mix of terror and seduction Rivera wrote about—and the alluring nature of an apocalyptic vision in which evangelicals' special status will become undeniable as they are literally evaporated into Heaven—leads some to work tirelessly toward the promised return. Others see the signs of that return scattered everywhere. An obsession with the Rapture also leads to a Christian culture that treasures images of persecution for faith's sake, the torments of the End Times, and the primacy of believers' purity in an unclean world.

Like Taylor Rousseau, American evangelicals have an almost fetishistic view of this persecution, which they spend an inordinate amount of time preparing for. The notion that Christianity will soon be outlawed on pain of death is omnipresent in certain theological circles. Online, you can find youth ministries peddling ideas for "Persecution Games" to play with Christian campers: adults portray secret police who capture and torture Christians ("The jailer can 'torture' them as much as you want, have the jailer dress up and look scary, make a scary jail, use black lights, whatever you want"); adult "Communists" seek to capture Christian children and steal their Bibles. It's in the context of this roiling persecution complex that a fantasy of being beaten to death for refusal to take a vaccine begins to make sense. It also explains in great measure the violent policies advocated by Christian Right politicians: a world in which Communists are out to capture your children and seduce them away from Christ is a world in which social change, from gay marriage to trans acceptance to the accurate teaching of America's checkered past, must be rooted out wholly from the country of the sacred.

Tracking Mark of the Beast scares, in particular, is a way to measure the perennial swellings of these anxieties—and the ways in which they have marked a concomitant reactionary drive born of fear among the believers of the Christian Right. While more pronounced in the modern era, Mark of the Beast scares go back a long way; as the medievalist professor Richard Landes told *Wired* back in 2006, Johannes Gutenberg's movable type was initially perceived as such a mark. The notion is intertwined with commerce—without the mark, you cannot buy or sell—so over the last century, changes to American commercial systems have created paroxysms of evangelical anxiety.[18] These cyclical panics can be roughly grouped into two types: the first concerns economic collectivism and the specter of godless communism and socialism, a fusion of scriptural and political preoccupations. The second concerns new commercial technologies; these waves of dread serve as pressure valves to ease anxiety about technological evolution and change. (Speaking of which: yes, there are plenty of people who believe that Bitcoin is the Mark of the Beast.)

Perhaps the most clearly political of these panics boiled over around Franklin D. Roosevelt's New Deal. Fundamentalist opposition to FDR was widespread, as it was believed that he was intimately allied with the atheistic forces of world communism. His social welfare policies, in the words of the historian Matthew Sutton, were "subverting God's order and assuming responsibilities that God had assigned to churches and local communities." FDR was considered by many in evangelical circles to be a forerunner of the Antichrist, if not the figure himself.[19]

Another of Roosevelt's initiatives that attracted an intense and lasting apocalyptic penumbra was the Social Security number (SSN), introduced in 1936. Because, over the years, SSNs have become indispensable for many jobs (without it you cannot buy or sell—or fill out a W-9!), fundamentalists have long raged against the concept, as expressed in periodic lawsuits. This has continued well into the twenty-first century: on June 28, 2021, the Supreme Court declined to address a five-year quest by an Idaho man named George Ricks to obtain an exemption from providing his Social Security number. "By forcing me to disclose an SSN in order for one to buy my labor or for me to sell my labor, is in essence the number of the beast and the card is a form of the mark," Ricks wrote in his filing before the court, to no avail.[20]

In his fascinating book *American Apocalypse: A History of Modern Evangelicalism*, Matthew Sutton depicted fundamentalist figureheads as defending against the "satanic forces [of] communism and secularism, family breakdown and government encroachment" besieging the United States—of which the New Deal, with its economic collectivism and support for workers' rights, was at the vanguard.[21]

Apocalyptic thinking became a particular Christian cause célèbre in the 1970s, following the wild success of a book by the premillenarian dispensationalist Hal Lindsey called *The Late Great Planet Earth*. The book was an entreaty for the faithful to look to Christ in the imminent time of Tribulation, heralded by the European Common Market, drug use, "Communist subversion," the establishment of the State of Israel, and "the alliance of the Arabs and the Russians," among other signs. It's difficult to overstate the influence Lindsey had; like many purely Christian phenomena, his influence might not have penetrated the mainstream, but it changed the tenor of fundamentalist Christianity, shifting its focus from the present to a near-term, apocalyptic future beset by omens of doom. Between 1970 and 1999, the book sold an estimated 35 million copies in more than 50 languages, warning direly of the "computerized society" that would enable "everyone who will not swear allegiance to the Dictator to be put to death or to be in a situation where they cannot buy or sell or hold a job."[22]

Following directly on Lindsey's apocalyptic vision (elaborated on in such sequels as 1972's *Satan Is Alive and Well on Planet Earth*; 1983's *The Rapture: Truth or Consequences*; and 2023's *Faith for Earth's Final Hour*), emerging commercial technologies became specific focal points for End Times panics.[23] Barcodes for scanning products with greater ease were introduced in the United States in the mid-1970s—and immediately ran into the rising apocalyptic fervor. Protests took place at grocery stores; an urban legend spread that the Number of the Beast, 666, was embedded in the lines of the code. One of the IBM engineers who invented barcodes, also known as

Universal Product Codes (UPCs), received an anonymous letter purporting to be from Satan himself, thanking the man for carrying out his wishes so precisely. It didn't stop in the 1970s—or with barcodes. In 1984, Pat Robertson averred that credit cards were a precursor to widespread Mark of the Beast hand and forehead microchipping, which became a surprisingly durable source of Revelation predictions for the next few decades. Radio-frequency ID (RFID) chips, which gained broad popularity in the early 2000s as a more durable and convenient form of identification than barcodes, sparked a surge of millenarian angst, particularly in 2004, when the FDA approved a chip that could be embedded in human skin called the VeriChip. Two devout authors wrote a book entitled *The Spychips Threat: Why Christians Should Resist RFID and Electronic Surveillance*, calling the new tech "surprisingly similar to the mark of the beast predicted so long ago."[24] The prediction that microchips would migrate from credit cards and smartphones into hands and foreheads has not manifested itself, but it was directly from those panics that the dual hypotheses underpinning Christian antivax sentiment arose: that the covid-19 vaccine is full of secret microchips and that it's the Mark of the Beast.

Anxieties about the mark and what it heralds—Tribulation, Rapture, the enemies of Christ consigned forever to a flaming abyss—were and are commingled with a certain eager anticipation. "I think we have to recognize it as a hopeful sort of terror," Anna Merlan, the author of *Republic of Lies: American Conspiracy Theorists and Their Surprising Rise to Power*, told me in an interview. "If you're a millenarian or not, the folks who believe in the mark of the beast also want to see it appear, since it marks the beginning of the period of time that ends with the Second Coming. That's why there have been so many false starts. It's a hope that their suffering—for example, being asked to get vaccinated—will be rewarded."

If you are a self-determined member of the elect, schooled to await the Apocalypse from your earliest days with a combination of fear and anticipation, the end of the world coincides with the destruction of your perceived enemies and your elevation to the ranks of the angels. The exultant reaction to the Israel-Hamas war, coupled with demonstrations of public support for Israel, typifies this duality of agony and ecstasy. In the early, bloody days of the war in November 2023, a group of Missouri-based, cowboy-hatted "farmhands" affiliated with the Christian Zionist organization HaYovel ("The Jubilee" in English) landed at Ben Gurion Airport in order to volunteer in the West Bank—during a period in which violence by Jewish settlers against Palestinians had been rising to epidemic proportions. "The time has come for Bible believers to stand," read a post on HaYovel's website on November 1, 2023. "Stand with Israel. Stand with Zion. Stand with the Jewish people. Stand with God's Kingdom."[25]

In 2 Peter 3:11–13, the apostle declares that Christians should act "in holy conduct and godliness, looking for and hastening the coming of the day of God, because of which the heavens will be dissolved, being on fire, and the elements will melt with fervent heat" (NIV). The act of "hastening the coming" is interpreted in many ways by different Christians: some extremists seek to establish a holy kingdom in the United States, others to usher in a bloody struggle that will explode into the End of Days. Whether this entails theocracy at home or militancy abroad, Christian eschatology is an underrated factor in US government policy—one that has a direct impact on the lives of millions of people in the here and now.

Many former evangelicals have written about the terror that the Rapture instilled in them as children—the expectation that any day, they or their parents would vanish into the arms of Jesus, never to return. That fear was intimate and present, a catch in the throat upon opening the door and wondering if your loved ones would be there or gone forever. The notion of martyrdom can be thrilling—thrilling enough to dramatize and act out on TikTok over and over again—but it also means that you have to die. Too many people, led by the fickle forces of prophecy and belief, have done just that, whether through the protracted glass-lung death of unvaccinated covid-19, via the religiously inspired skepticism of mainstream health care treatments, or in wars and conflicts eagerly cheered on—and funded—by American Christians. In seeking to hasten the end of the world, evangelicals often make it worse for others who do not anticipate being snatched up into the clouds to sit by Christ's side as the seas boil and Satan takes possession of the earth. For those who are not perennially looking out for signs of Armageddon and awaiting it as a child waits for a father to return, the drama of Apocalypse looks merely like a collection of people who, in waiting for the world to end, are actively worsening life in the present.

CHAPTER 5

SEX AND DEATH

In 2018, a woman walked free after twenty-three years in prison. In wire photos from her 1993 trial, the forty-six-year-old housewife Rachelle Renae "Shelley" Shannon has long dark hair, cut in an unfashionable fringe, and round Coke-bottle glasses; her head is cast down and her body bundled in a trench coat against the cold wind of a Kansas autumn. Months earlier, she had taken the bus from her home in Oregon to Oklahoma City and then driven hundreds of miles to ambush an abortion provider who had long been a target of antiabortion extremists. With a hail of bullets and through a storm of broken glass, she had shot Dr. George Tiller, one of the nation's few providers of late-term abortions, in both of his arms. He had gone back to his clinic the following day swathed in bandages; Shannon was arrested at Will Rogers Airport in Oklahoma City and later deposited in a Wichita jail.

During her incarceration, it would be revealed that she was responsible for an interstate string of arsons and butyric acid attacks targeting eight abortion clinics in Oregon, California, Idaho, and Nevada. Since 1988, she had become increasingly involved in the radicalized antiabortion movement, engaging in protests that had obstructed clinics and trespassing on their property, resulting in several arrests. Her commitment had become increasingly violent over the ensuing years, evincing a dedication to eradicating abortion in the United States by any means necessary, including murder. She had written dozens of letters to Michael Frederick Griffin, who had murdered abortion provider Dr. David Gunn in Pensacola, Florida, in March 1993.[1] Less than a month before her attempted murder of Dr. Tiller, Shannon had visited John Brockhoeft, who was serving a sentence in federal prison after firebombing multiple abortion clinics. (Decades later, Brockhoeft would participate in the January 6, 2021, insurrection at the US Capitol.)[2]

The Shelley Shannons of the world, along with an assortment of firebombers, arsonists, shooters, and the crowds that routinely picket abortion clinics, harassing patients and holding up placards splattered with gore, believe intensely in the notion that there is a war against the unborn and that they are fighting public murder. Ry Terran, forty, told me that she had been taught during her childhood in an evangelical Pennsylvania church that she was called by God to shoot abortion doctors when she grew up.

But abortion wasn't always at the heart of evangelical activism. As Randall Balmer, a professor of religion at Dartmouth College, has pointed out, opposition to abortion wasn't a central or even a fringe tenet of conservative evangelical activism until well after the *Roe v. Wade* decision in 1973.[3] Throughout most of the twentieth century, abortion was considered a Catholic issue, one viewed with either apathy or distaste by the majority of Protestants in the United States. As late as 1976, the Southern Baptist Convention—then and now a central organization in the evangelical landscape—passed a resolution calling for the legalization of abortion.

Future antiabortion firebrands at the center of the evangelical movement, such as James Dobson and Jerry Falwell, refrained from opining on abortion in the 1970s, even acknowledging the Bible's silence on the subject. At the time, the religious Right was engaged in a ferocious backlash against school integration, struggling to retain the tax-exempt status of the parochial "segregation academies" they had set up across the South. Balmer identified the stripping of Bob Jones University—a fundamentalist college in South Carolina infamous for its refusal to admit Black students and subsequent prohibition on interracial dating—of its tax-exempt status by the IRS in the 1970s, in particular, as the incident that truly galvanized evangelicals to become a political force to be reckoned with.

It took religious and political leaders such as Paul Weyrich and Jerry Falwell, acting in concert, to harness the newly inflamed political passion of evangelicals and redirect it to a cause that might win them more converts outside the fold of committed segregationists.[4] "Instead of the Religious Right mobilizing in defense of segregation, evangelical leaders in the late 1970s decried government intrusion into their affairs as an assault on religious freedom, thereby writing a page for the modern Republican Party playbook," Balmer wrote. "Opposition to abortion, therefore, was a godsend for leaders of the Religious Right because it allowed them to distract attention from the real genesis of their movement: defense of racial segregation in evangelical institutions."[5]

Throughout the 1970s, a conservative Christian movement spearheaded by the right-wing gadfly and activist Phyllis Schlafly agitated against expanding women's rights, successfully killing the proposed Equal Rights Amendment, which would have enshrined protection against sex-based discrimination in the Constitution.[6] Schlafly's rhetoric, influenced by her conservative Catholicism, was profoundly Christian: she identified herself as a "housewife" despite a long and lucrative career as a writer and public speaker and emphasized her role in raising six children. Her recruits, she said, were conservative Christian housewives who wished to constrain women's opportunities in the name of a more restrictive and godly performance of femininity.[7] In reality, her companions in the struggle against women's rights included far-right groups such as the Ku Klux Klan and the John Birch Society, along with a broad consortium of right-wing pastors, ministers, and priests.

"A staunch Catholic, Schlafly innovatively drew from different conservative and religious traditions to build a multifaith and geographically diverse coalition," wrote the historian Gillian Frank in a retrospective on Schlafly's antigay activism. "Drawing from longstanding opposition to racial integration, interracial marriage, and mixed-race families, her pamphlets and

articles transposed racial rhetoric onto fears of homosexuality."[8] Schlafly
herself documented a decades-long struggle, with the help of other far-right
activists, to reshape the Republican Party into the "pro-life" party—a shift
that at last began to become apparent in the 1980s. "Schlafly's pro-family
position represented what would become the core ideology of social conservatives: privileging the rights of heterosexual Christian parents over any
other social groups and viewing any deviation from this model as a political threat," wrote Frank. Her role in the Christian Right was emblem-
atic of another dynamic: the involvement of reactionary Catholics in an
evangelical Protestant-led movement. Catholics make up 21 percent of the
US population; 59 percent of US Catholics are white, and, according to
a Pew Research Center poll, 49 percent of white Catholics in the United
States are Republican.[9] The math adds up to a significant addition to the
ranks of the Christian Right. While evangelical Protestants were and are
the primary constituents of the Christian Right, reactionary Catholics
such as Schlafly have been more than happy to go along for the ride, even
if some of the theology involved disagrees with their creed. That alliance
has continued to this day; no matter the bloody past of the Reformation
in Europe, American hard-right Catholics and Protestants find that their
political goals are consonant, nestled under the aegis of "religious freedom"
for white Christians.

By the 1980s, the struggle for "religious freedom"—the freedom to
instruct children in all-white religious schools without paying a dime in
taxes—was transmuted by canny operators on the religious Right into the
more broadly appealing fixation on abortion rights. It looks more sympathetic to a wider segment of the public to express tragic concern for a
fetus—or, as Christian rhetoric puts it, "a preborn child"—than to mili-
tate for school segregation. This strategic political decision has been deliberately obscured by a half century of fevered rhetoric. Nonetheless, the
truth is that the rise of the Christian Right has its roots in segregationism
and has grown to accommodate a generalized backlash against the social
changes that accompanied the civil rights era.

To the faithful, the shift from anti-integration to antiabortion activism came from the same source, the wellspring their pastors led them to: the infinitely malleable, infinitely instructive Bible, an indispensable tool for the sophist and the power seeker as well as the believer. Picketing integrated schools and screaming invective at Black schoolchildren like Ruby Bridges melded seamlessly into blockading abortion clinics and burning them to the ground. Either way, the instruction came from God himself—by way of his most charismatic earthly messengers. It was a fortuitous time for the Christian Right to adopt a new cause célèbre. The civil rights movement had bypassed them; they had stood in direct opposition to it, in fact. The segregationist Alabama governor George Wallace had made overt appeals to a Christian audience during his 1968 presidential campaign. "Segregation now, segregation tomorrow, segregation forever" was his infamous slogan—and he actively courted the Christian vote, with some success. One Wallace campaign ad mailed to Wisconsin voters echoed subsequent Christian Right rhetoric down the decades. It read:

Dear Patriot:

Should we reelect the gang that takes Christ out of Christmas, prayer out of the public schools and may yet tax the tabernacles or temples of the Living God? Everything this outfit does is wrong and nothing is right!? Mt. 7:20. Time for a change to the Wallace Ticket. Pr. 14:34; Mt. 6:33; Acts 5:38–9.[10]

By the 1970s, the public association of southern white churches with segregationism had damaged the image of the Christian Right. In adopting the antiabortion struggle, evangelicals saw themselves as engaged in a battle for the civil rights of the unborn—a new conflict every bit as morally weighty as the struggle against slavery or Jim Crow. The struggle against abortion was the new abolitionism, and this time, they would be on the right side of history. That the adoption of an identity as abolitionists—explicitly, in some cases—was somewhat grotesque on the part of a group most famous for having stood squarely in the path of integration and civil rights was beside the point; it was a chance to redress a past moral failing by donning the very vestments they had once derided.

Comparisons between abortion and the Holocaust, slavery, racism, and other historical ills have been part of the Christian Right case against *Roe* from the very beginning. One early statement of the case was made by James T. Burtchaell, a professor at the University of Notre Dame, writer for *Christianity Today*, and staunch antiabortion advocate. In his 1984 book, *Rachel Weeping: The Case Against Abortion*, published by the mainstream publisher HarperCollins, he made these comparisons explicit. "At the yeoman's level...abortion facilities are picketed, prospective abortors approached, and clinics burnt. Some of this is illegal; all of it is bitterly resented. But it has an interesting precedent in the energetic efforts many antislavery believers made to thwart their racist adversaries," he wrote. "In a way, the freeing of the slaves and the burning of the clinics displayed— more clearly than published remonstrances—the smoldering vehemence of feeling against slavery and against abortion."[11] This line of rhetoric, with its florid moral justifications and implicit link with antiracist heroes such as Martin Luther King, Jr. (himself killed by a devotee of George Wallace), has continued to represent the Christian Right's approach to abortion over the past five decades. In 2021, in a speech at a rally outside the US Supreme Court as it prepared to decide the *Dobbs* case, which would overturn *Roe*, Marjorie Dannenfelser, the president of the antiabortion organization Susan B. Anthony Pro-Life America, again compared the antiabortion movement to the abolitionist movement against slavery. "Friends, life is truly the most important human rights cause of our time. From abolition to suffrage to the civil rights movement, principled women and men throughout history have always stepped up to lead at pivotal moments like this," she told the audience.[12]

Adopting the language of abolitionism—and the world-historical moral certitude it represents—is just one of a multiplicity of rhetorical strategies adopted by the Christian Right in its battle against abortion. In order to strengthen their arguments, antiabortion lawmakers often shore up their claims with a fixation on selectively applied biology. This cherry-picked embrace of science dates to the earliest years of the Christian Right's national abortion obsession. In 1979, a curious duo—the wild-haired preacher Francis A. Schaeffer and C. Everett Koop, then surgeon in chief of Children's Hospital of Philadelphia and future surgeon general of the United States—created a book and film series called *Whatever Happened to the Human Race?*[13] They toured the film series, a four-hour God-drenched critique of abortion, around the United States, converting the masses to the antiabortion cause. As the antiabortion doctor John Ling recalled in a revisiting of the film, it had three crucial components that led to its overwhelming success, first sweeping the United States and then embarking on a UK tour: "First, it identified a dreadful problem (rampant abortion, covert infanticide and threatening euthanasia), second, it explained the origin of that problem (the advance of secular humanism coupled with the decline of biblical Christianity) and third, it outlined the solution (Christians must believe that the Bible is true and live and act upon its teachings)."[14] The films—lo-fi, with the overall tenor of a training video for some ghoulish workplace—were peddled to millions of people, winning converts to the antiabortion cause through a combination of solemn preaching, "scientific fact," and a judicious helping of fire and brimstone.

In one surreal shot, Schaeffer intones to the audience about the methods of abortion as a choir sings in ominous, swelling notes in the background. The camera pans over a field of salt crystals, upon which are scattered nude baby dolls, their limbs contorted among the jagged whiteness of the salt. "Another common type is the saline, or salt-poisoning, abortion, or, as it is called, 'salting out.' A rather long needle is inserted through the mother's abdomen, directly into the sac surrounding the baby, and a solution of concentrated salt is injected. The baby breathes it in, swallows the salt, and is poisoned by it. The outer layer of skin is burned off by the high concentration of salt. The mother usually goes into labor about a day later and delivers a dead, shriveled baby," Koop intones solemnly as the strewn baby dolls—one thousand in number—lie inert in their salt bower. Wind sounds; the soundtrack skitters into a horror movie crescendo. The camera then pans to the preacher himself, standing on a small outcropping of rock above the toyland of carnage. "Salt: this is the site on which the city of Sodom once stood, here on the Dead Sea in Israel. Once here, under this surreal field of salt, Sodom was the most humanly corrupt city on Earth, a place of evil and of death. Sodom comes readily to mind when one contemplates the evils of abortion, and the death of moral law."

Koop, a passionate antiabortion advocate and Schaeffer's copresenter in the film and in the lecture tour that accompanied it, became surgeon general of the United States under Ronald Reagan and served from 1982 to 1989, presiding over the burgeoning antiabortion movement. He never stopped adding a scientific imprimatur to what he called a "moral" question, and in his time as surgeon general published a report that sought to demonstrate the harms of abortion from a scientific perspective.

Given the abundance of florid rhetoric on offer—from Burtchaell's comparison of abortion clinic arsonists to opponents of slavery to Koop's evocation of the bloody end of Sodom—it was a short step from speech to militant action. In the wake of the Christian Right's move toward opposing abortion, a wave of violence against abortion seekers and providers began that has not let up for half a century. One of many militant antiabortion groups, the Army of God, was a sprawling, leaderless network of would-be killers, and it made the 1990s the high-water mark of a half century of violence against abortion providers and their patients. In 1996, Eric Rudolph, a carpenter and member of several militant white supremacist Christian sects, set off a bomb at the Olympic Games in Atlanta, killing two people and injuring more than a hundred, in an attempt to curb the rise of "global socialism." When he was arrested years later, he admitted to prior bombings of two abortion clinics, one in an Atlanta suburb and another in Birmingham, Alabama.[15] In the name of Christ, people such as Shannon, Griffin, Rudolph, and Brockhoeft set out to burn down clinics and murder their staff as part of a divine mission to stop what they perceived as a perpetual holocaust of infant murder in the United States. On the Army of God's website, you can find the group's manual, which began to be circulated in the 1980s. "After Shelley Shannon, a.k.a. 'Shaggy

West,' shot Babykiller George Tiller in Wichita, Kansas, the resulting FBI investigation found a copy of the AOG Manual buried in Shelley's back yard," the site brags.[16]

The anonymous author of the manual claims that aborted fetuses inspired the text: "These ideas originated in the minds of the small but precious victims of the New Holocaust." The "covert activists" encouraged to blow up abortion clinics and murder care providers are instructed to think of themselves as "termites": anonymous members of a broader movement, engaging in leaderless resistance, exhorted to trust no one.

The Army of God makes no bones that their ranks consist of those who are willing to murder: "Our Most Dread Sovereign Lord God requires that whosoever sheds man's blood, by man shall his blood be shed. Not out of hatred for you, but out of love for the persons you exterminate, we are forced to take arms against you. Our life for yours—a simple equation. Dreadful. Sad. Reality, nonetheless. You shall not be tortured at our hands. Vengeance belongs to God only. However, execution is rarely gentle."

In a pamphlet describing an arson targeting the Catalina Medical Center in California entitled *Join the Army, or How to Destroy a Killing Center If You're Just an Old Grandma Who Can't Even Get the Fire Started in Her Fireplace,* Shannon had used the pseudonym "Shaggy West, A.O.G.," or "Army of God."

In 2009, a decade and a half after Shannon's attempted murder of George Tiller, another soldier in the Army of God, a Kansas convenience store clerk named Scott Roeder succeeded at what she had attempted. In the intervening years, right-wing media—in particular, Fox News fixture and Christian Right darling Bill O'Reilly—remained obsessively fixed on Tiller, targeting the doctor, who had already suffered an assassination attempt, for further violence. Between 2005 and 2009, Salon reported, O'Reilly referenced "Tiller the Baby Killer" on twenty-nine separate episodes of his show, comparing him to Adolf Hitler, Mao Zedong, and Joseph Stalin and accusing him of running a "death mill."[17] Roeder was one of many who listened to that invective—and drew it to what might be considered its logical conclusion. As Dr. Tiller worshipped at a Sunday service at the Reformation Lutheran Church in Wichita, Roeder shot him point-blank in the head and fled in a powder blue Ford Taurus. In 2010, Roeder was sentenced to life imprisonment for premeditated first-degree murder; he said in a parole hearing that he had "no regrets" about what he had done.[18]

The Army of God website is festooned with garish images of dead babies, with a slate of murderers and arsonists hailed as "Heroes who stood up for the unborn." As in most cases of extremist movements, Christians who take up the instruments of murder reflect the distilled essence of more broadly held views and inspire silent sympathy or open admiration on the part of those more inclined to remain within the law. Years before she picked up a weapon, Shannon took part in antiabortion protests at clinics that have, in subsequent decades, become so routine around the country that clinic escorts, whose goal is to shield patients from harassment or violence, are sought-after volunteers.

When Shannon was convicted for her string of attacks on abortion clinics, a federal judge declared her a terrorist.[19] She was and perhaps remains so—certainly according to the abortion providers quoted on record expressing their trepidation about her release. She was a part of one of the most sustained and successful terrorist movements in US history, a twentieth-century analogue of the racist reign of terror that followed Reconstruction in the South. The five-decade campaign of assassinations, arsons, bombings, stalkings, blockades, and death threats has made providing abortions, supporting abortions, and receiving abortions increasingly dangerous since the initial *Roe v. Wade* ruling. Looking back on Shannon's terror career and those of her associates decades later, what is most striking is how much closer to the mainstream her views have become, as an uncompromising embrace of violence becomes an indelible part of the religious Right. Shannon and her compatriots in the Army of God no doubt celebrated the culmination of their deadly efforts in 2022, when a new Supreme Court explicitly stacked with members of the Christian Right overturned *Roe v. Wade* and let loose a series of increasingly restrictive state laws criminalizing abortion providers, patients, and their supporters. That decision created a tide of maternal deaths that would put any individual firebomber, arsonist, or assassin to shame.

Routine antiabortion protests—such as the Summer of Mercy created by the far-right Christian group Operation Rescue, which blockaded Kansas clinics in 1991 and 2011—are filled with children trained from their earliest days to take part in the politics of obliterating choice.[20] Children and teens make up a large proportion of the crowds that flood Washington, DC, each year in the antiabortion movement's annual March for Life. Expressing the certainty of Scripture and bending scientific knowledge to their own ends, the terrorists and the movement from which they arose have created laws around the country that put doctors and pregnant women in fear for their lives. From arson to legislation is not so far a distance as those who maintain a veneer of conservative respectability would have you believe. If a woman dies in a bombing or if she dies of infection because a law prohibits the removal of a stillborn child from her womb, she is still dead. Terrorist violence and increasing legal jeopardy have combined to make control of their bodies something beyond reach for tens of millions of American women. All of it has been done in the name of God.

In the half century under *Roe*, antiabortion rhetoric has utilized strategic science—the dates of development of skin, of nails, of breath—to undergird a moral and religious argument. Placards of bloody fetuses have become banal, but their origins lie in the Schaeffer-Koop technique of marrying saline and Sodom. In the contemporary landscape, laws that none too subtly proclaim a divine origin often also claim to be rooted in science, natural law, or simply commonsense ideas about what natural law should be. These ideas have become fact without needing anything as crass and slow-moving as the cautious inferences or mewling objections of actual scientists. So laws that ban abortion after six weeks are called "heartbeat bills," although at this supremely early point in pregnancy, the embryo (the future fetus is called an embryo until eight weeks after fertilization by gynecological convention) has neither a developed heart nor any audible heartbeat, just a faint electrical impulse in the general future cardiac area that is just barely detectable on transvaginal ultrasound equipment.[21] To bolster the deluge of questionable science, the Old Testament, while conveniently discarded when it comes to things such as eating shrimp, prohibitions against making images of God, and the wearing of mixed fabrics, becomes both inerrant and a handy mold for retrofitted scientific truth. By extension, anyone who opposes these laws opposes both nature and God. Anyone willing to subvert all of that is by definition unnatural.

The jewel in the crown of Christian Right cultural warfare—its ultimate zenith, the apex it has striven for over generations—is the war on abortion rights. The overturning of *Roe v. Wade* in 2022 was both an overtly religious project and a seismic shift in the lives of the millions of Americans who happen to be in possession of a uterus. Not only did the ruling go explicitly against the will of most Americans—in almost every demographic, in every age-group, at every level of education, clear majorities supported *Roe*—it sprang a nationwide series of traps known as "trigger laws," ready-made to punish women and their doctors in the event that the protective precedent should be overturned.

How does such an idea take root—let alone become national policy?

The terror of the Army of God was a part of it, and, still more, the way the blockading and stalking and perpetual threats against abortion clinics became normalized over the five decades since *Roe*. Even before the 2022 decision, a Christian-led series of laws made the administration and reception of abortions more and more arduous and created desperation in patients and doctors, as whole states became abortion deserts. In 2021, the year before *Roe* was repealed, the National Abortion Federation recorded an explosion of antiabortion violence over the prior year, including a 600 percent increase in stalking; a 54 percent increase in acts of vandalism (which included numerous incidents of bullets being fired through clinic windows); an 80 percent increase in bomb threats; and a 128 percent increase in invasions, including instances in which antiabortion protesters forcefully entered clinics.[22] A Department of Justice summary of illegal antiabortion acts is both staggering in its scope—from Molotov cocktails in Missouri, Florida, and Delaware to arson and death threats in Maryland, Virginia, and Alaska—and numbing in the sameness and malice of the crimes. The tacit acceptance of this state of affairs by the general public, including the Democratic Party, which never used its legislative majorities to codify *Roe* into law, meant that abortion was imperiled or nonexistent for tens of millions of Americans even before the nominal constitutional right was deracinated by the court. For decades, terrorism achieved its goal in plain sight: to strike fear into the hearts of those who would provide or receive abortions, to infuse the procedures with danger and fear and shame, and to make providers, escorts, and patients live in fear for their lives.

On June 24, 2022, when *Roe* was repealed, the arsonists and their legislative counterparts rejoiced. "Pastors, evangelists, and other Christian speakers must speak up for life. They must stop equivocating or remaining silent on this subject. They must be willing to suffer the wrath of men, but have the favor and blessing of God," wrote the director of the Christian Action League of North Carolina, Reverend Mark Creech. "Their message should be that to destroy human life in abortion is to assault the very image of God—to declare worthless what God calls precious—to be responsible for blood-guiltiness."[23]

Christian nationalism, like other forms of nationalism, begins with the idea that the country, once thriving, has departed from the norms of a mythologized and ideal past. This is particularly and peculiarly reified in the Christian nationalist obsession with the nation's founding documents, in particular the Constitution, which is treated as sort of a subsidiary Bible, an inerrant sacred text that sinners are perpetually betraying. The contents of these documents are far less important than the act of believing in them: belief shapes things, turns civic texts into Holy Writ, selectively picks passages and rewrites them in letters of fire, wraps the cross in the flag. From Christian militias to sovereign-citizen sheriffs to apostolic preachers at political rallies, the notion that once there was a purity to this Christian nation that has fallen into the mire of sin serves as an irresistible spur to action. Just as man is perfectible through the purging of sin, so may a country be; and the "unborn Holocaust," as evangelicals refer to it, is the apogee of contemporary American sin, the eradication of which may be the country's salvation.

The makers and supporters of theocratic laws have a general notion that society has gone astray, has lost its way, is wandering in the wilderness. Much of that purported loss of national morale is blamed on the feminist movement and its success in securing women's rights. Since the purported triumph of women's equality, everything else has gone to hell and has to be clawed back from the maw of the abyss. As noted in Kathryn Joyce's book about the Christian patriarchy movement, *Quiverfull: Inside the Christian Patriarchy Movement*, the influential Christian author Mary Pride really did "see feminism as combining a range of ills from communism to self-worship to witchcraft" as early as 1985.[24]

The fact that a woman's right to choose—and the specter of forced pregnancy, forced parenthood, and the many mortal dangers these processes entail—forms the bedrock of the contemporary Christian nationalist movement is not a coincidence, nor does it stand alone within the Christian moral framework. It is part of a moralizing view that makes consensual sex out to be a potentially mortal sin. As Reverend Creech put it in his statement on *Roe v. Wade*'s overturning:

> Parallel with the emphasis on restoring the sanctity of human life, the sanctity of marriage between a man and a woman should be stressed. God gave the gift of sex to strengthen the marriage relationship. Sex is restricted to marriage and meant to bless the home with children. To seek the pleasures of sex without viewing it as a sacred responsibility to God and the possibility of a priceless child from the union is the chief reason behind the practice of abortion.[25]

Discussions about abortion that fixate on incest and rape—situations in which "the pleasures of sex" are not sought but brutally imposed on an unwilling body—miss the central horror of forced parenthood and unwittingly agree with the central premise of believers such as Creech: that consensual sex should potentially carry a death sentence, for it is in and of itself a mortal sin. Never mind that sex is as basic a human drive as the avoidance of death, or that abortion seekers are often mothers of other children constrained by economic circumstances; that prenatal care in this country is so precarious that maternal and fetal deaths are routine; that sex education is the subject of a separate and steady Christian Right barrage; and that any fiscal safety net for mothers and children in this country is tattered beyond recognition. Such is the Christian Right's fixation on sex that there have been evangelical drives against the legality of birth control for decades, supported by Speaker of the House Mike Johnson, among others.[26] It's worth noting that Johnson is a former attorney for the Alliance Defending Freedom, a Christian Right law firm whose chief function is providing model legislation to states on subjects evangelicals fixate on, including abortion, birth control, and gay sex. In the opinion that overturned *Roe v. Wade*, Supreme Court justice Clarence Thomas indicated that other legal rulings dependent on the legal concept of a "right to privacy" would be imperiled—chief among them *Griswold v. Connecticut*, which legalized birth control; and *Obergefell v. Hodges*, which granted gay people the right to marriage.[27]

In the eyes of evangelicals devoted to sexual purity, sinister influences that seek to undermine it—that celebrate birth control and abortion as the keys to sexual freedom and bodily autonomy—have combined to turn American culture into a swamp of sin. Like a dam across a mighty river, the interlinked movements generally grouped under "social progress"—antiracism, feminism, LGBT rights—have combined to stop the natural flow of God's will, and it is to be hoped that with sufficient seething, frothing, and boiling over, the warriors of God will sweep away the encumbrance once and for all. That's how they see themselves, as natural as water and as necessary, cleansing a society crawling about in its own filth. The stakes are high; the righteous brides and grooms of Christ must contend with enemies who are summoning Beelzebub every hour they go around with pink hair, uncovered knees, and anarchic gender-bending.

"Wives, submit yourselves to your own husbands as you do to the Lord," says Ephesians 5:22 (NIV); that's where things ought to have stopped. And they will be stopped: by fire, by sword, by law.

Especially by fire. Even since the repeal of *Roe*, the arson attacks on abortion clinics haven't stopped. In fact, they've accelerated: in 2022, the year *Roe* was overturned, the National Abortion Federation recorded a 100 percent increase in abortion clinic arsons over 2021. In May 2022, after the draft of the ruling that would go on to overturn *Roe* was leaked, a young woman burned down an abortion clinic under construction in Casper, Wyoming, saying that she had been visited by dark dreams. On August 15, 2023, the sole abortion clinic serving California's Imperial County—on the border with Arizona, which had mandated a fifteen-week abortion ban in 2022—burned to the ground, leaving a gap in care that crossed state lines.[28] In Peoria, Illinois, a thirty-three-year-old man burned down an abortion clinic in January 2023; he had, according to his guilty plea, broken a window and thrown a burning container into the building because he'd been reminded of an ex-girlfriend who'd gotten an abortion against his wishes.[29] The fire burns on, and its chief purpose is control.

Fire is a useful tool—it works well in conjunction with fear, and it is an instrument of the cleansing of evil, sometimes right out of people's bodies—but it isn't the only weapon the Christian Right has chosen to wield. The other one cuts sharper and deeper, and you don't even have to watch anybody burn.

Under an onslaught of antiabortion state laws, underage rape victims have to cross state lines—sometimes under the threat of legal repercussions—to pursue abortions, and doctors living in fear of prosecution routinely delay resolving ectopic pregnancies, despite excellent outcomes with early treatment. Approximately one in fifty pregnancies in the United States are ectopic; these pregnancies implant outside the uterus, in the majority of cases in the fallopian tube, are never viable, and have the potential to cause life-threatening hemorrhages. Under Texas's draconian abortion law, maternal-fetal medicine specialists told researchers that patients would have to be "on death's door" to receive abortion treatment—no matter how ill the mother or nonviable the fetus is.[30]

The Christian Right has fought against abortion even in cases when it is the only available option to save a woman's life. In 2024, the Supreme Court agreed to hear a case in which Idaho's punitive antiabortion restrictions, which posit that doctors who perform even lifesaving abortions are subject to criminal penalties, came into conflict with a federal law, the Emergency Medical Treatment and Labor Act (EMTALA), which stipulates that medically necessary abortions must be provided regardless of state regulations. Under the reign of the Idaho Republican Party (which boasts its "love of God" in a chipper YouTube video on its home page, as the camera pans over a cross), doctors fear to provide even lifesaving care in the form of abortion, forced to choose between imprisonment and saving women's lives.

Under current legal regimes, the endangerment and suffering of women are inevitable. As the indefatigable anti–abortion law chronicler Jessica Valenti has pointed out, this is intentional: for the Christian Right, to become a martyr in birth is a holy and fitting end for a woman. "If we were good mothers, we'd give up anything for our fetus, including our lives. Those who don't fulfill that role deserve disdain and punishment," Valenti wrote in January 2024, following the EMTALA ruling. "How dare we expect to live."[31] Our bodies, after all, are imperfect vessels for our spirits. We are all caught in a spiritual war, even if we never chose it, even if we didn't ever believe in it, and every body that can become pregnant in America is entrapped in a wild faith that would rather see us die in birth than live free. Even if martyrdom is imposed on a woman by law, her death is pleasing to God; even if the baby never draws a breath, even as she bleeds her lifeblood out onto the table, she praises the Lord.

CHAPTER 6

LET THE FIRE MAKE YOU PURE

It's a constant in this country that the people who make the laws love to talk about God when they take things from you. One example is Senate Bill 129, introduced in the Oklahoma legislature in February 2023 by state senator David Bullard, a church deacon and board member of a Christian organization called Patriots Ministries. According to an Oklahoma senate press release, the bill would "prohibit Oklahoma doctors from providing gender transition procedures or referral services relating to such procedures to anyone under the age of twenty-six. The bill would further authorize the state's attorney general to enforce the act and those found guilty of violating it would be guilty of a felony and subject to license revocation."[1]

The nickname Bullard coined for his bill—the "Millstone Act"—hints at darker penalties. "The Millstone Act," the press release continues, "was named in reference to Matthew 18:6, 'but whoever causes one of these little ones who believe in Me to sin, it is better for him that a heavy mill-stone be hung around his neck, and that he be drowned in the depths of the sea.'"

Medical care for trans youths, in other words, is a mortal sin—one whose penalty ought to be death, though a felony conviction will do in the interim. The bill passed both chambers of the Oklahoma legislature.

"Bullard typifies the modern genre of Christian Nationalist politician. Oleaginous facial hair—a pathetic grab at the masculinity conservative politicians are so desperate to cosplay these days—hides a weak chin, but the beard cannot camouflage Bullard's dearth of original thought," opined the constitutional attorney and vice president of strategic communications of Americans United for Separation of Church and State, Andrew Seidel, reacting to the Millstone Act. "The sole concern for Bullard and his dull ilk seems to be imposing their conservative version of the Christian religion on the rest of the state by abusing a legislative power that is, constitutionally speaking, entirely secular. This is Christian nationalism."[2]

Christian nationalism requires imposing a particular view of sex, sexuality, and gender on the public at large regardless of any individual's faith or lack thereof. In the case of gay and transgender people, this mandate is guided by bigotry and Leviticus; in the case of women in particular, it's guided by misogyny and Leviticus again, with its death penalties for various forms of illicit fornication. Purity culture—the Christian Right staple that in lieu of sex education provides endless fire-and-brimstone mandates about chastity, particularly for women—transmits the idea that seeking sexual pleasure is an inherent evil. As such, the mainstream belief of the Christian Right is that sex is God's domain, and it is his prerogative to make it result in death, if he so chooses. This may be odious to outsiders, but within evangelical theology, it is a culturally coherent conclusion.

Women steeped in purity culture—particularly during its peak in the 1990s—endured an education that postulated that their moral center lay between their thighs. "Call them evangelical, fundamentalist, or radicalized, over the past few decades, the more extreme adherents have leveraged an obsession with virginity (especially female virginity) into a purity movement with impacts that extend beyond their stained-glass windows," Melissa Mayer put it in a 2019 *Bitch* magazine article. "For fundamentalist youth, purity culture means virginity pledges, comparing women who aren't virgins to already-chewed gum, novelty underwear coyly prompting from a nubile pelvis 'stop because my father is watching,' and lavish balls where young women date their dads."[3]

In 1996, a reverend in Yuma, Arizona, named Denny Pattyn began selling silver "purity rings" engraved with 1 Thessalonians 4:3—"For this is the will of God, even your sanctification, that ye should abstain from fornication"—which inspired countless imitators and were often gifted to purity ball pledgers and Christian teen girls. (First Thessalonians 4:6 elaborates on the consequences of fornication: "Because that the Lord is the avenger of all such, as we also have forewarned you and testified.") Not incidentally, the rings were often gifted by their fathers, whose property they would remain until marriage, which, in the evangelical view, is more or less a transfer of property. James Dobson of Focus on the Family encouraged "daddy-daughter dances" and even "dates" between daughters and fathers to drive home the point. At the same time that the purity movement was driving chastity fever into the hearts of evangelical teens, abstinence-only sex education was receiving federal funding and becoming the law of the land in dozens of states—despite its documented failure at preventing teen pregnancy or STDs. It was yet another confluence between church and state, a tacit agreement between legislative authorities and Bible-thumping that young people as well as adults must avoid fornicating at all costs or be forced to pay a price in blood.

In 1997, a twenty-one-year-old evangelical and popular homeschool circuit speaker named Joshua Harris published a book entitled *I Kissed Dating Goodbye*, advocating that young Christians abandon the secular model of dating for a chaste and godly vision of courtship.[4] The book became not just a bestseller but a phenomenon, an immediate evangelical classic that crested the wave of the 1990s purity movement. A few years earlier, Christian teens had begun making "True Love Waits" pledges, in which they had signed three-by-five cards that declared, "Believing that true love waits, I make a commitment to God, myself, my family, those I date, my future mate and my future children to be sexually pure until the day I enter a covenant marriage relationship."

Harris's book, accessible if somewhat pedestrian in its prose, made a strong, folksy case for complete chastity before marriage, arguing that secular images of "love" were pale shadows compared to courtship in Christ's image. The book is salted with anecdotes about Harris's purported friends who have fallen victim to salacious attitudes and fleshly lusts, as well as the pure and the saved who have turned away from such temptation. Harris delved into theology with the flair of a bargain-basement St. Augustine: "Impurity is a grimy film that coats the soul, a shadow that blocks light and darkens our countenance," he wrote. "Without purity, God's gift of sexuality becomes a dangerous game. A relationship devoid of purity is soon reduced to nothing more than two bodies grasping at and demanding pleasure. Without purity, the mind becomes a slave to depravity, tossed about by every sinful craving and imagination."[5]

In 1998, a year after the smash success of *I Kissed Dating Goodbye*, a field director for the Christian Right Family Research Council named Randy Wilson came up with another way for teens to publicly pledge their commitment to abstinence. Utilizing "dramatic imagery," as the *New York Times* put it, Wilson's "purity balls" featured young girls performing ballet, placing roses before a cross, and ballroom dancing in gowns with their fathers.[6] Their fathers, in turn, committed to guarding their daughters' purity until marriage. Photos of purity balls around the United States are full of girls as young as seven in full faces of makeup, clasping their fathers' hands. The "couples" are attired as if for a prom or a date, and the girls smile in frenetic rictus.

In her memoir *Pure: Inside the Evangelical Movement That Shamed a Generation of Young Women and How I Broke Free*, Linda Kay Klein listed a dizzying array of metaphors for the nonvirginal female body, employed routinely in evangelical education.[7] Women who had had sex were compared to already chewed gum; an Oreo that has been bitten and spat upon; a licked lollipop; a piece of tape that has lost its stickiness from overuse; a derelict car; a used tissue; and grimy, adulterated water. So many of the metaphors focus on food, she noted, conveying a message that female sexuality is something to be devoured by others. "Based on our nightmares, panic attacks, and paranoia, one might think my childhood friends and I had been to war," she wrote. "In fact, we had. We went to war with ourselves, our own bodies, and our own sexual natures, all under the strict commandment of the church."[8] In evangelical societies, an impure woman is considered a danger to the community, a stumbling block in the path of the godly men whose righteousness upholds the church.

The small, godly men in good suits who work at organizations such as the Alliance Defending Freedom (whose chief interest appears to be curtailing freedom for anyone who isn't a white Christian man), the American Legislative Exchange Council (ALEC), the Family Research Council, and other organizations with carefully bland names and very long documents give model laws—fill in your state here!—to other small men in usually worse suits who sit on state legislatures in Montana and Arizona and Nebraska, Idaho and West Virginia and Missouri. The Republicans who sponsor these bills represent themselves as small-businessmen, ranchers, churchgoers, salt-of-the-earth men unsullied by politics, such as Barry Crago of Wyoming, who serves on the board of a private evangelical Christian academy and recently sponsored a ban on trans athletes participating in interscholastic sports. Or Adam Thomas of Kansas, the chair of a committee that sponsored a bill that would force trans children to sleep "according to biological sex" on overnight school trips, regardless of their presentation; he spends his weekends as a member of the Lenexa Baptist Church praise band.[9]

They call their acts by names such as SAFE—Saving Adolescents from Experimentation—and ban trans care; they ban abortion as early as they can, as often as they can, and their goals are limitless. They meet in quiet rooms with catering platter sandwiches on the table and their busy little clerks are everywhere, and it's only the public faces that bother with the invective, bringing a bit of fire and brimstone to the chambers of the law. Everything else is dry and quiet and done in a very civilized fashion. Without raising their voices, they condemn children to die of despair and women to bleed to death or face choices no person should have to make. They make laws that turn bodies into prisons and women into less than people, because people who don't own their bodies aren't really people at all. Perhaps they smile, if they can fit it into their busy schedules—there are always more laws to be written. Presumably they find time to pray.

"The Religious Right has been a ready and willing ally in efforts to overturn elections, stack the judicial system, and deny women bodily autonomy, among other things, all while providing a Christian rationalization for it all," explained the ex–evangelical writer Blake Chastain in a column. "The groups we now collectively call 'Christian nationalist' are very effective at leveraging those weak points. They are well-funded and well-organized. Groups like the Council for National Policy, ALEC, Alliance Defending Freedom, United in Purpose, and many others, are able to work on long timetables in order to achieve their goals."[10]

Part of the reason for the slate of laws being drafted and passed, the lawyers who argue for them in court, and the judges who uphold them is the process, begun in the 1980s, of the Christian Right capture of the US judiciary. A great deal of its power—and the reason that in the case of a Trump election win, any illegalities will likely be swept smoothly aside—has been accrued in the judicial branch of the government. The central figure behind this slow-motion coup is an ultraconservative Catholic named Leonard Leo, who cofounded an organization called the Federalist Society, whose branches, with two thousand chapters in law schools and member judges in courtrooms across the country, comprise some seventy-five thousand members. Founded in 1982, three years after the Moral Majority, the group has since aimed to destroy the "liberal orthodoxy" of the legal profession. "Backed by a who's who of right-wing money, the fledgling group quickly grew from a handful of grassroots chapters on college campuses into a million-dollar organization with headquarters in Washington, D.C., and at least 75 campus affiliates," the Intercept noted in a history of the society.[11] It was cofounded by Paul Weyrich, the so-called Robespierre of the Right, who the journalist David Grann noted was "the man who founded the Heritage Foundation, orchestrated the party's alliance with evangelical Christians, and, more than any other figure, organized the right inside the Beltway."[12]

Over the past forty years, the Federalist Society has established a coterie of committed hard-right judges and lawyers, often in prominent positions, and a close, cozy relationship with the Christian Right. It was a Federalist Society member, serving as chief counsel for the Christian Right organization Alliance Defending Freedom, that argued the *Dobbs* case that felled *Roe v. Wade*—before a Supreme Court of whom six of the nine justices were current or former Federalist Society members. *Roe* never stood a chance; it was the culmination of a half-century project of incursion into and capture of the nation's legal institutions that had scaled the ladder of ambition to the very top of the US judiciary. The Trump administration in its first term accordingly appointed judges, many of them youthful, extreme members of the Christian Right, to lifetime judicial appointments at record speed—234 judges in total, three of them members of the Supreme Court. These judges have gone on to uphold countless decisions that curtail the rights of women and children in the name of "religious freedom."

Religious freedom, for the GOP, means the ability to impose grotesque levels of control, particularly on bodies capable of pregnancy. Here are some things that can happen to the body in a normal and uncomplicated pregnancy: swelling of the face and extremities, nausea and vomiting, pelvic bone separation, frequent nosebleeds, increased hair growth, urinary leakage, loosened teeth, impaired memory and concentration. Complex pregnancies can be fatal; preeclampsia, a hypertensive disorder during pregnancy, affects between 2 and 8 percent of pregnancies worldwide and can result in death for both mother and child, extended hospital stays, and poor perinatal outcomes. Vaginal delivery entails significant physical trauma, with bleeding, called lochia, that typically lasts four to six weeks; cesarean section is a major surgery with lifetime scarring and the potential complications caused by any such incision.

Moreover, in states with restrictive abortion laws, it is not only pregnant women who fall under a vicious regime of state surveillance; any woman with the potential for bearing a child potentially faces restrictions on her medical care, including women of childbearing age who require cancer treatment that may be teratogenic and legions of autoimmune patients, particularly those with lupus, whose best treatment, methotrexate, is also an abortifacient. Thousands of patients have had their medical care disrupted because they were pregnant.

There's a certain vigilante aspect to many abortion laws that seems rooted in the antiabortion terrorism movement: in Texas, private citizens can report abortion providers or those who aid people seeking abortions and in the process collect a $10,000 bounty. In Oklahoma, people are encouraged to sue anyone who pays for an abortion.[13]

As red states have continued to curtail women's reproductive rights two years after the fall of *Roe*, these legal fetters have become ever weightier and more complex. The fight purportedly against abortion and for "religious freedom" has turned American women's lives into legal minefields; having a uterus is functionally not unlike possessing a controlled substance. In 2024, the Alabama Supreme Court ruled that frozen embryos produced during in vitro fertilization—a process undergone by parents eager to have children—are, legally, considered children. This means that should embryos (or, as one justice put it, "extrauterine children") be lost in lab accidents or discarded, care providers can be prosecuted for causing wrongful death. Immediately after the ruling, three IVF clinics paused procedures, attempting to sort out the legal snarl created by the sudden personhood of embryos in freezers—and causing patients seeking to get pregnant to scramble to find care.[14]

A 2024 report released by reproductive-rights organization Lift Louisiana revealed the extraordinary degradation of women's health care under the state's draconian abortion ban laws. The fear of criminal liability among medical providers has led to catastrophic consequences—some patients report delays in receiving prenatal care in the first trimester, when miscarriages are more likely, leading to potential complications later in the pregnancy. The laws have severely limited clinicians' options to effectively manage pregnancy loss, because many of the same procedures and medications are used for abortion. In other cases, patients were denied abortion care despite life-threatening conditions, such as cardiac disease exacerbated by pregnancy, or receiving advanced cancer diagnoses while pregnant. According to researchers' conversations with patients and doctors, patients with severe or fatal fetal diagnoses were forced to remain pregnant, and, when a pregnancy could not result in a viable outcome, clinicians felt pressured to perform invasive procedures, such as C-section, to end the pregnancy, or put patients at risk for infection by delaying delivery. One emergency medicine physician described a colleague "having to take [a patient] for C-section to preserve the appearance of not doing an abortion, even though this is not a viable pregnancy...subjecting the patient to unnecessary abdominal surgery." The abortion bans create both danger for patients and moral injury for doctors, who are torn between obeying the law and providing evidence-based medical care that would keep their patients safe.[15] It's a pattern being repeated in numerous states—and, if the Christian Right has its way, one that will soon engulf the entire country.

Trigger laws—laws already on the books but illegitimate under *Roe*—were immediately enacted in thirteen states where the Christian Right and its willing legislative partners had spent decades chipping away at access to care.[16] The extremity of this legal bonanza is in part explained by the deep roots of the antiabortion movement and the rhizomatic network of motivations and neuroses it taps into. Understanding the Christian Right's fixation on pleasure having deadly consequences; its obsession with the chaste, pure female body; the militant upholding of gender roles; and a half century of propaganda about an unborn holocaust explains in part why holy warriors are avidly pursuing several legislative paths to a total national ban on abortion. It's part of why trans care has been de facto outlawed in an increasing number of states. It's why there are increasing rumbles about dismantling gay rights in every possible fashion. Consider Reverend Creech's assertion that marriage is between "one man and one woman" on the day *Roe* fell, and his invective that sexual pleasure should be coupled with "sacred responsibility." But sex is and has always been messy and ungovernable, ill-suited to puritanical restriction, a titanic drive that manifests in each of us differently; it's dangerous, ecstatic, part of being alive. The Christian Right's obsession with controlling sex is why providers of birth control anticipate a campaign to eliminate the public availability of contraception and why the Trump administration rolled back access to birth control. A movement motivated by virulent anti-feminism and obsessed with wifely submission can do much to roll back a few decades of tenuous progress.

The specter of femicide haunts American political rhetoric from campaign stops to megachurches to school board meetings to social media posts.[17] Republican presidential candidates proudly tout their Christian values and the need for the United States to get back to its Christian roots, to wit, a time before women had even nominal bodily autonomy. Even when God isn't directly invoked, he—it's inevitably a he, a specific he to boot, usually the Jesus with ultramarine blue eyes and the soft, curling shoulder-length hair of an ancient-times shampoo model—hovers above the proceedings, and the subtext in the room is the kind that comes in chapter and verse from Acts or Proverbs or Philippians or some other sacred plural noun. Christian dominionism, Christian nationalism, and simple zealotry stand at the epicenter of US politics. When culture war, spiritual warfare, and public policy intermix in the minds of legislators, the results are inevitably corrosive to those who don't share their faith.

They're coming for all of it: everything outside of the framework of a submissive wife and a patriarchal husband and a *Cheaper by the Dozen*–style fleet of children. And like the family structure blessed by the Almighty, the headship of this society is male, Christian, and white. A zealously policed theocratic society is the goal, and it's not one the Right bothers to conceal, as the stakes are high and it is not a fight it is prepared to lose. There is a well-financed armature behind these laws, the result of a font of small-dollar donors and deep-pocketed megachurch impresarios; that's how they crop up in different states. The Right has a holistic vision—a kingdom to win—and it is pursuing it, and it is winning.

It's well and good to look piecemeal at each element of the destruction and what is being built in its place. It is also necessary to look at the whole picture and to recognize that what is being waged is a holy war, a war that will lead to deaths—of pregnant people and trans people and anyone else who won't fit into the kingdom of Christ on Earth.

At the moment, in the national political landscape, there is ample evidence that the Republican Party and its far-right fellow travelers seek absolute power at all costs. Consider, for example, that in November 2023 a majority of Ohioans voted to enshrine a right to abortion in the state constitution—only for the Republican state legislature to publicly vow, in a press release the same week as the vote, to override the popular will and even that of state courts if necessary.[18] Recent headlines across the nation underscore this principle: egregious gerrymandering in red and purple states that creates a firewall against majority rule; the deliberate restriction of voting rights, including purging thousands of voters from the rolls in Virginia, Wisconsin, and Arkansas; the continual insistence, central to party orthodoxy, that the last presidential election was a fraud; the January 6, 2021, storming of the Capitol. What does the GOP want? A kingdom of Christ on Earth ruled by his elect. In practice: to impose a nationally unpopular set of principles, many of them theocratic, and seal them into law; to purge the nation of undesirables; and to utterly dominate their inferiors.

In this pursuit, the GOP utilizes internally consistent logic, rooted in the ideals of the Christian Right, that advocates for the total elimination of a governmental social safety net for mothers, children, families, and the elderly. Lynn Fitch, Mississippi's attorney general, brought the lawsuit that overturned *Roe v. Wade* for good. She also advocates for private charities and churches to take the place of the United States' tattered public social safety net—in other words, the total elimination of programs such as SNAP, TANF, and even Medicaid. Of course, churches would be entitled and inclined to refuse care or services based on the undesirability of supplicants—including gender orientation or unmarried status. It's a dystopian vision, one in which women who are forced to give birth and their children will be left to free-fall. This is the world that Fitch and her cohort seem to desire, for the earthly glory of Christ. "We are a faith-based state and country," she said with regard to her lawsuit; the governor of the state announced that he was praying for her.

If control is the aim, it does not matter if there is a double standard or a flaw that can be highlighted. The more arrant the hypocrisy, the more brazen the contradiction, the stronger the party that continues to advocate those policies grows. Any flaw is null because the people pointing it out mean nothing; they're sinners, fallen from the grace of the one true burning path. Only the unborn, floating and hypothetical in their sacs, are sacred; the born are inconveniences; let them break, like earthen vessels, into shards.

They have so much in common, the arsonists and the lawmakers. For one thing, the threat of the former helps the latter ensure that they will be obeyed. They are as akin as the torch and the hand that wields it, as akin as the witch finder and the crowd gathered around the heap of straw. If you listen, you can hear the flames rising, reaching for a pair of bare feet belonging to a woman who didn't obey her betters. As they always have. As they always will—absent the thunder and the flood of opposition that ought by all standards of justice to oppose it.

PART II

FAMILY

CHAPTER 7

BROWNSHIRTS V. THE BOARD OF EDUCATION

This is a story of two organizations that arose in the same state sixty-nine years apart.

On October 26, 1954, five months after the monumental Supreme Court decision *Brown v. Board of Education* mandated the desegregation of public schools across the United States, the Defenders of State Sovereignty and Individual Liberties was chartered in Virginia.

"We believe," its founders wrote in a statement of purpose widely distributed across the state,

In the Sovereignty of the Several States;

In certain liberties for the individual citizens of these states;

In the preservation of racial integrity;

In an education for all children;

In a society based on racial separateness;

In the separation of church and state;

In the precious heritage handed down to us by our forefathers;

Very sincerely, that our objectives are in the best interest of both races.[1]

The organization claimed to be nonprofit and nonpolitical. But its objective was strident opposition to desegregation; its members included congressmen, ministers, and housewives. Husband-and-wife memberships were offered at $10 per annum, the same price as a single membership. The organization attracted some ten thousand members, becoming an important source of funding for new all-white segregation academies. Its members were "people from all walks of life," as the historian Brian Lee put it: white people engaged in a sense of "a shared fate among the white citizens in something greater than themselves." The organization presented itself as a union of concerned parents and public officials working for the welfare of children by preserving "racial integrity."[2]

But its principal and most influential members were local oligarchs in Virginia's Southside, such as the diminutive, cigar-chomping *Farmville Herald* owner J. Barrye Wall, who shaped his newspaper into a propaganda outlet denouncing integration, the Warren Supreme Court, and the NAACP.[3]

In the *Herald*, the specter of Communist influence on American youths was a perennial subject, and dark intimations spread across the editorial pages that civil rights activism and support for immigration were a Soviet plot. Its members infiltrated and then dominated school boards and raised hundreds of thousands of dollars to acquire land for segregation academies. Segregation academies were usually Christian schools affiliated with the South's white Protestant churches—one public school official in Charleston told the NAACP in 1972 that one way to identify a segregated academy was to look for the word *Christian* or *church* in its name.[4]

In one 1958 edition of the Defenders' newsletter, *Defenders' News and Views*, the broader political aim was made particularly stark—envisioning a future in which integration led to the complete dissolution of public schools. "Perhaps the day may come when private schools will replace all public schools," wrote an anonymous editorialist. "Let us never surrender our priceless heritage of freedom and independence."[5] The "priceless heritage of freedom" in question was segregation, and in Prince Edward County the entire public school system was closed down, leaving legions of Black children bereft of any educational opportunities at all. The Black residents of the county, led by the remarkable Reverend L. Francis Griffin, waged a fierce battle for their education; students walked out of inadequate segregated schools en masse, and the national NAACP joined the fight. Still, it took half a decade and another Supreme Court edict to force the public schools to reopen and to integrate. The effects have lingered: 20 percent of the county lives in poverty, its illiteracy rate of 16 percent is four points higher than the state average, and the chronically underfunded school district faces declining enrollment.

In the slow unraveling of the Jim Crow legal regime in the US South, a new phrase, now an indelible part of the lexicon of American politics, was born (or born again), and achieved ubiquity: *religious liberty*. It meant: If we nail a cross over the door and say our school is private, we're allowed to exclude Black people. And keep our tax exemption.

It was the latter bit that ultimately woke the sleeping kraken of the Christian Right, brought a new political force into its own, and turned churchgoers into politicians and politicians into holy guardians of a segregated Christian order. Prior to the mid-twentieth century, evangelicals had set out to create a world of their own, away from the grubby, sinful, and decidedly worldly realm of politics; they'd created their own churches, schools, and universities, their own books, even their own movies, such as the Rapture-oriented film series *A Thief in the Night*.[6] But having turned to God and away from the world, white evangelicals in the South nonetheless found the world looking in at them and the way the newfound parochial schools were whites-only and the evangelical universities were whites-only, too. After the passage of the Civil Rights Act of 1964, the world began to get interested. For that reason, a majority of Black Christians in the United States, although many are deeply devout and even eager to spread the Good Word, do not identify with the label "evangelical"; it was designed to keep them out.

⁓

ACCORDING TO THE HISTORIAN RANDALL BALMER, WHOSE BOOK *BAD Faith: Race and the Rise of the Religious Right* described the intricate path from the evangelical past to its present, the real awakening of the religious Right as a political force came not after the case of *Roe v. Wade* but after a different and far less famous one, *Green v. Kennedy*.[7] Outside the annals of evangelical history, it barely made a ripple; within those confines, it began a flood. It was a 1970 Supreme Court ruling on a case brought by a group of Black parents in Holmes County, Mississippi, who argued that three new all-white private K–12 academies being built in the aftermath of school desegregation should be denied tax-exempt status. By that point, white enrollment in the county's public schools had dropped to zero: segregation academies were cropping up in their place.

In 1971, the Supreme Court ruled that any organization engaged in racial segregation or discrimination was not a charitable institution by definition and therefore could not claim tax-exempt status—a status that had hitherto been claimed by the legions of religious segregation academies that had sprouted up like bad mushrooms after the *Brown* ruling. And the IRS, empowered under the Carter and Nixon administrations, began asking questions, sending letters even to the Lynchburg Christian Academy, run by the evangelical titan Jerry Falwell himself. Falwell wasn't pleased. Neither were the leaders of Bob Jones University, an evangelical institution made infamous for its obduracy on the question of segregation (to which its answer was: yes); BJU, despite having reluctantly admitted a few Black students—only married ones, so they wouldn't engage in race mixing; the school had a ban on interracial dating—found its tax-exempt status stripped away in 1976.

In 1971, the Supreme Court, prompted by a class action suit brought by the parents of two Black students barred from northern Virginia segregation academies, ruled that private schools could not discriminate on the basis of race. In 1978, the IRS proclaimed that it would strip the tax exemption of any school unless it could prove it had a "significant number of minority students."[8]

The prospect of the government laying its grubby hands on all those tax exemptions animated the evangelical bloc, which had been drifting gradually rightward in the Red Scare–tinted decades after the Second World

War. *Green v. Kennedy* and its associated rulings had a galvanizing effect on that drift: it turned it into a landslide, one that was suddenly aimed at crushing its opposition.[9] Canny political operatives who had been prodding the great mass of devout conservative churchgoers for decades, seeking any sign of the massive and powerful voting bloc they knew was in there somewhere, suddenly saw their opening.

But "Segregation now, segregation tomorrow, segregation forever" wasn't a slogan designed to win the hearts and minds of those who weren't inclined toward it already.[10] It took a special kind of mind to look at the white Christian parents arrayed at the school gates, determined to get their tax exemptions and never let a Black student in except over their (or preferably the students') dead bodies, and turn that rage into a cry of "religious freedom." Religious liberty meant that under a cross they could keep out anyone they wanted to. It meant, in fact, that anything they did or said came under the stamp of morality, because it was they who were saying it and they who defined themselves as the guardians of the true faith. It was a tautology—and a masterstroke in the quintessentially American art of marketing. In a single stroke, it whitewashed segregationists into crusaders for members of the Right to practice their faith unmolested.

It is Paul Weyrich who is most often credited with the creation of the "New Right," the muscular and powerful Right that propelled Ronald Reagan into the presidency and has kept social welfare programs skeletal ever since.[11] For the thirty-five years of his political career, which ended at his death in 2008, he helped cocreate some dozen prominent conservative organizations, among them the right-wing model legislation juggernaut ALEC—and, perhaps more significantly, united the free-market Right and the religious Right.[12]

Weyrich was the genius behind the alchemy that turned segregation academies into bastions of religious liberty; he, Phyllis Schlafly, and other canny figures who paired earnest religious zealotry with breathtaking cynicism realized that a legion of self-proclaimed moral guardians of the nation could come in very handy. The hostility to federal intervention on the part of the Christian Right could also be turned to serve the essentially libertarian ends of people who'd gotten filthy, stinking rich and wanted to stay that way. The people who could double-think so skillfully—who could advocate for laws that would surveil women until they were little more than chattel and for the return of sodomy laws that turned cops into bedroom-window peepers, while all the time trumpeting that they were the true and sole guardians of free speech, religious freedom, and every other form of liberty—were a useful bunch to keep around and keep fed on dark dollars until they grew bold enough to grasp the levers of power. Such people could be persuaded to care about abortion, to vote against gay rights, and, at the same time, to keep corporate taxes very low.

The Christian Right and the big-business lobby grew together and commingled, trading zeal for cash and spawning congregants in their thousands. It was worse than an unholy union; it was a holy one. In the Reagan 1980s, it grew fat and healthy on the corpses of AIDS victims, whose homosexuality meant that they were too sinful and distasteful to cure; in the 1990s, it fed on abstinence-only sex education; and in the early 2000s, it grew fatter still with post-9/11 wartime nationalism.

The election of Barack Obama to the presidency in 2008 sparked a renewed vigor in the Christian Right. It was the ultimate insult: the integration not just of schools but of the sacred and heretofore pure-white office of the US presidency. Accordingly, in October 2009, less than a year after Obama's inauguration, the Christian Right's struggle to control American society reached an inflection point. One hundred forty-eight clergymen—primarily evangelical Protestants, though Catholic and Orthodox priests participated—gathered in New York City to create and sign the Manhattan Declaration. The text plainly laid out the limits of Christian obedience to civil authority—and their willingness to defy it. The declaration was written a year before the Affordable Care Act, with its coverage of abortion, was passed, and six years before the Supreme Court decision on *Obergefell v. Hodges*, which legalized gay marriage throughout the country.[13] It was in part an anticipation of a cultural shift and, in greater part, a declaration to stand squarely against social change. An excerpt reads:

Christians are heirs of a 2,000-year tradition of proclaiming God's word, seeking justice in our societies, resisting tyranny, and reaching out with compassion to the poor, oppressed and suffering...

...Through the centuries, Christianity has taught that civil disobedience is not only permitted, but sometimes required...

Because we honor justice and the common good, we will not comply with any edict that purports to compel our institutions to participate in abortions, embryo-destructive research, assisted suicide and euthanasia, or any other anti-life act; nor will we bend to any rule purporting to force us to bless immoral sexual partnerships, treat them as marriages or the equivalent, or refrain from proclaiming the truth, as we know it, about morality and immorality and marriage and the family. We will fully and ungrudgingly render to Caesar what is Caesar's. But under no circumstances will we render to Caesar what is God's.[14]

The 148 men who signed the declaration, all powerful religious figures in their own right, ranging from pastors to priests to professors and Christian university presidents, were soon joined by legions more who added their names to the document. It was, in its restrained language, a masterpiece of politesse, but it was nonetheless a declaration of war. The document executed a neat three-point rhetorical turn: it positioned its signers and their flocks as the inheritors of a two-thousand-year-old tradition of principled suffering; it enshrined the US government as a sprawling, heathen, corruption-riddled modern incarnation of the Roman Empire; and it positioned the disobedience of laws, particularly those that barred discrimination and required the administration of health care to women, as a noble act, one that might, in the finest Christian tradition, require martyrdom. It contained a piece of the future: a prediction of the years of culture warfare that would follow, the acts of opposition to gay marriage, the continued building of judicial power until *Roe v. Wade* was toppled, and homophobia whipped to a fever pitch among the faithful. The Obama era saw a hitherto untold explosion of mythmaking and misinformation, the intimations of persecution made enormous from pastors' pulpits, of the careful cultivation of anger, fear, and faith. It was from that deliberate cultivation of the faithful that the Trump era arose, and in the present moment it is the faithful that seek its return.

If the 1960s presented their own unique perils to American public education, the present has no shortage of parallels. After the United States' stuttering and disconnected school year of 2020, during which teachers died in droves, mothers dropped out of the workforce in record numbers, and all-digital learning exacerbated preexisting inequities, the onslaught of protest roiled school boards already reeling from the impacts of the pandemic. In the following years, a right-wing movement funded by well-heeled national organizations exploited the panic and imbued it with a vicious, intractable certainty. During the pandemic, departments of education around the country faced interlinked and overlapping right-wing protest movements; those parents not fulminating against godless anti-racist curricula or the presence of transgender and gay students protested covid-19 precautions. The problem has since metastasized to become national. In practice, this is the biggest threat the public education system has faced since the 1950s; and, as the Republican operative David Avella put it on *Fox News* in 2021, the current strife will be "a boon for private schools, for charter schools": nouveau segregation academies.

In 2019, amid a flood of ten-year retrospective pieces about the Manhattan Declaration, Jonathan Lange, a Lutheran pastor and the leader of the Wyoming Pastors Network, built on the document's original intent in a piece for the Federalist. Marriage, he claimed, is a sacrament under threat in the wake of *Obergefell*, one that ties together Holy Writ with the biological orders written into men's and women's chromosomes. No-fault divorce had run riot, gay marriage was legal, and the nation was in peril. The declaration, he wrote, had made its uncompromising stance primarily in defense of children, those unborn and those already present, who could thrive only within the bounds of heterosexual marriage, as defined by both nature and God. "Since marriage so deeply affects the welfare of children, the Manhattan Declaration also calls upon every Christian to speak in defense of the life of every child conceived. While faith informs

Christian action, it does not limit it," he wrote. "The faithful do not do this primarily in self-defense, but in defense of all people. It is a duty of love to stand with any man, woman, or child who has been defrauded by a government derelict in its duties...Our grandchildren are watching to see how we respond."[15] It is a signature of Christian-Right rhetoric to position themselves as the defenders of children; by extension, this makes their opponents adherents of child predation, a danger to the innocent and pure.

The Defenders of State Sovereignty and Individual Liberties was founded to fight integration in Virginia in 1954. Nearly three-quarters of a century later, in 2021, 165 miles north of Prince Edward County, the generically named organization Fight for Schools was founded by Ian Prior, a former principal deputy director for public affairs in the Department of Justice under Donald Trump. Unlike the Defenders, whose composition has been demystified by diligent historical work over the past decades, the membership of Fight for Schools is more opaque, its chief and often sole spokesperson in the press being Prior, who has appeared on *Fox News* at least eight times, has attended rallies alongside Ben Carson, and has been a steady darling of the right-wing news outlet the Daily Caller. Nonetheless, its political aims are no less stark and echo those of the Defenders; it's headquartered in Loudoun County, a county with a checkered and brutal desegregation history of its own. (The year before Fight for Schools was founded, the county issued a belated apology to the Black community for an integration process that had taken fourteen years of bitter, massive resistance to overcome.)

Fight for Schools was founded to combat the nebulous specter of critical race theory (CRT), a phrase that nominally refers to an academic discipline that explores racism's role in social systems but has in recent years become a bête noire of the Right. In its dog-whistle-ridden "Why We Fight" manifesto, Fight for Schools lays out a sinister vision of public education, presenting itself as a critical bulwark against the indoctrination and diminishment of white children, insisting that by utilizing "critical race theory concepts," which hold that American meritocracy is systematically racist, schools are teaching children to see everything through the lens of race. In the face of this threat, Fight for Schools offers the bulwark of parental rights, and expresses its desire to strip public education of anti-racist concepts by electing "common-sense candidates" that support "meritocracy." The meaning of "meritocracy," as it howls through the gaps between the lines of the manifesto, is simply that the American status quo, in which white leadership dominates in nearly every sector, is not only just, but the natural state of things—and anyone who seeks to change that is a threat.

"Help support our cause to take back America's schools," they appeal.

Aided by an eager right-wing media, Fight for Schools has been featured in countless roundups of the "parent-led rebellion" against "indoctrination" that has swept across the nation. And it has made Loudoun County School Board meetings a raucous, nationally watched mess. Loudoun County parents have compared diversity initiatives to an "American version of the Chinese cultural revolution" and denounced its roots in "cultural Marxism." Numerous members of the Loudoun County School Board faced Fight for Schools–sponsored recall petition drives that have garnered thousands of signatures; one member, Beth Barts, resigned after a scandal caused by her membership in a group called Anti-Racist Parents of Loudoun County. School board meetings have become the sites of ferocious protests against anti-racist education and trans-inclusive policies: in June 2021, holding signs that read "Education Not Indoctrination," angry residents drowned out speakers with a raucous rendition of "The Star-Spangled Banner" at a meeting that led to at least one arrest. "Shame on you," they chanted, their white faces mottled with red.

This current, perilous moment in American education hearkens back to mid-century conflicts over school desegregation. The principal difference is that the era of "massive resistance" was largely, though not entirely, concentrated in southern states. In an era in which right-wing media are ubiquitous, national, and paranoiac and spread via memes, Facebook groups, and untethered dark money, such sentiments are more diffuse; they stretch countrywide. (When I mentioned writing a feature about school boards on Twitter, dozens of people reached out to me, asking me to look into meetings in their districts in Tennessee, Kansas, Texas, Idaho, Connecticut, Indiana, Maryland, Washington, and Ohio.)

The anti–critical race theory movement has compounded the pressure on depleted and exhausted educators, and is bolstered by state legislatures around the country. Dedicated right-wing activists have elected to run for school board en masse, potentially engulfing US public education in a reactionary miasma for years to come. The movement is well funded by organizations such as Intercessors for America, Moms for Liberty, and the Leadership Institute; principally organized around opposition to anti-racist education; and strengthened by years of pandemic paranoia. The year 2021 saw more recall efforts against school board members than any other year on record, and numbers remained high.

In practice, the anti–critical race theory protests are based on a cut-and-paste template of prior American moral panics: CRT will lead to the diminishment of white children's morale; it is a form of socialist subversion; it is a fundamental threat to the American way of life. These reactionary forces have plagued the United States in waves for a century, but when combined with the extraordinary circumstances of a plague, they burgeoned into an existential threat to public education as we know it.

The attack on school boards became a roiling affair in which moral panics past and present surged, a catch-all assault on public education. In 2021, in Brevard County, Florida, a school board member named Jennifer Jenkins recounted, in somber and even tones, the threats and harassment she had faced for her support of mask mandates in schools. Initially, her opposition had been antigay members of Moms for Liberty, a group linked to the Christian Right that has mounted campaigns to censor schoolbooks around the United States.[16] Things got more heated, though, when Jenkins sought to uphold a mask mandate in schools during the height of the pandemic. Protesters were seen carrying weapons in the church parking lot behind her home, burned the letters *FU* into her lawn with weed killer, even chopped down her bushes.

According to an editorial Jenkins wrote in the *Washington Post*, fifteen neighbors had gathered outside her house to chant "Pedophiles!" As she recounted, the chants had grown even more threatening: "'We're coming for you,' they yelled, mistaking friends standing on my porch for me and my husband. 'We're coming at you like a freight train! We are going to make you beg for mercy. If you thought January 6 was bad, wait until you see what we have for you!'" Jenkins said they had reported her, falsely, to the Florida Department of Children and Families, claiming that she had abused her five-year-old daughter. She hadn't. She had supported a policy that during a period in the pandemic in which no children under the age of twelve had been vaccinated, masks should be worn in the county's schools. While mandatory vaccinations and public health measures for plagues such as smallpox and polio have been met with resistance movements in the past, covid-19 arrived at the crest of a decades-long antivaccination wave—and in an era of increasingly well funded and immersive right-wing media.[17]

All across the country, similar stories have unfolded, with blocs of dedicated right-wing activists—some parents, some not—enacting an interlinked series of protests against the public education system. In Hampton Roads, Virginia, a man with a knife in his waistband screamed expletives at a school board meeting, and police investigated shooting threats directed at board members over covid protocols. In Kent County, Michigan, the Health Department director reported that a woman had repeatedly tried to run him off the road at seventy miles an hour following the establishment of a mask mandate in schools.[18] In Williamson County, Tennessee, health care experts who had testified in favor of masking were subjected to death threats by screaming parents.[19] In 2023, police were called on the family of a school board member in Dripping Springs, Texas, the allegation being that there had been a domestic disturbance in her home; there hadn't been.[20] School librarians across the state, facing record numbers of book bans, left their professions in 2023; those who remained were subjected to social media posts by community members calling them "pedophiles," "groomers," and "bearers of the millstone"—a reference to a verse in the Bible that condemns all those who tempt children to sin to be executed by drowning with a millstone around their necks.

The movement expanded to encompass other panics. In 2022 Florida passed a law, HB 1557, commonly known by its critics as the "Don't Say

Gay" law, and similar measures have been under consideration in many states. While certainly homophobic, the law is really an attack on queerness as a whole: it prohibits teachers from discussing gender identity and sexual orientation from kindergarten onward. This law and others like it force gay and trans teachers into the closet, keep students forcibly ignorant of their own and others' identities, and marginalize or endanger queer parents. Since the beginning, the rationale has been a ferociously bigoted, and deeply wrongheaded, conflation of queerness and the "grooming" of children. In the context of sexual assault and abuse, grooming is the act of readying a victim—through isolation, inappropriate physical contact, and other forms of behavioral conditioning—so that he or she will be less likely to resist or report such abuse. Like other terms (*woke* and *triggered* come to mind), the term *grooming* has been avidly adopted and warped beyond recognition by the right-wing media sphere. Needless to say, reading a book about trans rights or learning that your female teacher has a wife is nothing close to grooming, which is the careful cultivation of a victim to make him or her vulnerable to sexual abuse. The conflation of homosexuality or gender nonconformity with pedophilia is a shopworn, long-debunked avenue of prejudice.

Still, proponents of the new law argued that anyone who opposed it must, ipso facto, be a pedophile or sympathetic to pedophilia. In March 2023, Christina Pushaw, then press secretary for Governor Ron DeSantis, tweeted, "The bill that liberals inaccurately call 'Don't Say Gay' would be more accurately described as an Anti-Grooming Bill."[21] "If you're against the Anti-Grooming Bill, you are probably a groomer or at least you don't denounce the grooming of 4–8 year old children," she wrote. "Silence is complicity. This is how it works, Democrats, and I didn't make the rules."[22]

The Florida legislation, however, extends far beyond four- to eight-year-olds, stating that "classroom instruction by school personnel or third parties on sexual orientation or gender identity may not occur in kindergarten through grade 3 or in a manner that is not age appropriate or developmentally appropriate for students in accordance with state standards"—a

subjective consideration that covers all schoolchildren, caters to conservative parents, and can be enforced via monetary damages and administra-
tive retribution.[23]

Since Pushaw's statements, the "groomer" libel has snowballed. The
Walt Disney Company, a major Florida employer that faced internal
protests from employees and external pressure from fans for financially
supporting the authors of HB 1557, eventually came out against the bill,
stating that the law should be repealed and pledging a modest $5 mil-
lion to LGBTQ+ organizations. What followed was a surge of anti-Disney
outrage by the loudest bigots this nation has to offer. The neo-Nazi-
adjacent social media influencer Jack Posobiec promoted a T-shirt for
sale reading "Boycott Groomers" in Disney's signature font, with "bring
ammo" in smaller text.[24]

In April 2022, the swirl of conspiracies came to a head. Led by the
social media–savvy extremist pastor Sean Feucht, a motley but sizable
group of conspiracy theorists and far-right activists gathered outside Disney headquarters in Burbank, California, carrying an array of signs from
virulently homophobic slogans to Don't Tread on Me flags. Among the
slogans: "Boycott Disney and Their Attack on Our Kids: It's a Satanic
Agenda."[25]

More grimly, Robert Foster, a former GOP state representative and
gubernatorial candidate in Mississippi, tweeted that anyone who teaches
children that "men are women" should be "lined up against [a] wall by a
firing squad to be sent to an early judgment."[26]

QAnoners have long made clear that "pedophile" is synonymous with
their political opposition. Furthermore, QAnon's central fantasy is the
mass execution of alleged pedophiles at some point in the perennially near
future. Extending that paradigm to anyone queer or trans—and encouraging the enraged to "bring ammo"—is an open-source call to violence.
At stake in the Manichaean worldview that has spread throughout the
GOP is the necessity to protect the "innocence" of children—idealized,
middle-class, white children, anyway—which is an ideal worth killing for.

In general, this paranoiac worldview uses the safety of children as a cudgel against anyone who does not conform to a white, straight, fundamentalist Christian order.

The official title of HB 1557, "Parental Rights in Education," lifts the mask on its true goal: it weakens the power of public institutions to intervene in family abuse while consolidating power in the hands of those most likely to abuse kids—their relatives. (According to the Centers for Disease Control and Prevention, 91 percent of child sexual abuse is perpetrated by someone known to the child or their relatives, including parents.) In the United States, it is parents who are empowered to approve child marriage; only six states prohibit all marriages under the age of eighteen. In five states, there is no lower limit on marriageable age at all. Fifteen states require judicial approval for underage marriages, some of which will verify parental consent. In six more, the lowest age limit is below the age of sixteen, according to a 2019 analysis by the Tahirih Justice Center.[27] According to the anti–forced marriage nonprofit Unchained at Last, three hundred thousand minors were married in the United States between 2000 and 2018, some as young as age ten.[28] Most were girls wed to adult men an average of four years older. Of course, none of that had anything to do with queerness, and it left parental rights intact, so those three hundred thousand minors didn't fall under the aegis of the panic about protecting kids from sexual exploitation.

Abusers tend to utilize positions of power and community acceptance to hide their misdeeds: the Jimmy Saviles and Jerry Sanduskys of the world and the Margaret Thatchers and Joe Paternos who protect them; the neighbor, the father, the friend of the family, the pastor, the respectable businessman, the youth group leader, the coach.

⌣

FLORIDA GOVERNOR RON DESANTIS IS A FORMER LAWYER WHOSE MILItary service included providing legal advice to torturers at Guantánamo Bay; one former detainee claims that DeSantis personally oversaw his force-feeding, though the governor denies this. More proudly, he claims the mantle of defender of a Christian nation. In May 2023, during his brief but staggeringly expensive campaign to become the Republican candidate for the presidency, he made sure to stop by Cambridge Christian School in Tampa, a high-profile institution for evangelical Christian education established in 1964. Cambridge Christian had been the center of a legal battle in 2015, when it was barred from broadcasting prayers over the speaker system during a championship game against another school. "Next time Cambridge Christian returns to play for a state championship—and we will return—we will pray over the loudspeaker before kickoff," said the school's principal when introducing the governor.[29] One rule of a battle is to always choose your ground carefully and know who your allies are. In picking that particular evangelical redoubt, DeSantis had done both.

It was a useful place for him to sign a package of five bills into law. One bill, which he named "Let Kids Be Kids," banned gender-affirming medical care for any person under eighteen.[30] Another prohibited teachers from asking students about their preferred pronouns and expanded on a previous ban prohibiting any discussion of gender or sexuality so that now it stretched from pre-K to eighth grade. A third banned minors from attending drag shows on pain of the shuttering of premises providing "adult performances." A fourth required all public bathrooms to be restricted to use by people of the gender assigned at birth and forced juvenile prisoners to be assigned to facilities that matched their birth sex, regardless of any gender transition in the interim. The fifth allowed prayers before high school sports matches.

In short, it was a legislative gallop into the realms of censorship and the careful inspection of children's genitals, designed to evoke a pall of permanent fear in teachers, librarians, and queer youth. In August 2023, in response to the laws restricting the teaching of anything pertaining to gender identity, the College Board, which ensures students receive standardized advanced education across the country, announced that Advanced Placement (AP) Psychology would no longer be taught in the state. "We are sad to have learned that today the Florida Department of Education has effectively banned AP Psychology in the state by instructing Florida superintendents that teaching foundational content on sexual orientation and gender identity is illegal under state law. The state has said districts are free to teach AP Psychology only if it excludes any mention of these essential topics," the College Board wrote in a statement.[31]

It wasn't a fluke or an unintended consequence; it was a choice made by a small man in a big pulpit constructed by the zeal of his allies. The weakening of external authority only makes control of children within the family unit easier. It only makes the bubble less porous, the air inside thinner and harder to breathe.

⌢

HIGH SUMMER IN LOS ANGELES IS AT LEAST AS HOT AS ONE OF THE FIRES of Hell, possibly one of the smaller ones, the one on the level for, perhaps, petty thieves and overly creative accountants.

Nonetheless, it was there, in the dog days of August 2023, that a throng gathered outside the Los Angeles Unified School District building. Although they were gathering around a place of education, their shirts said "Leave Our Kids Alone." And they were shouting. They were also playing conservative rap, although this in and of itself, sadly, isn't a crime. The song they picked was called "God over Government," by Hi-Rez and Jimmy Levy, which has a beat like a store full of synthesizers exploding and lyrics like this:

> *They coming for children and all our traditions*
> *So get ammunition prepare for the war*
> *The revolution is in store*
> *I'm waiting for them at my door.*[32]

And so on. They were there to protest the purported brainwashing of their children by public schools, although at least one of their spokespeople was homeschooling hers prophylactically. Several had been involved in a contretemps over a book read to kids in a nearby school that mentioned gay people, in that it mentioned that some children have two mothers and some have two fathers; those particular concerned citizens had decided to demonstrate that some children have very loud parents. Now they were there with their banners, handmade by a woman who also provides similar services for the Proud Boys and other local far-right groups: a Christian flag with a blue cross on a white field and another flag, a pine tree on white embroidered with the words "The Appeal to Heaven," which signifies that the bearer will find no justice among authorities on Earth and must look higher. It is more or less the unofficial flag of Christian nationalism in the United States, and there it flew above the baking asphalt in the shimmer of heat and the chant of hate.

One of the participants, a man in white, was determined to have his say. "You guys cannot indoctrinate our kids," he shouted into a livestream camera. "That's our job as parents."[33]

That said, perhaps, more than he meant it to. In fact, it said nearly everything.

All over the country there have been laws passed censoring teachers and libraries. And all over the country this has led to a slew of consequences: teachers quitting, library books being removed from the shelves, lawsuits and countersuits, a push by conservative influencers to start homeschooling children, a miasma of threat hanging over school board meetings, and a fug of sullen ire hanging over schools themselves. And the accusation— the drumbeat of accusation, sometimes quiet, sometimes full bore, like the rough music of home-brewed justice—that schools are predatory, are hotbeds of pedophilia, are making your kids gay, are making your kids trans, are making your kids disobey you. That schools are taking your kids away, exposing them to ideas you don't approve of; there ought to be a law against it.

All that put together smells like a threat.

In Florida, under the leadership of DeSantis, one of a cadre of reactionary Catholics who form part of the religious Right, a bosom companion of every evangelical available, endorsed by a number of charismatic prophets, and the terror of teachers in the entire state, being a teacher or school librarian involves an increasing number of legal hazards.

Those aren't the only laws he's passed in the realm of education. Of particular note is the focus the Florida educational regime has placed on history, the sanitization of it; specifically the breezy notion that chattel slavery was a kind of skills program that ultimately benefited the people who endured a system of labor unto death, mass rape, and the routine theft of their children. In *Florida's State Academic Standards–Social Studies, 2023*, the curriculum for African American history is salted with "clarifications": clarifications that work to wheedle and push and insinuate a worldview in which hundreds of years of chattel slavery in America weren't that bad after all. One clarification, which drew particular ire from the NAACP and other civil rights organizations, is the following pernicious shard of text:

SS.68.AA.2.3: Examine the various duties and trades performed by slaves (e.g., agricultural work, painting, carpentry, tailoring, domestic service, blacksmithing, transportation).
Benchmark Clarifications:
Clarification 1: Instruction includes how slaves developed skills which, in some instances, could be applied for their personal benefit.[34]

In response to the controversy raised by the curriculum, DeSantis told NBC, "They're probably going to show some of the folks that eventually parlayed, you know, being a blacksmith into, into doing things later in life."[35]

Most people born into slavery died in it; there was no "later in life" in which to pursue other occupations. Enslavement wasn't a hobby. But the Florida Board of Education took pains to minimize it. Doing so made sense, for a particular reason: to preserve the founding myth of Christian nationalism, of a sinless state, the damning influence of history has to be dampened.

Some of these distortions are now codified into the curriculum standards of the Florida State Board of Education—with extra laws, with more teeth, to keep teachers in their place. Other states have other laws with similar "patriotic" goals. These laws are designed to wipe history cleaner than it ever was, but chiefly to stoke fear of the other, and to utilize the greatest tool of the religious authoritarian: absolute control from the beginning of life to its end—with a particular focus on the beginning.

Many evangelicals, in their careful, even selective, readings of the Bible, pay particular attention to Psalm 127, verses 4 and 5: "As arrows are in the hand of a mighty man; so are children of the youth. Happy is the man that hath his quiver full of them." The verse gave a name to the "Quiverfull" movement, a cultic strain in evangelicalism that encourages couples to eschew birth control in favor of creating an army for the Lord. They may, the verse continues, "speak with the enemies in the gate." Which are, in the evangelical mind, everywhere.

But the thing about arrows is that they don't start out that way. They start out as wood that needs to be whittled down to size, metal that needs to be forged and beaten, shaped into a weapon while it's soft. One bad wind, an errant surge from the bellows, and an arrow is useless, blunted. It has to be kept carefully under control.

Of course, the desire to keep the minds of children and young adults under control isn't limited to Florida; that state just happens to do it bigger and louder and hotter, as is its wont, and under the guidance of a cunning, unscrupulous man who never met a suit that liked him and never met an evangelical who didn't. Ron DeSantis has a special kind of reverse charisma—what the British author Terry Pratchett called charisn'tma—with a smile like half-melted rubber, a stiff gait, and a semipermanent defensive cringe in large groups. What he is good at, what keeps getting him reelected as governor and inspired him to run for the presidency, is his ability to engender fear of those who are designated as "other"—trans people, immigrants, gay people—and create whole new categories to spurn.

DeSantis isn't unique. All across the country, big corn-fed men, little men who feed on their own zeal, and women with bouffant hairdos iron hard with hairspray and righteousness work to undermine the notion of public education and the common good it implies. A *Washington Post* analysis in 2022 found that 283 laws had been proposed in 45 states—64 were signed in 25 states and ultimately affect 42 percent of the American population—censoring curricula to restrict what teachers can say about race, racism, and American history; to change what instructors can teach about gender identity and sexuality; to boost parents' rights over their children's education; to limit students' access to school libraries and books; to circumscribe the rights of transgender students; and/or to promote what legislators defined as a "patriotic" education.[36]

Some educational outlets have begun to anticipate these legal threats and individualized harassment and have capitulated in advance. In 2023, Scholastic, the nation's largest children's book publisher, began building a collection of "diverse" children's books that "engage with the presence of racism" and deal with LGBTQ topics. It also offered an option for school districts to opt out of carrying those books at any particular event, in a move that critics called the installation of a "bigotry button." With one click, school districts could make their children's book collections white, straight, and diversity-free—a capitulation to a loud and bigoted minority driven by hate and zealotry to delimit their children's imaginations for the sake of their "parental rights."

"There is now enacted or pending legislation in more than 30 U.S. states prohibiting certain kinds of books from being in schools—mostly LGBTQIA+ titles and books that engage with the presence of racism in our country," Scholastic said in an October 2023 statement. "Because Scholastic Book Fairs are invited into schools, where books can be purchased by kids on their own, these laws create an almost impossible dilemma: back away from these titles or risk making teachers, librarians, and volunteers vulnerable to being fired, sued, or prosecuted...We cannot make a decision for our school partners around what risks they are willing to take, based on the state and local laws that apply to their district."[37]

PEN America, a nonprofit devoted to literary education and human rights, identified 392 censorship-related laws proposed between 2021 and 2023, of which 38 had been enacted. "Increasingly, bills that exert direct censorship on public educational institutions by prohibiting specific topics or content are being complemented by a different kind of bill—one whose provisions do not censor schools *directly* but rather cast a chilling effect that creates the conditions for censorship *indirectly*, threatening the freedoms to teach and learn with death by a thousand cuts," PEN noted in its report.[38]

A thousand cuts, a thousand arrows, a thousand empty library shelves. The face at the pulpit says, "Yes." And parents say, "Only we can indoctrinate our children."

They are ready to do so. They've been ready for a very long time. That's what the "school choice" bills, the homeschool lobby, and the federal subsidy dollars for parochial schools all add up to: an alternative structure and source of funds for when public schools collapse. Then nothing will be left but the iron dome of indoctrination. It's been their goal for so long that some of the godly may have forgotten that it's where they started from; they never strayed far, and now they have returned.

It's not a coincidence that the assault on public education has an overt veneer of Christian faith—the idea of saving children from godless gays and Communists who want to victimize white children by teaching the history of a country riddled with racist violence. The sound of protests at school board meetings is the sound of the Christian Right returning to its roots.

It all started with schools—with the segregation academies of Virginia, with all those parents bristling with their parental rights who dressed up their hatred in the decorous language of individual liberties. Even now the echoes sound: the odious, astroturfed Moms for Liberty are at the forefront of every ugly attack on education, and the repetitious vocabulary evinces an unbroken chain across seventy years and a whole country's neck. *Liberty* is such a flexible word. It's also a disarming one; who, after all, wants to stand in opposition to liberty, one of the values on which this country was ostensibly founded? It's like going out and declaring that you're against sunsets or world peace. But liberty, as used by those who go around painting it on banners and starting groups with Liberty in capital letters in their names, can also be a weapon.

The slogan "Defend children" is the battle cry of the Christian masses, the justification for every piece of zealotry and bigotry and mythmaking that came before it and any that will come afterward. The last half century has been the story of the transformation of the pious, whose hate turned the fight for segregated schools into a political crusade, into the self-proclaimed arbiters of the nation's conscience and the great moral army whose task is to safeguard its soul. They aim to do it under the armor of defense of children.

In those ranks are people who will tell you that the people who are "grooming" your kids—who pose them great danger—are men who dress up in glittery dresses, kids who want new names to match the way they feel inside, or people who look different, because different is dangerous. They will tell you that sin is something you can see, that, as among reptiles or amphibians, bright colors are the mark of poison. They stand out. They aren't your parents, your pastor, or your youth group counselor—no matter what has happened to you.

The truth is that grooming isn't telling kids that there are different kinds of people in the world; it's telling them that they're worth nothing if they're different, that they are fundamentally alone, that no one will help them, that they shouldn't understand what's happening and why it hurts. Increasing the amount of shame kids feel increases the likelihood that they won't speak about their wounds. That's the vision of the "Don't Say Gay" bill and its world, and it is one that will hurt children and make it easier to silence them. Even now you can't hear them, the kids who are being hurt, over the din of protests by the people who claim to be saving them.

That din is everywhere if you listen for it. It's the sound of power uncoiling and trapping the women and children who are least likely to be able to fight back. All over this country the army of the godly are on the march. Look, and you will see their battle standards unfurled; listen, and you will hear their ram's horns sounding. Their weapons are the cross, the rod, and the wooden spoon. Their objective is to gain complete control of the family sphere, to exact complete obedience. Their desire for control masks itself in piety, godly concern, and disingenuous beatitudes, but in its heart is murder, the snuffing out of all that is other and degenerate, all that is disorderly.

The rhetoric of the Christian Right, which militates so strongly against the rights of children, couches its rhetoric in the language of their defense. Christian titans such as Home School Legal Defense Association cofounder Michael Farris have laid out in no uncertain terms that they believe the right of parents to control their children is both absolute and of divine origin. It is the heart of the Christian Right's plan to gain control of this country from the blood and the bone of its youth. "Parental rights" is a feather-light euphemism for something much darker: a world of hidden pain and absolute control.

While much of this book has concerned itself with evangelicals' efforts to make the entire United States conform to their views of morality—sexual, spiritual, and nationalistic—perhaps the most instructive way to examine the totality of their belief system is to look within the walled gardens of evangelical societies. Set apart from, yet determined to take charge of, American society writ large, these communities operate under strict moral codes that engender tremendous suffering—and are a preview of the dystopia they seek to usher into the country at large. With the aid of more than a hundred interviews with former evangelicals, as well as examination of primary source texts, I was able to get a glimpse into this insular world and in particular its views of what men, women, and children should be. The voices of my interviewees serve as a kind of Greek chorus, echoing the pain inscribed into every line of evangelical doctrine: living tributes, with the scars to match, of what they bore under the yoke of God.

CHAPTER 8

GOOD CHRISTIAN FATHERS

Growing up in northern Illinois in the 1990s, Eddie K. was told exactly who his role models should be. They were swaggering, macho types heavily salted with a dose of public holiness: the pioneering revival preacher Billy Sunday, Ronald Reagan, Confederate general Stonewall Jackson, and Eddie's own dad—the meanest, toughest brawler in town, a mechanic who evangelized at his job at the Illinois Tollway. Eddie confided to me in an interview that he had been told he walked like a fag and been called a sissy, instructed that men didn't show emotions even if their loved ones died. As a Christian man, he would be responsible for his household— God's placeholder in the family; women were objects to guide and to guard, to be kept, as he said in an interview, "like a bonsai tree." Lust might bloom in him, but if it did, it was the fault of women, who were "snares" for him to stumble into. He was told he should be willing to die for his faith, just as Confederate soldiers had died for their freedom. All that, he said, was a promise in exchange for a malleable, virginal bride— one he would protect and control in the name of Christ for the rest of his life as a good Christian husband. And he would never, ever divorce her; divorce, he had been taught, was "satanic."[1]

One of the signature feminist legal achievements of the late twentieth century—that of no-fault divorce, meaning that with a minimum of legal fuss women could free themselves from oppressive, abusive, or simply unfit marriages without having to prove misconduct or infidelity in a court system, is a popular subject of Christian ire. It took a four-decade fight, from 1969 to 2010, for no-fault divorce laws to be enacted in all fifty states. The laws resulted in dramatic decreases in domestic violence, suicide, and femicide—and in certain states, they are under attack.[2]

In its 2022 platform, the Republican Party of Texas, which holds majorities in both chambers of the state's legislature, inserted a clause asserting, "We urge the Legislature to rescind unilateral no-fault divorce laws, to support covenant marriage, and to pass legislation extending the period of time in which a divorce may occur to six months after the date of filing for divorce."[3]

"Covenant marriage" is a legally distinct form of marriage in which couples agree to undergo premarital counseling that emphasizes that marriage is for life and that effectively dispenses with no-fault divorce laws. Those married under covenant marriage are able to divorce only under certain conditions, such as legally provable adultery or sexual abuse, or after two years of legal separation. At present, covenant marriage is legally binding only in Arizona, Louisiana, and Arkansas. Louisiana representative and Speaker of the House Mike Johnson is part of such a marriage, along with his wife, Kelly, who is an outspoken proponent of conversion therapy. In the same platform, the Texas GOP strongly asserted its Christian character, not just in its condemnation of homosexuality as an "abnormal lifestyle choice" and its declaration of pornography and pedophilia as "public health hazards," but also in more explicit ways. Asserting its belief in "Judeo-Christian principles," the party declared its "acknowledgment that the Church is a God-ordained institution with a sphere of authority separate from that of civil government, and thus the Church is not to be regulated, controlled, or taxed by any level of civil government."[4]

Under such a mode of government, femicide is merely an incidental issue, one that certainly does not usurp the sanctity of marriage between, as the GOP so fondly and frequently repeats, one man and one woman—with the man firmly in charge.

Across the country, other state Republican parties have adopted opposition to no-fault divorce in an overall platform built of God-drenched planks that ooze bigotry, zealotry, and a general air of holy roller opprobrium. The Nebraska Republican Party, for example, offers its opposition to no-fault divorce as an integral part of a defense of civilization and hostility to the federal government couched in religious values. On the "Family" page of its party platform, this interrelated series of Christian values—the right to ignore federal law for the sake of religion; the notion of an indivisible, heterosexual nuclear family as a kind of societal self-defense, in which women free from male control are in essence hostile free agents—rolls out in plain white text against a red-and-blue background, American as anything, and staunch, uncompromising, and militant in its mindset:

> The Nebraska Republican Party affirms the family as the natural and indispensable institution for human development...We believe no-fault divorce should be limited to situations in which the couple has no children of the marriage...We believe that the institution of marriage is crucial to the American family and that marriage should be defined as the legal union of one man and one woman.[5]

The Republican Party of Louisiana also considered adopting opposition to no-fault divorce and an option for all couples to engage in covenant marriage in its 2023 platform. The proposed draft language asserted that "Louisiana marriage laws have destroyed the institute of marriage over the past thirty to fifty years." Similarly, but more drastically, a motion to oppose no-fault divorce as a federal stance was considered during the 2016 Republican National Convention, the very same one in which a twice-divorced real estate charlatan became the party's nominee for the presidency. "Children are made to be loved by both natural parents united in marriage," read the proposed platform language. "Legal structures such as No Fault Divorce, which divides families and empowers the state should be replaced by a Fault-based Divorce."[6]

As the historian Caroline Shanley put it when addressing GOP attacks on no-fault divorce laws, the whole crusade is part of a broader attempt to place women firmly under male control, and to determinedly annihilate both their bodily autonomy and their equal citizenship. "Women of the 21st century are currently living through direct, concerted attacks to their rights including reproductive choice," she wrote for CNN in 2023, a year abortion bans rolled through states about as often as tornadoes and left more destruction in their wake. "This renewed assault on divorce shows how quickly purported concerns about marriage can become a proxy for a conservative agenda that wants to reinforce women's subordination to men."[7]

EXTREME POSITIONS ABOUT DIVORCE ARE ECHOED BY—OR ORIGINATE from—the beating heart of evangelical Christianity's largest institutions. "God hates divorce in every case," Gary Chapman, a Baptist pastor and frequent content contributor to evangelical lobbying juggernaut Focus on the Family, intoned into a microphone in a 2019 YouTube video for the organization's half-million YouTube subscribers.[8]

There's a diagram that's instantly familiar to a good many people who have been educated as evangelical Christians, even those who weren't homeschooled. It was originally designed and disseminated by Bill Gothard, an accused serial sexual predator, the former titan of Christian homeschooling, and the founder of the infamous Institute in Basic Life Principles (IBLP). (Gothard resigned his decades-long stint as leader of the IBLP in 2014 after thirty-four women came forward to accuse him of sexual harassment and molestation, though he was never convicted of a crime.) His vision of Christian patriarchy has shaped and permeated generations of the Christian Right. The image he repeated in diagram after diagram is simple: a downpour cascading over three umbrellas of decreasing size, each one sheltered by a larger one. The largest one is labeled CHRIST; the second HUSBAND (underneath the HUSBAND umbrella, the texts PROTECT FAMILY and PROVIDE FOR FAMILY provide helpful pointers);

below the husband, a smaller umbrella reads WIFE (under which the labels CHILDREN and MANAGERS OF HOME appear). In other cartoons, he labels the umbrella GOD-GIVEN AUTHORITY and the rain "Destruction."[9]

Gothard's diagrams are as simple as a knife and cut to the heart of the evangelical movement more broadly. His arguments reached thousands of evangelical parents, and his curricula helped raise their children; although he personally has fallen from grace, his ideas retain a potent influence over the tens of millions of members of the Christian Right. The ideas Gothard presents are profoundly patriarchal, and they have significant staying power: in November 2023, the Christian influencer "The Transformed Wife," a proud antifeminist who advocates for women to be expelled from church leadership, posted Gothard's umbrellas diagram to her fifty thousand Instagram followers, garnering twelve hundred likes. In the grid of her posts, it lay between photos of a pumpkin pie and chicken soup. According to the doctrine relayed by Gothard and its many followers, without a husband's God-given authority, a wife is doomed to destruction, as are her children. Only Christ reigns above the husband, shielding him; to step out from under the umbrellas of protection, as he calls his model, is to face annihilation. Setting up a patriarchal hierarchy, through which a wife's access to God is only through her husband and the children reside somewhere below them both, is as simple as the few lines in an IBLP "wisdom booklet" distributed through Christian households. For evangelical men, the reality is simple: adhere to a model of forceful masculinity, control and dominate women in the guise of protection and provision, and make damn sure not to step out of line, or else, as God once said to Adam, thou shalt surely die.

Gothard's teachings were made famous by the Duggar family, the stars of a long-running reality show on TLC called *19 Kids and Counting* (the title kept changing over the years as the family's matriarch, Michelle Duggar, birthed more kids). The IBLP distributed "wisdom booklets" that provided the framework for the makeshift homeschooling of their nineteen children.[10] The curriculum is a motley collection of homilies, proverbs, anachronistic math, and frankly racist sketches of history (such as the idea, promoted in certain Christian curricula, that the Trail of Tears, an act of genocide in which thousands of Native Americans died while they were forced to relocate en masse, was ultimately a good thing because it led them to Jesus). At the center of many Christian homeschool curricula is a continual fixation on sexual purity, which forms part of studies from a very early age. In the one example of a wisdom booklet featured in the 2023 documentary *Shiny Happy People*, which examined the Duggars and the broader culture of child abuse within evangelical communities, children were encouraged to identify "eye traps" in the outfits of cartoon women: features such as low necklines and sheer sleeves that were designed to draw sexual attention and were, therefore, the very fabric of sin.[11]

But the IBLP predated the Duggars by nearly half a century, and its origins are deeply entrenched in the conservative backlash to the feminist movement and the rising divorce rate that accompanied the slow adoption of no-fault divorce throughout the 1970s and '80s. Its models, and similar groups' teachings, have percolated throughout fundamentalist communities in the United States, providing a rigid and unbending godly model of the family, a model that millions of Americans were raised in—and are emulating as they raise their own families.

For many years, opposition to women's rights and no-fault divorce has been central to the way fundamentalist sects have influenced broader evangelical culture. But the IBLP and groups working in harmony with its aims are not just concerned with denouncing the evils of the world; they are also interested in affirming ideas about masculinity and biblical headship that conflict with societal changes that have taken root over the past half century. Generations of men and boys have been nursed to resent and seek to overturn a "feminized" society, not just in courtrooms but in church groups and militia units. Their goal is to create a kind of parallel society composed exclusively of ideal Christians in ideal marriages, in which women are subject to the will of men and men are subject only to the laws of God.

Even beyond the bonds of marriage—which are solid as iron and quite as restrictive—contemporary evangelical Christianity in the United States has plenty of ideas about what being a Christlike Christian man is all about. It will come as no surprise that most of them have very little to do with, say, developing skill at carpentry.

There are many definitions of being "Christlike" across the broad spectrum of Christianity, but in fundamentalist contexts, the qualities held up as being necessary for young men to emulate aren't all contained in sermons, parables, or tragedies of Christ's martyrdom. To be a man of God, one must be a leader on Earth: a leader of one's family; a leader in the church hierarchy—rarefied heights where no women reside—and a leader in society at large. This entails embodying a straitened view of godly masculinity.

One example of a kind of near-cartoonish masculinity is the curious troupe known as the Power Team, a group of extremely burly men who travel among churches and schools, bedecked in brightly colored muscle shirts and performing feats of strength often involving either lifting or breaking large pieces of wood, along with devotional skits.[12] They call their performances "crusades" and proudly declare that they are second only to the Billy Graham Evangelistic Association in the total number of salvation of souls. (Graham, too, called his preaching tours "Crusades.") "Each night features 90 minutes of illustrative sermons, Christian dramas, feats of strength and more, as The Power Team communicates Biblical truths and scriptures to your attendees," they explain to churches curious about booking their services. "Whether you are a Baptist, Methodist, Lutheran, Assemblies, Presbyterian, Non-Denominational church or beyond, God has something great in store for you and your community, and The Power Team is here to help."[13] The team's photo gallery is full of bulging muscles, flashy sweatsuits, and smoke machine fog. The power of God can melt hearts, it seems, but it helps if it can also shatter blocks of concrete with a meaty, sunburned fist.

A less flashy, if better known, example of Christian manly virtue comes in the brotherhood–cum–social movement known as the Promise Keepers, an organization for faithful Christian men willing to renew their bonds with Christ in a particularly masculine way. Founded by a former football coach in 1990, the group routinely holds large, ecstatic meetings across the country, filling stadiums and halls usually used for the less godly pursuits of sports and rock concerts.[14] The men-only organization holds its brethren to seven promises, among them "practicing spiritual, moral, ethical, and sexual purity." Promise 4 asserts that "a Promise Keeper is committed to building strong marriages and families through love, protection and biblical values." The verses cited to support Promise 4 are unsurprising: Proverbs 22:6, which instructs parents to "train up" their children; and Psalm 127:3–5, which compares children to arrows in a warrior's quiver, and blesses the man who fills his up.

"There's nothing inherently wrong with wanting to be a better father or husband. The problem is that it was all couched in men as authority over women; therefore a man has to be the head and lead his family toward a deeper relationship with God. It was toxic masculinity cloaked in Jesus," said Matthew, forty, a former Southern Baptist who remembers his father attending several Promise Keepers meetings in the 1990s. "Men would come home and suddenly want to take spiritual authority in the house after being a shitty husband for years."

Among some fundamentalist sects, the notion of "manly men"—what the scholar Kristin Kobes Du Mez describes as the John Wayne model of cowboy Christian masculinity—takes on darker tones. In her book *Jesus and John Wayne: How White Evangelicals Corrupted a Faith and Fractured a Nation*, Du Mez explored the model of fierce, authoritarian masculinity that has permeated evangelical communities for decades, expanding exponentially in the reactionary, militarized atmosphere of post-9/11 America, when a societywide sense of civilizational warfare made evangelical men look back to models of militant Christianity, the Crusaders of the medieval world chief among them.[15] Along the way, preachers and ministers began emphasizing that a man of God is a warrior—not just in the spiritual but sometimes in the literal sense. You can see it in the ways the evangelical Right embraces law enforcement—a cross and a Thin Blue Line flag are common lawn ornaments—and a military-first foreign policy; you can see it in the ways Christian movements are often married with showy acts of violence, as when, in protest of a marketing campaign that utilized a popular trans woman influencer, conservative Christian commentators videoed themselves shooting up cases of Bud Light with machine guns. You could see it on January 6, 2021, when a crowd—with legions of evangelicals among them, the whole heaving mass spurred on by the ram's horns preachers were blowing—bum-rushed their way into the Capitol and the foundations of the country rocked and swung and trembled like the hemp-rope gallows that had been set up on the Capitol Hill lawn. You could hear it in the chants in that very loud crowd—the ones that, having objected to the results of a democratic election, filled the air with a new chant: "Christ is King!"

Sometimes God's warriors are organized ahead of time, and the notion of spiritual warfare takes on a physical form. Just ask Mark Rogers, a former pastor at Harvest Time Church in Fort Smith, Arkansas, known online as "The Christian Gun Owner," the proprietor of a YouTube channel with thousands of subscribers. He's someone who'll give you honest reviews of handguns and firearms—without all the foul language, in case his good, Christian audience objects to cursing. "The fact is that millions of responsible Christians across the U.S. enjoy shooting and hunting," Rogers wrote on his website. "The true Christian gun owner believes he/she is to be a servant to humanity. **But that belief does not extend to being a doormat to those who refuse to live by the rules of reasonable human behavior.**"[16]

Addressing his fellow Christian firearm enthusiasts as "patriots," Rogers offers guides to strikers, decockers, steel sights, ammo, and how to protect your church against mass shooters. He even sells a guidebook for would-be volunteer armed church security: *Your Guide to Armed Volunteer Church Security: Protecting Your Faith-Based Congregation in Today's Threatening World of Violence with Weapons*. It costs $9.99 and contains helpful tips such as the use of full-sized semiautomatic weapons as opposed to "trendy pocket pistols." Drawing on his faith, Rogers declares that Christianity need not be equated with passivity—nor does being fully armed at church detract from one's faith. "Civil law and order is Biblically assumed to be something we are all to be participants in," he wrote in the *Guide*. "That civil law and order involves the use of weapons by police and the utilization of weapons by all citizens where legal." Make sure your security team is experienced with SIG Sauers and Berettas, acquire a bevy of tactical holsters, and be sure, along the way, that each armed church member knows that his "spiritual condition will be monitored." After all, in the United States, even the time of "worship and service to God" might "have to transition immediately into a violent confrontation." In a section dedicated to would-be armed security leadership, Rogers reminded the reader, "That confrontation could result in them having to take a life. Would they be able to do it if necessary? Discuss this from every perspective."[17]

And pray, if you can fit it in.

Other group leaders are even better organized than Rogers, whose imagination is crammed with armed bands patrolling the 120 churches in Fort Smith, Arkansas, and all across the country. To return to the infamous Bill Gothard: alongside his umbrella diagrams of protection and homeschool materials emphasizing the inherent sinfulness of women's bodies, the man had another task at hand for the many Christian boys who fell under the influence of his Institute in Basic Life Principles; it was to join his militia. ALERT (Air Land Emergency Resource Team—the man loves his acronyms) has the tagline "Forging Men," implying the application of searing, quenching, and hammering in order to create, as it's put in the marketing materials, "extraordinary men who influence their world for Christ." (The ALERT Cadet program, designed for younger boys to bond with their fathers, offers such experiences as "local unit meetings where iron sharpens iron."[18] A heavy emphasis, of course, is placed on discipline.)

According to its website, ALERT has some twenty-seven hundred alumni all over the world in positions of professional prominence and public service. Targeted at young men seventeen or older, basic training is a $5,270, nine-week program that is "modeled after military boot camp." It's physically and mentally demanding, biblically so—after all, it's designed to help you, young Christian man, "root your life in the Gospel."

The glossy photos on the website show something of a mix between *Full Metal Jacket* and church camp: Bible Study and Scripture Memorization are two major facets of the program, alongside Physical Training (swinging from ropes) and Drill & Ceremony (wearing identical paramilitary uniforms with shiny, shiny black boots). If you've made it through basic training—Bible in one hand, uniform donned, hands stung by rope burns, bunked up with all the other young men sent for a few thousand dollars to have their errant ways burned from them by the power of the Word—you may proceed to become a member of an elite "cadre" that will "lead the Unit" under a "grueling schedule."

Molding people like clay into preestablished gender roles—whether imbuing boys with macho swagger or girls with passivity and submissiveness—is in and of itself a violent process. People aren't clay, bones aren't malleable; children differ wildly from one another and change as they grow; if they don't fit in, they can suffer for it along the way.

In the case of ALERT, this unaccountable organization run by religious authorities responsible for not just the spiritual salvation but also the corporal needs of a large group of young men has run into trouble now and again. The advertising of grueling schedules and strict discipline has, in the experiences of some attendees, been, if anything, undersold. Jeri Loftland, a former Gothard disciple who ran the website Heresy in the Heartland, deconstructing and investigating Gothard-aligned programs for more than a decade, alleged that students in the ALERT program were subjected to extreme punishments, such as being tied together by the feet, as well as medical neglect.[19] In one case, she described "a unit of under-dressed teen boys standing outdoors in subfreezing temperatures at night until one confessed to a minor infraction."[20] Other, anonymous alumni have reported medical neglect—such as being forced to hike on a knee so swollen that a doctor outside ALERT subsequently administered steroids—and abusive training consisting primarily of yelling and screaming, honed to a fine pitch designed to shatter a boy and remold him into a more obedient image. (Gothard and the IBLP did not respond to the allegations.)[21]

At ALERT, men march into the ceremony as graduates and leave as Units. The program is modeled after the military, after all, though it isn't accountable to any government, any civilian payroll, nor, indeed, any oversight whatsoever outside a sprawling campus in Big Sandy, Texas. They are responsible to Christ alone, and he isn't known for personal intervention no matter how serious the infraction. Let loose on the world, *forged* into men by all that severe discipline interleaved with gospel truth, they are ready to take up the positions of authority and power they have earned through all those ropes and verses. They number in the thousands, and the number keeps growing. Every thirty weeks a Unit graduates (graduation followed by banquet), ready to spread the Word by any means necessary; ready to march.

Evangelical masculinity isn't all macho swagger; sometimes its essential violence is contained, constrained under an outward appearance of gentle godliness. For Jonathan Rueger, forty-one, an exceptionally eloquent writer and former evangelical who grew up in a missionary family between Indiana and Indonesia, the model of masculinity he was taught wasn't John Wayne, precisely, or even Ronald Reagan. If he now had to put a finger on a man in the public sphere who embodied all he'd been taught as a child about what makes a strong Christian man, he said, that man would be Mike Pence.

Pence, the erstwhile vice president chosen for his immaculate credentials with the evangelical crowd, the better to smooth away the vulgarities of Donald Trump; a man with a perfectly contoured silver head of hair, still and manicured as a crown of thorns; a man who, during his career as a radio host, called himself "Rush Limbaugh on decaf," without the ragged energy and the cussing but with all the hate, each syllable dropping into place just so;[22] a man who looks awkward standing next to a horse in publicity photos but does so anyway because that's what men are supposed to do; a man who was a candidate for president in the 2024 contest despite the avowed desire of a great proportion of the Republican base to hang him as a traitor to his former master, because Christian men don't back down; a man who once held power over an entire state—Indiana—and who did what a good Christian man would do in that circumstance: he created a plague among the unrighteous. HIV rates in Scott County, Indiana, shot up when budget cuts he instituted closed the only clinic that provided testing for the disease, which happened to be a Planned Parenthood; he also resisted the recommendations of experts to provide a needle exchange until hundreds of people had been infected, leaving the small town of Austin, Indiana, with a higher HIV rate than any country in sub-Saharan Africa.[23] Rueger calls him an embodiment of the "genteel paternalization of evangelical chauvinism"—a calm mien belying violent actions.

Pence instituted draconian abortion bans, among the nation's strictest at the time, and symbolic punishments, such as a requirement that any aborted fetus be formally buried or cremated. Shame is a weapon, too, especially when it comes in the form of a tiny grave. He did it all without raising his voice, with that air of preternatural, godly calm that comes easily to men who believe unshakably in their own righteousness and believe they hear the voice of God speaking to them personally. That is one zenith of evangelical manhood: poor, perhaps, at aping the swagger of the ungodly, which is only a sop to the public on the campaign trail anyway, but very good at wielding the reins of power and even better at inflicting pain under an unwavering veneer of tranquility. "Instead of reckoning with this 'other' person as a whole being whose feelings and desires matter, they seek to eliminate those feelings and desires by punitive force," Rueger explained of the evangelical paternal figure. In himself, the evangelical man sublimates his own feelings, pushes them downward into seeming tranquility. All control starts with the self. And control is always the aim.

For Calvin Bushman, twenty-seven, growing up in a church with Baptist roots in New Jersey, masculinity was a way of being: men were to lead, and women were to follow. It was taught in church and Sunday school, but more than that, explicitly patriarchal ideology suffused the milieu of his evangelical community. "There was always an assumption that men would be the leaders and that there was a clear hierarchy of God, men, women, children," he told me. "I always knew that as a man I was seen as someone who would be above and superior to any woman. Men were dominant, unencumbered by emotions, logical, and strong. Women, on the other hand, were delicate, needed to be protected, nurturing, and emotional. That wasn't always said, but it was how our whole evangelical ecosystem operated. The men who were uplifted in our community were the men who had the appearance of that form of masculinity and wives who fit into that form of femininity."[24]

If marriage is both institution and sacrament, it's clear who is both head and CEO: it is the man in the union, and no union is legitimate besides that of one man and one subservient woman. For men as well as women, that expectation can be crushing. "I constantly feel like a failure for not being able to provide more for my wife, and I always feel like I'm not enough," Bushman told me years after he had moved away from the precepts of his evangelical upbringing. "I can't stop feeling like I should be someone else, but that someone else is something I absolutely despise."

As the feminist journalist Katha Pollitt put it in an analysis of the GOP's opposition to no-fault divorce, it's impossible to extricate this position from a deeply Christian, and deeply patriarchal, authoritarianism. "For right-wing Christians...both divorce and abortion represent social decay," she wrote in the *Nation* in 2023. "Families should pray together and stay together, with the woman firmly under the man's thumb."[25] The nature of the thumb under which a woman is pinned is linked to the nature of the man who wields it.

For Joel Stanley, part of what it meant to be a Christian man was to look down upon women from the great height God had placed him on. "Misogyny was ever present, albeit sometimes well masked, in purity culture's prurience and general obsession with sexual innocence and perversion," he said, "and of course in rabid antiabortion sentiments that generally entailed a total lack of bodily autonomy." He expressed it, too, in his first marriage, after getting engaged at the age of sixteen. "I was demanding, hot tempered, and impulsive and went along for quite some time just trying to replicate whatever signals I had picked up along the way about being a man, being a 'good' husband, et cetera," he told me. "Strong and stoic, always needing to have 'the answer,' expecting to be listened to, obeyed, even, expecting parades in my honor when I lifted a finger towards domestic upkeep, and incredibly touchy and sensitive in the face of any kind of criticism." The process of moving away from those teachings caused a great deal of collateral damage, including the collapse of that first marriage. "The arc from a boy raised to be a kind of a fanatical tyrant-king to a man that has aggressively recanted that entire worldview was painful and long, both for myself and for others," he said.[26]

This country is full of petty little tyrant-kings who never bothered to unlearn it. Some of them are making laws, others are breaking them, and to still others, mere earthly law is nothing in relation to the great fiery codex of divinity. If it's true about that strange tree of liberty—the one that drinks blood, they say, the one always eager to spill it—it must be thirsty. It's probably time to call in a phalanx of gardeners to take a careful look. Gardeners split the earth with their spades, but they heal it afterward. It took many years and the love of an extraordinary woman for Eddie K. to heal himself of the views of manhood he'd been raised with. Afterward: the renewed, turned soil of possibility.

Growing up, Eddie realized that his hero in life wasn't Ronald Reagan, John Wayne, Mike Pence, televangelist titans, or any of the other larger-than-life, swaggering, sanctimonious figures put into his mind by a childhood of evangelical indoctrination. It was his grandmother, who was kind to him, who was his best friend. The church teachings about manhood had left him feeling that he would never measure up: "I felt that I was too fat. That I was too happy or sad. That I was too friendly. That I was too shy. That I was too needy. That I was too poor. That I was too educated. That I was too stupid. That my curly hair was a weakness. That other men were better. That other men should be worse," he told me. "Masculinity has a lot of bad cops and just enough good cops to sometimes add to the numbers, but it's so overboard that I burnt out and just want to be a human being again."[27]

Now, he said, he's married to a woman who faced her own journey away from strict Catholicism, and he has only one, heavily earthbound piece of advice about how to be a man. "Consent requires autonomy, comfort, and knowledge," he told me. "I've seen how miserable the opposite of that freedom is."

CHAPTER 9

GENTLE, SMILING MOTHERS

When Ruth* was twenty-one, she donned a wedding dress; it was high time, her parents and everyone else around her had said, for her to be married.

Growing up in the 1980s and 1990s in a hard-line evangelical church with branches throughout Pennsylvania, she had been told over and over again what it meant to be a woman—and marriage was at the center of all she'd been taught. In Sunday school and Bible study, she had been taught that a wife's role is to be submissive and to accept her husband's headship. Women were not allowed to address the congregation at her church. The faith she had grown up in was a "dark and bloody" one, she told me; in her Sunday school lessons, she had been taught to expect an imminent apocalypse that would annihilate the faithless and to wreak vengeance on God's foes in the wider world when she grew up.

At home, her parents were both active in the ministry, cultivating new "church plants" that would become active evangelical congregations of their own. In her community, dating was forbidden before the age of sixteen; at that point, young congregants were permitted to engage in strictly marriage-minded "courtships." At a Bible study for teens and young

---

* Name changed to protect a victim of abuse.

adults, she watched her female peers ask for prayers that they could be more submissive to their husbands. Her sex education, such as it was, consisted primarily of the *Sex, Lies &...the Truth* video series put out by Focus on the Family, featuring James Dobson and the evangelical darling Kirk Cameron.[1] All sex outside of marriage was a sin, and the only alternative was total chastity. Even kissing was to be reserved for the wedding night.

At nineteen, she met the man she would marry—the first one who had ever asked her on a date. Over the course of their courtship, the man, whom she had met at her Christian high school, became sexually abusive to Ruth—a terrifying and traumatic experience for anyone but doubly so for someone so inculcated in the culture of purity, and who had only the faintest notion of the mechanics of sex. He began by groping her; she refused his advances, but they only became more forceful. In Dobson's teachings, men cannot control their lust, and the burden is upon women to ensure that they do not fall into sexual sin. Even as the assaults escalated into forcible rapes, Ruth felt—and was encouraged to feel by her future husband—that the "sexual sin" was hers; even as he had pinned her down, she had not fought back hard enough, she had not screamed loud enough, she had not overpowered him, and she was to blame.

Faced with a life-rupturing event, she began to view herself as a sinner, someone stained by the sin of enabling a man's lusts, someone impure and undeserving. When her future mother-in-law discovered condoms in her son's room, Ruth's parents were told that their daughter was living in sin. In the ensuing months, her parents, future in-laws, and fiancé pushed her heavily toward the sole solution they could see, ending the sin through the sacrament of marriage; donning the dress and marrying the man who had raped her.

Ruth was an A student. "I was a really good kid, always followed the rules," she told me. She had, until that point, been an obedient Christian girl; she had internalized years of relentless teaching about sin, purity, and submission. Maybe the white dress and the holy bond of husband and wife could erase all that had happened. Maybe marriage felt inevitable in light of the intolerable pressure she faced. "The church's teachings made me feel it was also my fault," she told me. "Marriage would help make it right." Her future in-laws gave her a marriage manual called *The Power of a Praying Wife*—a manual offering a cure for women who suffer in marriage: prayer.[2]

By the time of Ruth's wedding, she had already begun to question the often violent education she'd received about what it meant to be a woman. But it takes a long time to uproot a lifetime's worth of indoctrination. So when the time came, she walked down the aisle toward the man who had assaulted her, the man who, according to all she had been taught—through beatings and fire-and-brimstone sermons, through books and tapes and quiet Bible study sessions—ought to lead her and guide her through a life of wifely submission and child rearing, whether she wanted that life or not. Perhaps their marriage would be different. Perhaps it wasn't a cruel and inevitable fate but a new beginning. She had bought herself a dress tinted ivory rather than virginal white to show everyone that she had sinned, a quiet act of nascent rebellion—one she performed while still unable to speak about what she'd endured. "I was trying so hard to assert myself," she said. Despite everything, she hoped that the sacrament of marriage would be curative, would fix what was broken in him and in her. And so she said yes that day.

What led Ruth to say yes in that moment—and what led her parents and church community to tell her to accept her abuse and repair it through submission? Was it divinely ordained, something innate to human nature since the misty prehistory of creation? Or was it something more socially mediated, something that had arisen in the reactionary Christian movement that spanned the second half of the twentieth century?

Some stories begin with a beginning, and to an extent, this is one of them. The Bible has its own version—several versions, really—of the creation of the earth and the creation of man and woman. The first three chapters of Genesis are a complex and at times self-contradicting story, combed apart by so many generations of theologians, scholars, and believers that the naked text bereft of interpretation feels puzzlingly bare. It contains two separate narratives of the creation of human beings: "Male and female created he them" appears in Genesis 1, alongside the creation of everything else, without any further caveats or additions. In Genesis 2, Eve is created because God decides—on his own, apparently—that it is not good for Adam to be alone. Some impromptu heavenly surgery occurs (complete with spiritual anesthesia!) and a rib is extracted from Adam, which God transforms into Eve, so that she may function as "an help meet" to Adam, as the King James Bible, the urtext of evangelical orthodoxy, translates it. Adam recognizes her as the flesh of his flesh and bone of his bone; the text asserts that it is thus a natural inevitability for man and woman to cleave to each other. The chapter concludes: they were naked and without shame. Two beings created for one another, hanging out naked in a garden, having just been granted dominion over all the earth and every being in it? Not a terrible situation overall.

It is only in Genesis 3—the infamous story of the snake and the forbidden fruit (unspecified, later retconned as an apple)—that the ideas of separate gender roles and the subordination of woman to man are introduced. Eve has her terrible encounter with the "subtil" serpent, who convinces her to partake of the fruit of the tree of knowledge of good and evil; he plies the naive new creation with the lure of knowledge, saying that she shall be as a god, with open eyes. Eve desires to be wise; she eats; she gives to her husband that he may eat, too. Instantly they are afflicted with a flood of sexual shame and God gives them some bespoke rawhide clothes to hide it. They hide from God in their shame (later in the Bible, Jonah will tell you that this rarely works), and he punishes them both.

- From now on, sexual shame will be compounded by pain and grief in birth for Eve.
- Adam must now labor to till the soil (no more free fruit).
- Both become mortal, returning to the dust; Adam must till thanklessly amid thorns and thistles all his life.
- As the final, pointed dictum of the matter, Eve (and therefore all of femalekind), for her decision to seek wisdom and her

leading role in the fruit-theft incident, is cursed to be subordinate to her husband for all of time.

- They are evicted from Paradise at flaming sword point. Nobody is having a good time.

Mortality, sexual shame, death in childbirth, agricultural labor, and gender-based subordination are introduced together in a heady swirl of narrative that runs a terse if complex twenty-four verses.

The Genesis creation myth has the dreamy feel of the ancient legend that it is; it happens to have had a great deal more staying power than analogous texts, such as the ancient Mesopotamian creation epic Enuma Elish (dating to the second millennium BC), which features 100 percent more deicide, sea goddesses, and lightning-bolt-based weaponry.[3] Nonetheless, I linger on Genesis because it has shaped so very much of the history of the West; the fruit, the temptation, the wrath of God, and above all an overriding ethos of punishment and shame has governed the relations between the sexes in a Christian context ever since.

Fast-forward some thousands of years, and Eve's condition as a "help meet" has formed the basis of countless guides to Christian marriage, ones that heavily emphasize the submission of women to their husbands and furthermore advance the notion that a woman without a husband is both incomplete and untrue to her "created nature."

Just ask Debi Pearl, a nationally famous Christian figure and the wife of the infamous right-wing pastor Michael Pearl, who laid out her stark vision of femininity in her book *Created to Be His Help Meet: Discover How God Can Make Your Marriage Glorious*.[4] It's the companion to her husband's book *Created to Need a Help Meet: A Marriage Guide for Men*,[5] and it is a large-font, sweetly decorated instruction manual on how to build yourself a lifelong prison. The book has sold some five hundred thousand copies in twelve languages, according to its ten-year-anniversary copy; originally published in 2004, it was reissued in 2014 and 2019. One friend who grew up in an evangelical context disclosed that she had been gifted no fewer than three separate copies of Debi's marriage manifesto upon becoming a bride. Another woman told me that her mother had given her the book as soon as she began to menstruate, to preview her future as a bride. "It was traumatizing," she said.

Pearl's view of femininity is derived from a smattering of Scripture with a heavy focus on the punitive. Drawing from Genesis, she asserts that women who are not married to men—and furthermore women married to men who do not assume the submissive role of help meet—are not just straying but forsaking the role for which God created them. Such departure is aberrant, abhorrent to God. Women who work outside the home are also forsaking their role of help meet by assuming that role for someone other than their husband; it will, Pearl writes, lead marriage "to ruin." A woman may not lead her household; she is instructed to accept her husband's leadership, even if it is poor, as being superior to her own more effective assertion of self.

The perfect Christian woman Pearl envisions is always happy; her smile (much emphasis is placed upon the necessity of a constant smile and a merry heart) is what draws her husband to her. "Being pitiful, hurt, discouraged, and even sickly is one side of a 'bad marriage' coin," she wrote. "Men, in general (your husband in particular) are repulsed by women who project this image...he will react with anger." Women who are being abused must neither fight back ("with the voice of a shrew and the demeanor of a feminist") nor "cower" and "brainlessly submit"—but rather display honor, reverence, and obedience to their husbands. In the spirit of Christ, they must "put on the whole armor of God" in order to "endure abusive words without feeling abused," and "live in the love of God when you are not getting love from your husband." Women who complain about their abusers, who leave relationships, or who do not marry are addressed in a section entitled "Disappointed Old Failures."[6]

Pearl's writings are generally viewed as an extreme vision of the doctrine of complementarianism—the Christian view that men and women were created to fulfill different roles and can find God's mandated fulfillment only in the relationship between husband and help meet. Nonetheless, Christian marriage guides with similar messages—even if delivered in softer tones, adorned with rose-blush pink covers and images of couples embracing—are legion; they fill bookshelves with their messages of submission and obedience, of the meek and quiet spirit, of the wife who never leads and only follows. These books are neither particularly old—many of the "classics" currently in multiple reprints were released in the mid-2000s—nor obscure; though aimed at a Christian audience, they seek to appeal to any woman who wishes her life or relationship to be better and offer, in answer, a theological straitjacket lined with the faux softness of gentle advice.

In *Captivating: Unveiling the Mystery of a Woman's Soul*, rereleased in 2021 in an expanded edition sixteen years after its initial publication, the popular Colorado-based husband-and-wife ministers John and Stasi Eldredge couched a brutally confined view of sacred femininity in soft-edged prose and bland pop culture references.[7] Since the expulsion from Eden, the Eldredges wrote, "woman is cursed with loneliness (relational heartache), with the urge to control (especially her man), and with the dominance of men." Despite the book's conversational tone—that of a gentle friend and confidante—the warning of the book is stark: when a woman is "grasping, reaching, controlling"—when she seeks to control and dominate her environment and those around her—she is "falling prey to the lies of our Enemy," Satan. "By living a controlling, domineering life, we are really refusing to trust our God," Stasi wrote. Women who are too needy, vulnerable, or desolate—women who hide their "true femininity" in acts of self-protection—are also fallen from grace; they, like Eve after accepting the serpent's gift, sin through self-concealment. There is no way to run this gauntlet successfully except to surrender one's control and safeguards, trust only in God and husband, and "return to our God with desperate, broken hearts." All other paths lead to the beguilement of Satan, to sin, misery, and ultimately divorce and damnation—options presented as equally devastating.[8]

This pink-hued surge of rigid rhetoric did not emerge from nowhere, and it is amplified by sermons in megachurches, marriage seminars and workshops, podcasts, radio broadcasts, and ultimately legislation that aim

to lay out and then mandate a stifling view of femininity. The life they advise women to undertake is viable only within heterosexual marriage. It demands that a woman carve from her own heart any ambition to lead or to employ her own skills for worldly success and requires her to constantly scour her soul for the many character flaws that equate to mortal sin. A woman on a path like this is theologically barred from advocating for her own rights. Even to think of them is to sin; there are only the headship of men and the cheerful, self-annihilating obedience of women. This view of femininity is not inherent to Christianity but rather is culturally mediated—the Eldredges hold up Renée Zellweger's pathologically self-effacing character in *Jerry Maguire* as a model; Debi Pearl cites a home economics textbook from 1950—yet it is bulwarked by carefully chosen verses, chains of domestic servitude disguised as the armor of God.

The role of women outlined in the Bible has been interpreted in many ways over the centuries, and its contemporary stringency on the Christian Right is a direct response to the feminist movements of the twentieth century. One of the most important books in the "Christian femininity" library, *Let Me Be a Woman* by the wildly influential missionary Elisabeth Elliot, was originally published in 1976 explicitly as a rebuke to the women's liberation movement. In the revised foreword for the 2004 edition, she said as much: "This book was written at the height of the strong feminist movement that swept through our country in the seventies and eighties. Women were told that they ought to get out of the house and do something 'fulfilling.' They listened, and many discovered what men could easily have told them: that by no means is fulfillment necessarily to be found in any job...any more than in the kitchen. I knew that real satisfaction and joy come in response to acceptance of the will of God and nowhere else."⁹

In the book, Elliot rebuked the women's liberation movement as a monument to "immaturity": its members, she said, have turned from the "only true and full freedom" of God's grace, which demands a "call to serve" others and acknowledgment of the "vast significance of the sexual differentiation." Women's liberation is an evasion of responsibility, and assertion of the self—a woman who "defines her liberation as doing what she wants, or not doing what she doesn't want"—is not only rebuking God but has forfeited her humanity. "By refusing to fulfill the whole vocation of womanhood," Elliot wrote, "she settles for a caricature, a pseudo-personhood." A woman who is a feminist—who seeks her own liberation—is a selfish, immature, and craven creature. She is not meek, and she will not "give up all [her] own plans and purposes, all [her] own desires and hopes, and accept Thy will for my life." She is not God's creature. She is not even fully human.[10]

Elliot went on to be a mainstay in evangelical Christianity for decades, influencing the purity movement and other vital segments of right-wing Christian culture. But she was hardly the only Christian to respond with repulsion to the feminist movement. Throughout the 1960s, '70s, and '80s, a tide of activism among women worked to chip away at the armature of oppression that had long restricted the material and social possibilities of female life. Throughout those decades, feminists built power and popular sentiment in order to create the changes that formed the basis of the world young American women were born into. They secured women's rights to obtain a no-fault divorce; to own their own credit cards; to access housing without sex-based discrimination; to obtain contraception, whether married or unmarried; to serve on juries. In 1970, marital rape was legal in all fifty states; by 1993, all states had withdrawn the "spousal exception" to rape laws. In 1973, *Roe v. Wade* secured the federal right to obtain an abortion. But Elliot and her ilk objected to the whole of the movement—to each right obtained, to each piece of economic security won. Abortion became the focal point of the Christian backlash to feminism, but the initial conservative Christian objections neither began with abortion nor made it the primary focus of animus. Instead, the very notion of a woman whose principal goal was not submission within the confines of heterosexual marriage was an affront to God, a tool of the enemy that must be confronted—and eradicated.

Conservatism as a whole, but Christian conservatism in particular, benefits from the construction and adulation of an imagined, purer past. That is why these marriage manuals fixate on the Garden of Eden, old-school Hollywood fantasies, and 1950s home ec. They are evoking a time unsullied by feminism, before the world was complicated and women's rights were enumerated and demanded. On the secular Right, the appeal is often to "Western tradition," a phrase fraught with heavy undertones of racism; one piquant example is a Trump-era executive order mandating that all future federal buildings in DC and all federal courthouses nationally be constructed with "the architecture of ancient Athens and Rome," a physical embodiment of the rejection of degenerate modernity. In Christian contexts, cherry-picked history coincides with cherry-picked Scripture; what is, in fact, a concrete reaction to social change has become recast as a divine mandate—the inerrant word of God, the essential and unchanging nature of humankind since its very creation.

Retconning the Word of God is nothing new. The parchment of Scripture has always been a palimpsest of interpretation, shifting as politics shift, with verses emphasized and de-emphasized as necessary in pursuit of power. Christian antifeminism is no different, and far from being immovable and unchanging since the time Eve was formed from Adam's rib, it is recent, it is virulent, and it is gaining traction every day.

Even the term *complementarianism*, which puts a name to the notion that men and women have inalienably different and divinely ordained roles, wasn't coined until 1987. In 1986, the Supreme Court made a ruling that established a precedent that discrimination on the basis of sex could entail a hostile workplace. The following year, in Dallas, a group of influential evangelical theologians—two of whom were named Wayne, all of whom have had long and influential careers on the Christian Right—met to create a new organization, the Council on Biblical Manhood and Womanhood. According to the council's statement of its history, that influential meeting was inspired by "the spread of unbiblical teaching" during the burgeoning and expanding feminist movement. Under the leadership of John Piper, a theologian and pastor and the founder of the Desiring God ministry, the group "drafted a statement outlining what would become the definitive theological articulation of 'complementarianism,' the biblically derived view that men and women are complementary, possessing equal dignity and worth as the image of God, and called to different roles that each glorify him."[11]

The following year, the group laid out just what complementarianism meant—and would come to mean—in the coming decades for right-wing Christianity in the United States. In Danvers, Massachusetts, they promulgated the Danvers Statement, a response not just to feminism in the culture at large but to the nascent Christian feminist movement, which had sought to reimagine gender roles within evangelical churches. Expressing their concern with "the increasing promotion given to feminist egalitarianism with accompanying distortions or neglect of the glad harmony portrayed in Scripture between the loving, humble leadership of redeemed husbands and the intelligent, willing support of that leadership by redeemed wives," the group laid out a definitive image of Christian manhood and womanhood that would thoroughly repudiate any vision of a Christian feminist future. "Ambivalence regarding the values of motherhood [and] vocational homemaking" was excoriated, alongside the emergence of roles for women in church leadership that were "crippling to Biblically faithful witness."[12]

In response to those purported societal cataclysms, the group laid out principles that they believed would lead all Christians from a path of damnation back into the loving arms of God: "In the family, husbands should forsake harsh or selfish leadership and grow in love and care for their wives; wives should forsake resistance to their husbands' authority and grow in willing, joyful submission to their husbands' leadership (Eph 5:21–33; Col 3:18–19; Tit 2:3–5; 1 Pet 3:1–7)…some governing and teaching roles within the church are restricted to men (Gal 3:28; 1 Cor 11:2–16; 1 Tim 2:11–15)."

The impact of the Danvers Statement on major Protestant denominations is impossible to overstate.

Not content to simply issue such a proclamation, the various ministers

and theologians who created it set about ensuring that it was adopted by
as many millions of Christians as possible. In 1989, the group published a
full-page advertisement containing the entire Danvers Statement in Christianity Today, a flagship evangelical publication founded in 1955 by the
legendary evangelist Billy Graham; in the 1980s, each issue of the magazine reached thousands of Christians.[13] A concerted pressure campaign,
including a 1991 anthology called *Recovering Biblical Manhood and Womanhood: A Response to Evangelical Feminism*, led to the nationwide spread
of complementarian theology.[14] Eventually, the council would claim that
its "gospel-driven gender roles" had been adopted by major Protestant
denominations, including the Presbyterian Church in America and the
Southern Baptist Convention, which together represent more than 10 million parishioners. The notions of biblical manhood and womanhood, so
recently invented, acquired a retroactive patina of divinity, folded into sermons, marriage counseling for young couples, and education for future
brides. Only in service, submission, and obedience could women fulfill
their divine mandate to be women; any other path, particularly one influenced by the hard-won victories of the women's movement, was a rejection
of grace.

While the submissive role of wives has, perhaps, a bit more textual
justification—Ephesians 5:22, "Wives, submit yourselves unto your
own husbands, as unto the Lord" is easy to point to—the role of single
women in a religious community is on its face a bit trickier to contend
with. Back in the 1970s, Elisabeth Elliot, a widow, defined the role of the
single woman as a call to "serve"—to dedicate one's life to others without
compromising the essential, tender femininity that is the ticket to God's
grace. In other Christian contexts, the nature of that service has become
literal. In fundamentalist communities, the so-called stay-at-home daughters movement has spread widely. The movement was initially promoted
by Doug Phillips, a hugely influential pastor whose Vision Forum Ministries, dedicated to the "restoration of the Christian household," produced
voluminous homeschool curricula used to teach millions of children. Phillips publicly resigned in 2013 after confessing to a "lengthy inappropriate

relationship" with a woman not his wife. That year, the woman, Lourdes Torres-Manteufel, the family's former nanny, sued Phillips for what she claimed had been a nonconsensual, coercive relationship based on sexual exploitation in which a man who was the "dominant authority figure in Ms. Torres' life" had used her for sexual gratification against her will.[15] Within the "total institution"—the closed and insulated world— that Phillips had created within Vision Forum and its associated ministry, Torres-Manteufel claimed, "obedience to Phillips was as obedience to God," rendering her vulnerable to the loss of her entire social world if she refused his sexual coercion. Phillips denied all claims, and the lawsuit was later dismissed, but by then the titan had fallen and his institution with him.[16]

But in the decades prior to his resignation, Vision Forum was a key building block of the burgeoning Christian patriarchy movement, a widespread push to embrace radically and proudly anachronistic gender roles in the name of Jesus. Phillips suggested that the proper role of daughters before marriage—at any age—was to remain at home under the aegis of, and in service to, their fathers. "Daughters aren't to be independent. They're not to act outside the scope of their father," he said. "As long as they're under the authority of their fathers, fathers have the ability to nullify or not the oaths and the vows."[17] And before their father-sanctioned marriage—more or less a transfer of property from one man to another—women are to forgo careers, in order to cook, clean, and help take care of the family.

The implied consequences for daughters who choose not to stay home can be dire—both spiritually and physically. One hugely influential source for the stay-at-home daughters movement was a widely distributed DVD called *The Return of the Daughters: A Vision of Victory for the Single Women of the 21st Century*, released in 2007 by a pair of early-twenties, glossy-haired sisters named Anna Sofia and Elizabeth Botkin.[18] The pair had authored a book in their teens about the role of daughters that encouraged young girls to obey their fathers in all things. The video describes itself as a guide for young women who "have dared to defy the

feminist culture in pursuit of God's plan for daughters"—a blow against
the "antifamily" stance of a godless world. The result is what the sisters
call "visionary daughterhood." The "vision of victory" laid forth was one
that encouraged daughters to prepare for wifehood by remaining in the
family home, cooking, cleaning, and taking care of any (and likely many)
younger children. This life of domestic labor would be a shield against
promiscuity, the corrupting influences of the outside world, and any roles
for women that deviated from a life of submissive service.

The Botkin sisters laid out their agenda for young women clearly in
2018 on their website Botkin Sisters: Thoughts on Womanhood, Christianity, & Culture.[19] In a series of posts addressed to victims of sexual
abuse, the sisters lay out a theological system in which responding to sexual abuse is simply part of women's ministry. "Dealing with men who are
sinners is an important part of the spiritual battle we're called to fight,"
they write. "Whether it's fighting back against creepy, inappropriate attention at church, grooming by a relative, or physical attacks on the street,
we should see this as part of the ministry and spiritual warfare of being a
Christian, rather than as a defect in His plan for our lives."[20] More often
than not, women who are victims of abuse—by relatives, church authorities, boyfriends, and loved ones—are not, as they put it, sufficiently soaked
in the Word of God. It is this lack of divine marination that makes them
stumble and fail and be raped and groped and groomed. "The failure to
confront men's over-steppings at the beginning is often the first inch that
we give. Perhaps we are flattered by a man's attentions and allow them…
or perhaps in discomfort or fear we deflect them in a way that sounds as
little like 'no' as possible—we turn it into a joke, we laugh, we change
the subject, we try to ease out of the situation in a way that won't make
things uncomfortable," the Botkins write. "Whatever the cause, if we fail
to clearly say 'no' at the little stages at the beginning, we are likely setting
ourselves up for failure at the crisis point—potentially training ourselves
in surrender."[21] Women who hate evil and love righteousness enough
will know to remove themselves from abusive situations, will know to be
armed, will know to be ready, will know to report, will know because God

told them. All this comes with the unspoken caveat that those who are unprepared have failed not only themselves but God.

In the film that made their names in the Christian fundamentalist world, the Botkins offer the example of Dinah, the only daughter of Jacob, who had gone out to visit with the young women of the city of Shechem. The prince of that city, overcome with lust at seeing Dinah, abducted and raped her. It's a grim little Bible tale that ends with the slaughter of all the men of the city—and according to the Botkin sisters, it was all Dinah's fault. If only she had stayed home under the protection of her father. If only she had not gone out to visit the women of the land, she would have been safe. Freedom is anathema to safety; to leave the home is to face peril and to earn its consequences by doing so. It is a stark vision, one that offers little by way of freedom to become who you are and much in the way of danger—danger you deserve—if you depart from the model carefully laid out for you by those wiser and closer to God, including the pure sisters, their faces in the portrait bathed in soft light like saints in icons, their hair perfectly teased, their gazes clear as purest water.

There have been many female leaders within the Christian Right: women such as the Botkin sisters, Elisabeth Elliot, and Phyllis Schlafly, a titan of Christian Right politics before them. They include legislators, school board members, and Moms for Liberty activists. They are flint-jawed, irrepressible in their activism, steely in their rhetoric, and inexhaustible in their efforts to push women toward a submissive role in society. They are Valkyries in the charge toward submission; they blow the great trumpet that calls other women to chaste silence. If looked at with an outsider's eye, there might be a sense of contradiction here: What kind of woman works all her life for churches that bar women from being ordained or leads a harrying crowd to coerce legislators into signing laws that turn women into chattel? The answer is found in what they say about the ways a woman can serve the Lord, become his tool. Earthly power is as nothing before his will, and its temporary acquisition in the service of the faith means little if its ends are good. They leverage the power of familial roles: mother, daughter, wife. One woman speaks for motherhood, others instruct all daughters, and still more—many more—give instruction to the ranks of wives. In doing so they use their labors to construct molds into which all other women must be fitted and they use their authority as women to assure the world that these prisons are properly constructed, by those who know exactly how closely the iron should lie against the flesh.

Femininity, along with masculinity, is central to the ideology of the Christian Right. The gender norms it prescribes, using a mix of the Bible and half-baked biology, form the moral center of its ideal society. Their rigidity cannot be overstated, nor can the Christian Right's punitive fixation on the enforcement of gender-appropriate behavior. It is, in its own way, a force of nature, with its best parallels deep in the past, in a time of legends.

Greek mythology tells of a bandit named Procrustes, a rogue who had once been a blacksmith. From a house along the pilgrims' path from Athens to Eleusis, Procrustes expressed his depraved urges by means of pretended hospitality. He would invite travelers on the Sacred Way to rest for the night in an iron bed of his own devising. Once a guest was lying down, according to Pseudo-Hyginus's *Fabulae*, the host would spring his trap: "When a guest came to visit him, if he was rather tall, he brought a shorter bed, and cut off the rest of his body; if rather short, he gave him a longer bed, and by hanging anvils to him stretched him to match the length of the bed."[22] Procrustes was killed by the hero Theseus, who was on a quest to rid Greece of its bandit scourge, in the same manner: decapitated, the better to fit his own cruel bed.

The story of Procrustes is instructive about the subject of people who offer false welcome; about people who smile as they break your bones to fit into the shape they want. Procrustes, the mad son of Poseidon, might appreciate the laws being proposed and passed across this country some three thousand years after his chroniclers lived.

For example: on the eve of Valentine's Day 2023, South Dakota's hard-right haircut of a governor, Kristi Noem, took it upon herself to sign a piece of pernicious legislation. House Bill 1080, dubbed the "Help Not Harm" act, betrayed much of its inner cruelty in its name: it is a bill designed to prevent trans kids from receiving routine health care procedures, such as puberty blockers and hormone replacement therapy.[23] It also legislates against all gender confirmation surgery, rare among minors in the first place, as part of a nationwide campaign of fearmongering and control.

Before the bill passed, South Dakota trans teens and their parents vociferously demonstrated that it would harm, not help, their ability to survive. The bill's primary sponsor, former Ted Cruz clerk Bethany Soye, crowed about 1080's success at a news conference at the South Dakota statehouse, accompanied by representatives of a nefarious Christian Right organization called the Family Heritage Alliance. The baby-faced Soye, moonlighting as a state legislator while holding down a day job as a lawyer for a bank, uttered a stream of vitriol of the type that has become her stock in trade. "Under the guise of medical treatment, children are being mutilated, sterilized, and being turned into permanent medical patients," she said.[24]

Soye was, of course, misrepresenting the case. In reality, under statute before the bill passed, if transgender teenagers' parents, who already have an inordinate amount of control over their health care, agreed, they could begin the extremely difficult process of accessing treatment. That consists primarily of therapy, hormone treatment, and rarely, for teens, mastectomies. On the other hand, fundamentalist lawmakers seem to display an inordinate amount of passion about teenagers' genitals or breasts or the lack thereof. The breasts of strangers' children bother them so much that they make laws about them. They believe they know the proper shape of a body and will enact any violence, use any coercion, to enforce it.

Soye's bill is being pushed by Family Heritage Alliance, a Christian Right lobbying organization that proclaims openly that its legislative agenda is driven by a commitment "to defending the freedom to live our Christian faith in every aspect of public life."[25] These are the people who militated for the crushing of *Roe*. Not content with endangering the lives of anyone with a uterus and causing a spike in the nation's already scandalously high maternal mortality rate, they are now interfering in extremely private decisions among kids, parents, and doctors, because to them the free exercise of their faith is an exercise in control over other people's bodies.

Their freedom is the unfreedom of others, and they know it. They revel in it. There is no such thing as hypocrisy in a holy war. Bethany Soye, who proudly proclaims to be an advocate of religious freedom and writes that she is on the "praise team" at her church, is at war with trans teens and their families. Their discomfort and pain are her joy, because she believes she will succeed at forcing them back into the closet, the better to fit into the Procrustean bed of Christian gender norms. "Eighty to 90% of children who are struggling with their identities will come to accept and thrive as their biological sex," she claimed at the FHA press conference. "That is why this bill is needed now."[26] The statistic has no basis, but it doesn't matter—truth doesn't seem to matter to her in this or any other context—and what she was making was a statement of intent. She wants kids who are questioning their gender to be pressed back into the rigid molds her faith dictates. And if they're too brittle to be so mishandled and they break, it's of no concern to her. Casualties are a fact of war, if not its purpose.

The freedom to exercise Christian faith as defined by the FHA and its many, many fellow travelers—in pulpits and state legislatures and sitting at home letting *Fox News* whip them into a lather—is the freedom to nullify their enemies, to obtain and retain complete control over every aspect of public life. They have creepy guys with sunken cheeks to work out the polysyllabic theories behind the "social tyranny" of the "secular progressive establishment." They have invented some very powerful enemies that they are pretending very hard are the ones doing the persecuting, and as a result they will stop at nothing to punch these phantoms to shreds.

It is the nature of reactionary movements to claim that their power is negligible until it is absolute; it is the nature of right-wing American Christianity to nurture a martyrdom that was never theirs and never will be theirs and use its sentiments to feed their animus. It is the nature of reactionaries, too, to hurl others forcefully back into an imagined, ideal past.

In his classic *A History of Fascism, 1914–1945*, Stanley G. Payne noted that fascists have a "complete horror at the slightest suggestion of androgyny," a fixation on male virility, and an obsession with female submission.[27] I have frankly neither the expertise nor the patience to conduct a one-to-one comparison between Benito Mussolini's *squadristi* and the holy rollers of Savannah, but fascist horror of androgyny has remained unchanged in the century since Il Duce's March on Rome. Why else let loose a flood of laws designed to regulate the gender presentation, pronouns, and genitalia of children?

The same people are banning books by Black and Native American authors at unprecedented rates, cleansing the past of all they find indecorous, performing profligate osteotomies on the hard bones of truth, and braying all the while that their opponents are too censorious. Holy warfare is waged any way it can be; in its service reality is malleable as shadow, and pain and ignorance are weapons of convenience.

Suffice it to say that it's no coincidence that laws designed to destroy the security, autonomy, and safety of people with uteruses are being rolled out across the country at the same time as laws mandating that gender identity be fixed as if in amber. Sadistic as Procrustes, the crusaders behind these laws will break bones and cut limbs until everyone fits snugly and everyone hurts.

The pain isn't incidental. It's meant to both prevent and punish misbehavior. Even the deaths caused by the withholding of necessary medical care aren't incidental but cautionary. It is not a matter of simply striving for the evangelical Right to recognize the humanity of people who, say, need a D&C to clear a miscarriage or who want, after years of struggle to achieve self-knowledge, to receive the hormone treatments that might allow them to live more comfortably in their own bodies. There is no humanity in a holy war, no subtlety in a crusade, just servants of light and servants of darkness.

These are people who are willing to storm a children's library because there's a gender-nonconforming performer in it, who are willing to call in bomb threats to hospitals and schools, who are willing to let women across the country bleed out and die from miscarriages and botched deliveries and perforated uteruses and all the myriad ways ill luck can pierce a birthing body. Their minds are smooth and narrow and pointed as bullets, ready to spill blood.

The Procrustean bed laid out for women—submission and obedience, labor and servility—has as little flexibility as the bandit's iron; any deviation is a fall from grace and into mortal sin. But submission and obedience without question are easily abused. The pliant Christian wife suffers; when she is abused, she turns not to earthly authority but to God for her answers. Though some manuals offer caveats in cases of severe physical abuse, anything short of bruises is readily explained; in Pearl's telling, a husband who feels insufficiently adored can become angry and violent, and the solution is not to escape or even fight back but to become a limitless font of grace. To fall short of this is to fall short of God's desire for a woman's life; to fall into sin, with all its eternal consequences.

By the time Ruth was a teenager in 1990s Pennsylvania, the biblical womanhood prescribed by the Danvers Statement had been transformed from the adages of pastors to the timeless wisdom of God. She was taught all her life that submission, obedience, and purity were the highest values a woman could hold, and as she married the man who had raped her again and again, she had yet to fully reject the teachings so deeply and deliberately ingrained in her. He became verbally abusive as soon as they signed a lease together. She would endure his abuse, both verbal and sexual, for eight years.

During her engagement, Ruth was given a book called *The Power of a Praying Wife* by Stormie Omartian, a Christian manual that teaches women how to endure suffering during marriage. In the foreword to the book, Stormie's husband, Michael, a Christian musician with three Grammys to his name, told a little joke he has become fond of telling over the decades. "It's been forty wonderful years for me and forty miserable years for her," he wrote lightly.[28]

One chapter in, it becomes clear that this isn't much of a joke—if it ever was. "I confess right now there was a time when I considered separation or divorce," Stormie Omartian wrote. "The last thing I want to do is grieve God. But I know what it's like to feel the kind of despair that paralyzes good decision making...I've felt pain so bad that the fear of dying from it propelled me to seek out the only immediately foreseeable means of survival: escape from the source of agony."[29]

Her husband, the flagship music producer for Campus Crusade for Christ, had, she alleged in her book, wounded her over and over. "The only ones that were ever the object of his anger were me and the children. He used words like weapons that left me crippled or paralyzed," she wrote. "A husband can hurt your feelings, be inconsiderate, caring, abusive, irritating, or negligent. He can say or do things that pierce your heart like a sliver."[30]

Stormie found her solution in what she described as a kind of death. Clutching her Bible on her bed after once again considering separation, she decided instead to let her own will be extinguished. "As I sat there, God impressed upon my heart that if I would deliberately lay down my life before His throne, die to the desire to leave, and give my needs to Him, He would teach me to lay down my life in prayer for Michael."[31]

And she did so for those forty years—so wonderful for him, so miserable for her, and so full, so very full, of prayer.

As for Ruth? The seed of rebellion that had begun with buying her off-white dress continued to grow within her. Despite pressure from her husband, church community, and parents, she refused to bear children for her abuser. She had decided she would not inflict on her children what had been inflicted on her: threats and beatings, with implements and without, for reasons so small, she told me, that they would "break your heart." Throughout nearly a decade of marriage, her husband berated her; he abused her sexually; he shamed her in the church community and among their families for her failings as a wife. She stayed with him like the good Christian woman she'd been raised to be, even as she worked to unravel the internal bonds that kept her tied to that image of suffering femininity. She endured it all—until she didn't anymore.

Ruth left the faith she was raised in, and then any faith at all, and then the husband who had used God as a weapon against her. She refused to die to herself, to let her own will die. She left him without a prayer on her lips but with hope in her heart. She is in her forties now, and as she spoke to me, her lively children interrupted her. She works to help other people who have left evangelicalism to root out the pain and shame instilled into them. It took her a long time, she told me, to figure out what a healthy relationship looks like. But she did.

CHAPTER 10

TRAIN UP A CHILD IN THE WAY HE SHOULD GO

Where do the inner maps that guide us through life originate? This emotional cartography is drawn from our earliest memories and carves grooves of nerves and sinews that lead our steps for the rest of our days. The landscape can be sunny or forbidding, depending on what we've experienced; it can lead us toward love or toward pain.

Corporal punishment of children is, of course, not new. It is as old as the Bible itself, and older. Many people have experienced some form of corporal punishment in their childhood, but it is comparatively unlikely that they would have undergone such treatment daily, let alone for the sake of God, in the full belief that should the rod be spared, the child risks being consigned to Hell. The latter, however, is the reality for many evangelical Christian children, pinned under an unsparing theology that has developed in best-selling books, charismatic ministries, and homeschooling curricula over the past fifty years.

In Holocaust survivor Alice Miller's book *For Your Own Good: Hidden Cruelty in Child-Rearing and the Roots of Violence*, Miller considered German pedagogical texts of the nineteenth and early twentieth centuries—the principles that guided the childhoods of Adolf Hitler and Hitler's disciples.[1] In the "poisonous pedagogy" of fin de siècle Germany, the child was trained, by means of consistent physical punishment from infancy, to suborn her own will entirely, to idealize authoritarian parents, and to accept violence as a normal part of life's course. "The men and women who carried out the 'final solution' did not let their feelings stand in their way," wrote Miller, who escaped a Nazi ghetto in Poland, "for the simple reason that they had been raised from infancy not to have any feelings of their own."[2] Under such a parenting system, the family itself is a totalitarian state in miniature, she wrote, the mirror of a fascist society. This does not mean that all abused children will grow up to be fascists, merely that authoritarian parenting creates the preconditions for that transformation and arises out of a social context whose principal methods are punishment and obedience. A childhood in which cruelty is the norm renders cruelty far easier to perform, or, as the poet W. H. Auden put it on the eve of World War II, "Those to whom evil is done / Do evil in return."[3]

Reading Miller's book in the United States in 2024, it quickly becomes clear that the world she describes—a world of people who, parented in an authoritarian fashion, become would-be authoritarians—is not so far from our own, a nation that is trembling on the brink of authoritarianism. The amount of violence in Christian homes is perhaps most directly reflected in the violence of the American Christian Right—and a contributing factor to just how violent a place the United States is in general. At Trump rallies, "Lock her up!" has remained a gleefully repeated refrain for nearly a decade; fatal shootings, carried out due to both domestic conflict and political extremism, condition our lives in the public sphere. Police kill daily and en masse and destroy protest movements with orgiastic savagery, public policy is austere to the point of cruelty and beyond, and wealth and authority are worshipped without question. It is a place where violence is part of the social fabric, seeping into all of us, and its epicenter is a right wing whose blood thirst has become more and more open over the past seven years.

In the harsh German pedagogy of the nineteenth century, parents were instructed to extinguish the will of the child utterly, to love and embrace the physical violence of the "rod of correction," and to value obedience above all things. For anyone who grew up in a certain subsection of the evangelical Christian faith in the back half of the twentieth century, these instructions are terribly familiar. The older texts are in another language and perhaps a bit stiffer in their vocabulary, but for a reader of evangelical parenting guides, there is a sonorous echo down the years. If you had to put that echo into words, it would be a refrain matching exactly the ghoulish lines from a 1752 German parenting tract by one J. G. Krüger:

> If he cries with the intent of defying you, if he does harm in order to offend you, in short, if he insists on having his own way,
>> *Then whip him well til he cries so*
>> *Oh no, Papa! Oh no!*[4]

This is also the ethos embodied in popular Christian child-rearing manuals, some of which have sold tens of thousands or more than a million copies: an uncompromising struggle for dominance with physical violence as a principal tool. Over the course of more than a hundred interviews with former evangelicals and a crash course in the central texts of Christian pedagogy over the last half century, I glimpsed a world that had left indelible scars in those who lived within its bounds—and has in turn inflicted tremendous harm on the social fabric of America.

In October 2021, I posted a tweet asking people who had had abusive evangelical childhoods to reach out to me for a research project. Within forty-eight hours, a hundred people reached out to me, sharing pieces of their stories on email and DM. Within seventy-two hours, fifty more reached out. The respondents' ages ranged from twenty-two to sixty-five; many were my age, in their early thirties. Above all, they were grateful that someone was paying attention to them, someone wanted to talk about what had happened to them. People who have left evangelical denominations have formed communities online—in Facebook groups, on websites such as Patheos and Recovering Grace, and on podcasts such as *Kitchen Table Cult* and *Exvangelical*. I wound up designing a twelve-question survey: What was your experience of corporal punishment like? What parenting books or doctrines do you recall your parents using? Do you feel childhood corporal punishment has affected you as an adult? The responses were intense and contained so much candid anguish it felt as though they would etch holes in my computer screen. I have included many in this chapter, with the names of my respondents changed to protect their identities.

Within many evangelical homes, violent abuse of children is cast as a direct act of service to God, and eschewing it a grave, even mortal sin that puts children in peril of losing their eternal souls. In tens of millions of American homes, over the last decades, an encore of Miller's "totalitarian family" has recurred: a structure in which the father dominates over his wife and children with unquestioned brutality and the wife's limited sphere of authority over the children is used to inflict further violence. It may seem anachronistic or even absurd to suggest that these are the values that contemporary Americans aspire to—and that it is from families such as these that the authoritarians of the Christian Right have arisen.

But according to survivors of violent childhoods under the aegis of Christianity, the fascism permeating the electorate stems from a system of conditioning that demands absolute obedience—and little more— from the children it controls. This system has morphed into a totalizing one over the past fifty years and continues to wound countless lives, in addition to irreparably marring the fabric of American civil society. It is a cycle that Miller laid out in stark terms: those who continue to justify the violence they experienced as children deprive themselves of the ability to empathize with others; and so "from their ranks are recruited the most reliable executioners, concentration camp supervisors, and torturers."[5] There are many who inflict pain in this country and even more who seek it, fantasize about it, and center it in their political ideologies. And there are as many childhoods filled with pain that lie veiled under those violent fantasies—in many cases, pain inflicted in the name of a merciful and loving God. It often begins at the kitchen table.

Evangelical Christian corporal punishment is a common practice in millions of American households, and while evangelicals might protest that its intended effect is virtuous instruction, in the moral universe of evangelical parenting, the ideal child is not necessarily smart, ambitious, or even kind or loving. Above all, he or she is obedient.

Nearly every survivor I spoke to emphasized that obedience was strongly emphasized in their homes—central, mandatory, and necessary, extending not just to outward behaviors, such as making a bed or cleaning a table, but even to the facial expressions of the child performing these duties, which must always be cheerful and compliant. As the novelist and former evangelical Kristen Arnett told me, "Defiance included rolling your eyes, back talk, or even using a sour tone."

Rachel, forty-four, who recalls being beaten with electrical cords, belts, yardsticks, willow switches, Ping-Pong paddles, and fishing rods, told me that obedience—and the consequences of disobedience—extended far beyond external behavior. "Not only should you obey but obey willingly with no rebellion in your heart and with a cheerful attitude," she said. "I got spanked for not cleaning my room fast enough once, and when I went back to cleaning after my spanking, I had a depressed—or 'rebellious'— attitude, so my dad made me sing a cheerful hymn while I cleaned, and if I didn't sound happy enough, I would be spanked again."[6]

Wooden spoons recurred in countless interviews. If you strike a child enough times and with enough force with a wooden spoon, it will shatter. Many of the people who wrote to me about their childhoods had had spoon after spoon broken on their thighs and backs. At twenty-three, Abigail refuses to have one in her house. "I don't even keep them in my kitchen for cooking purposes," she said. "They're not allowed in my house at all."

"My mom wasn't averse to carrying around a wooden spoon to hit us with," Rebecca, forty-six, told me. "She broke that wooden spoon on me more than once."[7] For thirty-two-year-old Sarah, a wooden spoon beating was routinely used until she showed sufficient "repentance." To this day, she says, "Being struck causes me to feel sick to my stomach, even if it's something as small as being brushed by a paper airplane."

Spoons were the least of it. "In our house the whip hung on a nail in the pantry and was used often. We'd be told to go to our rooms, strip completely naked, and bring the whip to our parents in the living room," said Anna. "They stuck to the forty-lash rule given in the Bible, but that was for each whipping. We might receive several at the same time, so eighty or one hundred and twenty lashes were not unheard of. My first memory at three years of age was receiving one of these whippings after having my clothes and underwear taken off. We would get it from head to toe, front and back. Neither me nor my siblings have a relationship with our parents today. Where they really belong is jail and then straight to Hell."

The beliefs that shaped those childhoods—belief that obedience to God requires doing violence to children—has shaped, and continues to shape, American public policy toward children, including in public schools. In March 2023, the Oklahoma legislature was presented with a bill that would have outlawed the physical punishment of disabled students, including slapping, spanking, and paddling. One Republican legislator, Jim Olsen, presented a fierce mien on the statehouse floor as he advocated against the statute. "God's word is higher than all the so-called experts," he said. "Several Scriptures could be read here. Let me read just one, Proverbs 29: 'The rod and reproof give wisdom, but a child left to himself bringeth his mother to shame.' So that would seem to endorse the use of corporal punishment."[8] The bill to protect disabled children failed, 45–43.

The regularity and implacability of physical punishment are two features that abuse survivors remember keenly. "I was young, probably around age 4, and I remember this experience very clearly yet remember almost nothing else from that age," Mary, age thirty, wrote to me. "We had been out in public. I'm pretty sure that the initial infraction was I started crying when my dad went to zip up my coat...By the time we got home the punishment being dealt was 100 hits without any pants or underwear. My dad didn't skip a single one. I just remember hearing my own screaming and wondering if it would ever end."

Leah, forty-three, told me that ADHD had prevented her from always accurately understanding the orders she was given; as a result, she had been beaten three to seven times a day for years.

In 1970, a child psychologist named James Dobson published a book, *Dare to Discipline*, that would galvanize a movement toward "biblical parenting."[9] He positioned it as a necessary curative for the permissive, sinful culture that had swept through the United States in the 1960s. Dobson's vision was undergirded by repulsion at widespread social chaos, and at its core was his solution: the enforced submission of children to absolute authority. His vision of molding legions of hyperobedient Christian children was not divorced from politics; not only did its modern iteration arise as a counterreaction to the liberalization of the 1960s, but the children produced by this brutal upbringing would go on to be key instruments in the politics of the Christian Right.

"The parent's relationship with his child should be modeled after God's relationship with man," Dobson wrote. "This same love leads the benevolent father to guide, correct, and even bring some pain to the child when it is necessary for his eventual good." He recommended squeezing the trapezius muscle at the back of the neck to control children of all ages. Several people I interviewed said that as a result, any touch on the shoulder still makes them flinch. But Dobson's book says that God created pain "as a valuable vehicle for instruction."[10]

The emergence of evangelicals as an active right-wing political force on the American scene came into full power in the 1970s, largely as a backlash to the civil rights movement and school integration. In tandem, and in ways that are complexly intertwined with an overweening political agenda, a new vision of the domestic sphere arose in popular books, ministries, and churches. Raising the specter of student-led activism—the antiwar, civil rights, and feminist movements—a new generation of evangelical leaders portrayed strict discipline in the home as a solution to social disorder.

"In the last half-century, conservative evangelicals were coalescing as this partisan political movement and coalescing around a particular cultural orientation, and child rearing is right at the center of that," Kristin

Kobes Du Mez, a historian and the author of *Jesus and John Wayne: How White Evangelicals Corrupted a Faith and Fractured a Nation*, told me.[11] "Out-of-control children were unraveling the social fabric of the country. So it was absolutely critical for parents to get their kids in line. It started in the home: you discipline your kids, and then your kids will grow up to be functioning members of this social order, which was always understood in a hierarchical sense. In the 1970s, disciplining children became thick with meaning in evangelical spaces as part of this political mobilization but also more fundamentally as part of this oppositional cultural identity."[12]

Dobson's *The Strong-Willed Child* (1978; reissued 2004) divides children broadly into "strong-willed" and "compliant"; it is primarily a guidebook in how to transform the former into the latter, creating pliant, submissive children through judicious blows.[13]

"I remember reading my mom's letters or diary about how she wasn't sure what to do about my 'strong will' and she just couldn't break it," said Bathsheba, thirty-seven. "Looking back, I have no idea what I did that was so strong willed. I remember her telling me a story about her telling me not to touch a plant when I was crawling and that I grinned a big 'knowing' grin and went and touched it anyway. I would tense myself up to endure hours of spankings. I felt that showing pain would mean they won."

"Almost every spanking I've ever received was a result of me asking 'Why?'" said Chloe, thirty-four, of her parents. "I think they really tried to break me of 'defying authority' because they felt it was necessary for me to be a good Christian and a productive member of society and a good wife."

Authoritarian parenting in a religious context, asserted Janet Heimlich in *Breaking Their Will: Shedding Light on Religious Child Maltreatment*, serves to perpetuate a worldview that devalues individualism for the sake of the collective and the church.[14] Weakening the bonds between parents and children subsumes both into the religious collective.

By the end of the 1980s, the Dobson view of child rearing had permeated American society to the point that when confronted with a choice to reject cruelty to children as a society, Americans and their government responded with a resounding rejection. In November 1989, the UN General Assembly ratified an international treaty known as the United Nations Convention on the Rights of the Child (UNCRC). It was an effort that had been thirty years in the making, expanding upon 1959's Declaration of the Rights of the Child. The 1959 document is simple—its ten principles take up a scanty two pages, including the preamble—and heartbreaking in its simplicity: a child is granted the right to a name; to a nationality; to an environment in which he or she is loved, protected against neglect and cruelty, and guaranteed an education.

These are basic things, but the document emerged out of a time of profound turmoil, in the aftermath of World War II. By 1959, the world at large and Europe in particular had endured the worst refugee crisis in history, in which a great many children had suffered namelessness and statelessness, cruelty and neglect. The 1989 convention extended the ten articles to fifty-four, largely extrapolations from the earlier, terser text: a child shall not be subject to torture; the jailing of a child should be a matter of last resort; children have the right to adequate medical care and to a free and compulsory primary education.

As of this writing, every UN member state has ratified the UNCRC except one: the United States. (Somalia and South Sudan, the previous lone holdouts alongside the United States, ratified the treaty in 2015.)

This is a stark reality, though it doesn't mean that, inter alia, children enjoy freedom—from cruelty and neglect, from filicide and abuse, from educational deprivation and hunger—everywhere else in the world. Wherever there are children, there are those who are cruel to them. But the CRC is an aspirational document, a set of standards that every other UN member state has agreed are worthy of adopting. The CRC would require a two-thirds vote of the Senate to be ratified. It hasn't come close.

The idea that children have rights that require enshrining separately from those of their parents is not a winning proposition in this country. In 1989, the George H. W. Bush administration refused to bring it before the Senate over "concerns of sovereignty." Bush's son George W. wasn't much better: in the delicate wording of the Congressional Research Service, "The George W. Bush Administration did not support ratification of CRC, citing 'serious political and legal concerns' with the treaty. It questioned the impact of U.S. ratification on state and federal laws and argued that the treaty was at odds with the emphasis of the United States on the duty of parents to protect and care for their children."[15]

By the 1990s, Dobson's ministry, Focus on the Family, was a media empire with book sequels, family-oriented radio programs, educational materials, and newsletters—a parallel culture that existed alongside but apart from secular Americana. As Du Mez put it, Dobson was "a fixture in the homes of tens of millions of Americans."

Legions of imitators followed, some more fixated on pain and others more faith-centric than Dobson's neighborly, folksy persona. They continue to shape evangelical parenting culture by emphasizing the perils of "sparing the rod." Dobson popularized a vision of parenting as a battle for the subjection of the child's will, with pain a central tool. His immediate successors include Michael and Debi Pearl, whose work through No Greater Joy Ministries includes the infamous *To Train Up a Child: Child Training for the 21st Century* (1994; 1.2 million copies sold), a work that, to me at least, is best described as a child abuse manual.[16] There are also gurus such as the pastor Tedd Tripp, whose *Shepherding a Child's Heart* (1995) seemingly erases the line between physical abuse and parental love.[17] Christian child-rearing guides have become no gentler in the ensuing decades. In 2017's *Grace Based Discipline: How to Be at Your Best When Your Kids Are at Their Worst*, a book currently offered for free to Kindle Unlimited members, Karis Kimmel Murray, a daughter of Tim Kimmel, the founder of the internationally popular Christian ministry Family Matters, emphasized the centrality of causing pain in imposing obedience on children. "Remember that pain is necessary for correction. You cannot discipline without it. Pain plays a loving role in discipline, and it has its rightful place," she wrote in an appendix advocating the use of "grace-based spanking." "After all, God uses pain to discipline us. If you disagree, your argument is not with me; it's with Him."[18]

"I specifically remember my mom paraphrasing sections of *To Train Up a Child* while she was spanking me," said Ophelia, thirty. "Nearly every time my mom spanked me, she'd cry and beg me to give in so she could stop spanking me because she hated doing it so much."[19] This touches on the most sinister parts of corporal punishment advice in Christian circles: the idea that a parents' instinct to shield their child from pain is ungodly and that instead the best parents will intentionally inflict pain.

Millions of children have been raised with these principles and this pain. At least three killings have been circumstantially linked to the parenting doctrines of the Pearls in particular: between 2006 and 2011, Sean Paddock, four years old; Lydia Schatz, seven; and Hana Grace-Rose Williams, thirteen, all died brutal deaths at the hands of parents who followed the teachings of the Pearls' *To Train Up a Child*. Sean died of suffocation in North Carolina, wrapped too tightly in blankets as a punishment; Lydia died after being spanked for several hours without pausing in California; Hana, emaciated, was left naked outside in the cold under the guise of punishment in the chilly winter weather of Sedro-Woolley, Washington.

The theology represented by Dobson, the Pearls, Tripp, and others is one of total obedience. It is vital, each of these authors says, to start early, utilizing violence as early as five months (per the Pearls) or fifteen months (per Dobson); to train often, consistently, and relentlessly; to extinguish undesired behaviors completely; to subject not just behavior but the will.

The books describe children as tyrants, anarchists, belligerents, and hardened revolutionaries. The texts are filled with palpable disgust, even rage, toward children. In *The Strong-Willed Child*, Dobson wrote, "The child has made it clear that he's looking for a fight, and his parents would be wise not to disappoint him!"[20] Both Dobson and the Pearls aver that children who cry too hard, or too long, after spankings are being manipulative and should be spanked again to silence their tears.

There is a theological root to this attitude: the child is a representative of fallen man, subject to the lusts of the flesh and the depravities of sin.

Among the general populace in the United States, support for hitting children is quite high—35 percent reported using spanking as a punishment in 2017—though it has lessened in recent decades.[21] The overwhelming scientific consensus is that physical punishment offers no benefits to children whatsoever and puts them at significant risk of both mental and physical health issues throughout their lives. But there remains a broad and widening gap between evangelicals' perceptions of spanking and those of the general public. Roughly half of evangelicals support spanking, and those who do seem to believe in it fervently.

According to the Public Religion Research Institute, evangelicals make up 14 percent of the American population. Half of that is 24 million people.[22] They are an enormously influential bloc, both culturally and politically. Yet too often coverage of the group is an odd mix of undue deference—uncritically reproducing the propagandistic notion that fundamentalist communities are the epitome of "family values"; conflating white evangelicalism in particular with a kind of "real" Americana—and dripping, aw-shucks condescension that views the ideas and experiences of evangelicals as fundamentally ignorant and unserious.

Whether or not it's recognized in major media, the Christian Right has enormous influence in the halls of power—and that influence is reflected, strikingly, in the transpartisan rejection of the CRC. Neither Bill Clinton nor Barack Obama brought the CRC before the Senate, either, due to Republican opposition; the mere specter of its ratification led Michigan representative Pete Hoekstra to introduce, in June 2008, a resolution "proposing an amendment to the U.S. Constitution stating that the 'liberty of parents' to raise and educate their children is a 'fundamental right,' and that no treaty may 'supersede, modify, interpret, or apply' this right."[23]

In lieu of the rights of the child, the Right has developed a parallel but opposing movement: the campaign for "parental rights." It is a campaign with deep roots in the Christian Right that extend to its origins in segregationist parochial schools. Commingled with the language of religious liberty and with the practice of punitive child rearing that permeates the evangelical sphere, it is a clarion call for control over children that is absolute and unbending.

As construed by the American right wing, "parental rights" is the most milquetoast way of expressing that children are their parents' property, subject to absolute control, and not accountable to any standard outside the nuclear family unit. In an interview with Slate, "parental rights" was the phrase used by the president of a charter school board that forced the principal of a local charter school to resign after an art teacher showed sixth graders an image of Michelangelo's *David* on the grounds that a tiny marble penis on a world-famous Renaissance sculpture is pornographic. Incidentally, the school is called the Tallahassee Classical School.[24]

The idea of "parental rights" obviates the notion that society has a collective responsibility to secure the welfare of children. As former Republican presidential candidate Rick Santorum put it in a screed entitled "Children Belong to Parents, Not Government" in April 2013, "So we go from telling the small-business man that 'you didn't build that' to telling parents that 'they don't belong to you!' It harks back to Marxism's trumping of the family in favor of the state."[25]

Freedom from cruelty or danger, access to health care, and not being locked up in solitary in juvie are all more or less irrelevant to this movement, whose sole principle is control. As "parental rights" rhetoric has reached new prominence in public discourse, child labor has returned in a big way, as Republican governors throughout the country roll back limitations on child labor under the guise that teenagers have just as much right to lose their arms in industrial accidents as anyone else does.

There's a laundry list of abuses that are permitted daily under the aegis of parental rights: physical and sexual abuse; the deprivation of education under the guise of homeschooling; and the denial of any outlet, in school or otherwise, to talk about what's happening at home.

Parental rights also enables child marriage, which is legal in thirty-nine states. Children, though able to wed as young as age ten, often to much older partners, are not allowed to file for divorce; they must do it through a legal guardian. That's "parental rights" in action.

ParentalRights.org is a right-wing nonprofit whose president served in the Trump administration and whose chairman is also a vice president of the massively powerful Christian lobbying group Home School Legal Defense Association. The boards of the organization and its associated foundation are loaded with a galleon of right-wing lawyers, legislators, Grover Norquists, and the president of Salt & Light Global, a ministry committed to "speak of Jesus in the Public Square."[26]

Unsurprisingly, ParentalRights.org really, really hates the Convention on the Rights of the Child. In a 2020 post, the site laid out its opposition in a way that paired the maximum of contempt toward children with fearmongering tactics about globalist overreach. Here's why children shouldn't have rights:

The CRC contains some "poison pills" that we must not accept.

The worst of these is a provision that states, "in all matters concerning children, the best interest of the child shall be the primary consideration."...

Consider, for instance, the prohibition of corporal discipline...

Ratifying the Convention would leave it to that elitist, foreign committee to decide when or if our treatment of children was acceptable under the CRC.

But you and I know that parents, except in extreme cases, are the ones who love their children most and know what is best for them.[27]

Three kids were shot and killed in school the day before that post was published, and ParentalRights.org had nothing to say about it.

Children are not property. They should not be nameless or stateless, forced into marriage, shot in homeroom, or denied vaccination against measles and rubella. Children should have rights, even when their best interests supersede the desires of their parents. We may be the only country in the world that disagrees.

For Dobson, the Pearls, and Tripp, physical punishment of children is not optional; it is central to child rearing, and it comes directly from God. Each of these authors quotes extensively from the Old Testament's book of Proverbs: "He that spareth his rod hateth his son: but he that loveth him chasteneth him betimes" (13:24); "Withhold not correction from the child: for if thou beatest him with the rod, he shall not die. Thou shalt beat him with the rod, and shalt deliver his soul from hell" (23:13–14). Their interpretation is literal. On Amazon, you can buy a wooden "Child Discipline Paddle" with the words "Proverbs 29:15" on it: "The rod and reproof give wisdom: but a child left to himself bringeth his mother to shame."

In *Dare to Discipline*, Dobson recounted an anecdote of his childhood that appears to be both foundational to his parenting approach and deeply Freudian. The day, he wrote, "shines like a neon light in my mind": he had sassed his mother, she had reached out to grab the nearest object, and her hand had landed on a girdle. "Those were the days when a girdle was lined with rivets and mysterious panels. She drew back and swung that abominable garment in my direction, and I can still hear it whistling through the air. The intended blow caught me across the chest, followed by a multitude of straps and buckles, wrapping themselves around my midsection. She gave me an entire thrashing with one blow!" It was the last time he sassed her, he says, though he has shared that story "many times through the years" on his way to becoming one of America's foremost proponents of corporal punishment in the home.[28]

In the world of this theology, a happy child is one whose will has been surrendered utterly, first to the authority of parents and then to the authority of God; a child whose will has been broken. Broken-willed children grow up, though. And sometimes they mourn what they lost in the process.

"I don't know what it was about me that made me so 'strong-willed' and difficult to control," Susannah, thirty-seven, wrote to me. "But I fucking want it back."

CHAPTER 11

AND WHEN HE IS OLD HE WILL NOT DEPART FROM IT

Once a violent childhood ends, what happens to the child who was and the adult he or she now must be? The trauma that thrums through body and mind remains; for those who stay in the evangelical community, it is passed on to their children. For others, those who leave the faith or adopt a new attitude toward their upbringing, it is the work of a lifetime to excavate the pain inflicted in their earliest years.

Many evangelical parenting authors declare that after inflicting physical pain, the parent must declare that "the slate is clean"—that the sin has been forgiven and parental opprobrium has gone along with it. But in the body and the mind of the child, the nerves sing against tabula rasa.* The pain you carry in your body as a child grows with you; it changes how you see love, how you see violence, how you see yourself in relation to the two. The parents of my correspondents may not remember administering beatings or may justify them still.

As one proverb puts it, "The ax forgets, but the tree remembers." My inbox is full to bursting of memories: I remember...I remember...I remember my father...my mother...beatings experienced now as vividly

---

* A blank slate.

as they were at four, at seven, at twelve. The reasons behind those beatings originated decades in the past, among pastors and ideologues whose peak influence came during the Nixon and Reagan administrations but whose effects are still felt keenly every day.

Many people who wrote to me said that after a childhood of obedience training, they were unable to assert themselves at work, make decisions, raise their voices, or initiate even healthy conflict with friends or spouses.

"I have a constant fear of failure and a lot of anxiety around succeeding. It damaged my ability to be creative and to be willing to stand up for myself or set boundaries," Jeremy, thirty-seven, told me. "I have felt as though I had no real goals of my own without someone telling me what to do. I still struggle mightily with taking initiative and fear of punishment."[1]

What does it feel like to be struck as a child? Children feel pain, as any human being does; there is no stage of development at which nerve endings are less sensitive, at which the wires that connect pain to fear and fear to survival are unformed. To be struck as a child is to experience pain and fear.

To be struck as a child by a parent is to experience a different kind of pain, an entanglement of emotional and physical suffering. It is a violating and bewildering moment, and the lessons it imparts are rarely those the parent sought to convey: to go to bed on time, to refrain from sibling conflict, to get better grades. Memories of the infraction fade, but a sense of betrayal lingers, as well as the sense that love and pain flow from the same font; that the child, through his or her fundamental flaws, caused the violence he or she endured from the idolized parent.

Most of the people who wrote to me experienced corporal punishment as a physical and psychological violation—as violence and as emotional pain. But some had more to say. For girls raised in an evangelical culture with a primary focus on modesty and purity, the prospect of having to strip bare before their fathers to be struck was humiliating, a source of profound shame and discomfort. In a kind of Greek chorus underlying the many, many books that advocate for corporal punishment, women in particular told me that they had experienced spanking as a sexual violation:

Rebecca, forty-six, recalled the sexualized humiliation of one specific beating. "I don't know what precipitated this particular assault. What I remember is being taken down the basement and my dad grabbing an old two-by-four and beating me across the ass with it," she said. "The rough edges and the nail heads in the old wood made a bloody mess of me, despite my clothes. Afterwards, once he'd calmed down, he had me lay on my tummy on my bed and exposed my bare ass and spread ointment on the bruised and bloody skin. I couldn't sit in a chair for some time, but the revulsion of him touching my bare ass when I was eleven or twelve years old stayed with me far longer."

For other respondents, the connections were more vivid, even from an early age. Dinah, thirty, recalled that being forced to strip created guilt and confusion—an extreme form of immodesty. "I had separately 'figured out' masturbation as a toddler (obviously without knowing what it was) and would often use it to self-soothe before and after getting spanked," she wrote to me. "The combination of authority figures forcing me to get naked and endure pain; blood rushing to the general area from the spanking itself; and masturbating afterwards to calm down created early connections between shame, pain, and sexual pleasure that were definitely inappropriate. I don't remember how early it was, but I know it was before the age of six. As an adult, I believe corporal punishment is virtually always physical abuse and often sexual abuse as well."

"There's something about being beaten in such a religious, ritualistic, intimate way that feels almost sexual, even if it's not intended as such," said Abigail, forty. "Child me picked up on that, too, and started having sensual feelings about it. And felt extremely guilty for that and wanted it to stop, but those thoughts intruded in my head, so much that I asked God to kill me. He didn't."

"Every position I was put into as a child to be hit is also a sexual position that adults use," Esther, thirty-two, told me. "The muscle memory is still very linked, and there are times that my partner and I have to stop interacting because I am having a flashback."

In the world of child rearing, "spanking" is a frequently used euphemism for striking a child. In the adult world, spanking is an exclusively sexual term. Well-administered slaps on the ass can add fervor to foreplay; in the context of kink, slapping can be only a start and sex, for some fervent fetishists, an amuse-bouche compared to the act of erotic punishment. Online, a search for "spanking paddles" results in an array of items, some overtly fetishistic—black leather, embossed red hearts—and some clearly designed for hurting children. The helpful, algorithmically assisted autofill on Amazon adds two options to guide your "spanking paddle" search: the first is "spanking paddle for sex"; the second is "spanking paddle for kids."

Among adults, spanking is either consensual and thrilling or nonconsensual and abusive, a crime of sexual battery. By contrast, in many of the states in which some 160,000 schoolchildren are subjected to legal corporal punishment each year, parents must sign consent forms signaling their willingness to have their children spanked by strangers with hands or wooden paddles—absent the child's input about their own body. It is easily surmised that a child whose parents consent to such punishment will not find respite from it at home or anywhere else.

Spanking a child and spanking an adult are fundamentally the same act—the deliberate infliction of pain to the buttocks—but socially, they are worlds apart. Because spanking is so common in American households, this aspect of corporal punishment is rarely discussed.

Jillian Keenan, a self-identified spanking fetishist, wrote in her memoir *Sex with Shakespeare: Here's Much to Do with Pain, but More with Love* that given her proclivities, the vicious spankings she remembered from childhood felt to her like a profound sexual violation. Memories of being spanked with a hairbrush caused her, many years later, to vomit violently at the recollection. Parents may not intend to harm their children sexually through spanking, but that, Keenan argued, doesn't matter when compared to its effects; parents who protest that they don't beat their children but only spank them are in fact "nonconsensually assault[ing]" an "erotic body part" in their children's developing bodies. Moreover, with regard to that lack of sexual intent, she asks, "Are you sure?...How much would you gamble on that certainty?"[2]

The buttocks and genitals are anatomically very close to each other, and the percussive contact of a hand or a paddle causes a flush of blood to the region. The same blood courses down the same, bifurcated artery during arousal. As Keenan put it in her memoir, "Children have emerging sexual identities—and if even 1 percent of them perceive spanking as a sex act, *we are violating too many kids*."[3]

When pleasure, pain, and love are mixed too hard and too early, they leave children who are abused vulnerable to yet more abuse. Painful love is the only love they have ever known. This can lead, in adulthood, to a propensity to seek out abusive relationships—or not to realize, until it is too late, that they deserve more from a partner than pain.

When she was very young, Hannah remembered, her parents often sent her to the copse of weeping willows beside her home. There she was instructed to pick her own switch—a short length of willow that would be used to beat her. When she grew older, plastic hangers and dowel rods from Home Depot were the tools of choice, but in her youngest years, she was made to participate in the ritual of her own punishment.

Hannah left home at seventeen, winding up with a man twelve years her senior who strangled her, beat her, and attempted to throw her out of a moving car. "I was denied autonomy, told I was evil and defiant, isolated from the world, denied friends, told I was an abomination, and beaten daily for at least twelve years of my life," she said of her upbringing. When it came to finding a partner, "I did not know what love was supposed to feel like, I didn't know what safety or security felt like, and I found myself in abusive relationship after abusive relationship."

Dr. Patrick Carnes, the founder of the International Institute for Trauma and Addiction Professionals, popularized the term *trauma bond* in 1997 in his book *The Betrayal Bond: Breaking Free of Exploitive Relationships*.[4] It's a recent term for an ancient phenomenon: "dysfunctional attachments that occur in the presence of danger, shame or exploitation." According to Carnes, the condition of the trauma bond is to feel "at the same time deeply cared for and deeply afraid":[5] it is present in both abusive childhoods and abusive romantic relationships, and it stems from the alternation of loving and violent behaviors. A young child cannot flee his or her parent; the inner paths formed in early years become the emotional geography of a lifetime.

"Early attachment patterns create the inner maps that chart our relationships throughout life," wrote Bessel van der Kolk in his groundbreaking work *The Body Keeps the Score: Brain, Mind, and Body in the Healing of Trauma.* "Our relationship maps are implicit, etched into the emotional brain."[6] The carefully performed infliction of physical pain, followed by declarations of love and gentle touch, create a concretization of the trauma bond, an indelible crevasse in one's emotional topography. Under these circumstances, the source of love and the source of pain—of hope, comfort, and intimacy, as well as physical punishment—are the same. It is a lesson that can echo down the corridors of a life.

Many fundamentalist Christian parenting guides lay out a bleak and often vicious vision of children. J. Richard Fugate's *What the Bible Says About Child Training: Parenting with Confidence* recommended beating children from ages one to twenty, starting with the "Tot Rod," a 3/16-by-24-inch dowel rod. Fugate described children as "sinful, dirty and selfish." They are born, he wrote, in a state of "spiritual death." The shocked look and tears of the baby, he wrote, will indicate that you have gotten his attention.[7] A 2017 *Journal of Pediatrics* longitudinal study of 758 adults found that children who were spanked—even when controlling for other types of physical abuse—are more likely to be involved in violent romantic relationships, often as the aggressors. Other research suggests that undergoing violent experiences during childhood makes people more prone to both perpetration and victimization of violence in romantic relationships. In each case, the wires that link pain and love have become soldered together, manifesting in either the instinct to violently dominate another person or the instinct to accept cruelty.

"Hearing my parents say over and over that they hit me because they love me, that they wouldn't have broken that spoon across me if they didn't love me, I have love and pain entangled in my psyche," Deborah, thirty-four, told me. She remained in an emotionally abusive marriage for ten years, she said, because her childhood had primed her to accept it. "I felt defective and unlovable because I was told by my mom during punishment sessions during my whole childhood that if I didn't shape up my character and behavior, nobody would ever want me for a wife."

Martha, twenty-four, was beaten with paint stirrers and a two-by-four with a handle shaped like the top of a picket fence. After her father beat her, he would tell her he loved her; he made her say she loved him back. "I was in an abusive marriage for years because I believed I deserved to be hurt by figures of authority," she said. "I thought it was making me a better person or keeping me safe from myself somehow. That's inextricably linked to corporal punishment for me."

Joanna, thirty-eight, was beaten on a weekly basis with wooden spoons and spatulas until she was twelve. She was told that it was the only measure that could correct her innate sinfulness. "I stayed with one guy who would throw me around when I 'acted wrong,'" she said. "I knew it wasn't right, but I couldn't articulate what wasn't right about it. I was so used to being punished for my wrongness that he just sort of fit the pattern. I only left after he raped me."

There's an unmistakable sensuality, even a certain lasciviousness, with which the authors of these parenting manuals fixate on the physical aspects of godly punishment whose locus is the buttocks. This can lead to passages that read somewhere between comical and horrifying, particularly given the endless repetition of the word *rod*. "The rod is somewhat of a mystery in how it works," wrote Ginger Hubbard in her 2004 book *Don't Make Me Count to Three! A Mom's Look at Heart-Oriented Discipline*, "but we can be confident that while we are obeying God and working on the buttocks, God is honoring our obedience and working on the heart."[8] Both Roy Lessin, the author of at least three books on child rearing, including *Spanking: A Loving Discipline* and *Spanking: Why, When, How?*; and J. Richard Fugate, the author of *What the Bible Says About...Child Training*, specify positions for children to take during the administration of blows.[9] Fugate, who went on to lead two separate Christian homeschooling curriculum companies, suggests specifically using a narrow rod on the bare back or buttocks, because "the more a child braces himself, the more he tightens up and increases the sting. The most sensitive layer of skin is close to the surface where the nerve endings are located. The only way to stop the sting of a rod is to submit."[10]

Men face their own challenges in building healthy romantic relationships after a childhood of enduring corporal punishment. Both men and women who had avoided physically abusive relationships wrote to me of enduring struggles in building and maintaining emotional openness, hindered by fear that love and vulnerability would invite further pain. Some had never had a successful relationship; others struggled to feel anything but fear.

"I carry a paralyzing fear of screwing up, being less than perfect, having thoughts which I find immoral," said Paul, who grew up in a Baptist church in Virginia. "I find it extremely rare to feel safe in any environment, even my home."

While violent upbringings scar individual lives, the accumulation of them—and the institutionalization of violence across generations—accrues into societal harm. Pain left unaddressed can turn to anger, shame curdle into rage, the memories of hurt turn into a desire to hurt others. And the particular elements of violation that accompany a culture of corporal punishment can render sexual abuse common to the point of banality—an inevitability rendered invisible by its own ubiquity.

In the mid-1970s, Larry Tomczak, a charismatic, clean-cut neo-Calvinist pastor, met a peripatetic, long-haired "Jesus freak" named C. J. Mahaney in Washington, DC. Tomczak and Mahaney shared a love of impassioned worship, filled with music and speaking in tongues. They began to collaborate on Sunday services and in 1982 founded Sovereign Grace Ministries, an evangelical denomination that would eventually encompass some hundred churches and twenty-eight thousand adherents.

In the same year Sovereign Grace Ministries was founded, Tomczak published his first book, a manual on biblical parenting entitled *God, the Rod, and Your Child's Bod: The Art of Loving Correction for Christian Parents.* The book, which was purchased by his congregation, emphasized obedience, lamented that in modern homes "everything is controlled by a switch—except the children," and focused heavily on the innate sinfulness of people of all ages.[11]

In 2012, eight plaintiffs brought a class action lawsuit against Sovereign Grace Ministries, alleging that Tomczak and Mahaney had carefully orchestrated a wide-ranging cover-up of child molestation and abuse throughout the 1980s and 1990s. "Defendants taught members [of the church] to fear and distrust all secular authorities, and expressly directed members not to contact law enforcement to report sexual and physical assaults on children," the plaintiffs alleged. A woman using the pseudonym "Carla Coe" alleged that Tomczak had imprisoned and starved her over a twenty-five-year period extending from her childhood to her early adulthood. The complaint stated, "On multiple occasions, including occasions after Carla Coe reached the age of majority, Defendant Tomczak forced Carla Coe to strip out of her clothing against her will, and be beaten on her bare buttocks. Defendant Tomczak continued to engage in this forced undressing and beating of Carla Coe until she fled and escaped from the abuse." The lawsuit was dismissed in 2013 on the grounds that all but two of the plaintiffs had exceeded the statute of limitations for child sex abuse cases. No court ever examined the truth of the allegations; Tomczak denies them, and Sovereign Grace Ministries has not admitted that its pastors ever perpetrated or covered up sexual abuse.[12]

"Where should the rod be administered?" asked Tomczak in *God, the Rod, and Your Child's Bod*. "God, in his wisdom, prepared a strategic place on our children's anatomy which has enough cushiony, fatty tissue and sensitive nerve endings to respond to Spirit-led stimulation. The area is the base of the back, above the thighs, located directly on the backside of every child. All children come equipped with one!"[13]

Sovereign Grace is not a house church. The organization has 132 churches in twenty-one countries, and an associated vocational school for Christian ministers called Pastors College.[14] Though it is no longer affiliated with any denominational governing body, from 2012 until 2014 Pastors College boasted a direct relationship with Southern

Baptist Theological Seminary, the flagship seminary of the Southern
Baptist Convention, which has trained pastors and theologians including countless presidents of the convention and public intellectuals such
as Russell D. Moore.[15] Students at Pastors College could take more than
a third of their required credits toward an official ordination as a Southern Baptist minister from Pastors College. Observers sounded the alarm
about Sovereign Grace in 2013 after the complaints of sexual misconduct had been filed and Mahaney had stepped down, citing his own
"sin" and "pride," but the seminary did not cut ties with the group for
more than a year.[16]

This is par for the course for the Southern Baptist Convention, which,
in recent years, has been plagued by claims of perpetrating and mishandling incidents of sexual abuse. In 2018, former SBC president and
conservative political heavyweight Paige Patterson was accused of mishandling sexual misconduct and summarily fired from his position as president of the Southwestern Baptist Theological Seminary. Though Patterson
declined to respond to the allegations, documents in a lawsuit brought
against Patterson claim that he had exerted considerable psychological
pressure on a rape victim who had been a student at the seminary, leading
her not to report the incident to the police. The lawsuit also included an
email purportedly from Patterson that was widely reported from *Baptist
News Global* to the *Washington Post*, in which the seminary president said
of the victim, "I have to break her down."[17]

The prior year, influential Baptist layman and GOP political power-
house Paul Pressler had been accused of not just enabling, but perpetrating abuse. In a lawsuit that targeted Pressler and the Southern Baptist
Convention itself, a male defendant accused Pressler of sexual abuse. The
lawsuit caused seven other men to come forward, revealing Pressler had an
alleged forty-year-long history of abuse, including the sexual abuse of children, although he has denied all allegations. The 2017 case took six years
to settle for an undisclosed amount. In the initial lawsuit, the accuser
alleged that "when it came to sexual abuse, the [conservative Baptist fac-
tion] of the 1980s, 1990s, and 2000s adopted a clear policy of institutional

silence that had the effect of enabling abusers and discouraging or even blaming victims," though the SBC denied these claims.[18]

In 2022, the SBC released a sprawling third-party investigative report of its own mishandling of sexual misconduct that revealed the staggering truth that it had kept a secret list of seven hundred pastors and church personnel accused of sexual misconduct, shuffling them from congregation to congregation rather than dismissing them from leadership over vulnerable parishioners—and enabling countless acts of sexual abuse in the process.[19]

Against that backdrop of broader misconduct on the Christian Right, Mahaney was reinstated as president of Sovereign Grace Ministries but later resigned the executive directorship of the church network, though he remains at the helm of Sovereign Grace's flagship church in Louisville. Mahaney has denied sexual abuse allegations and has stonewalled any independent investigation; during his presidency, the organization called any outside investigation of sexual abuse claims against the church network "unjust" and "impossible" and said that it would "dishonor Christ."[20] Still, despite the ignominy, men such as Tomczak and Mahaney continue to repeat the same creed: to strike your child is to express God's purest love.

"They hit me because they love me" bears a remarkable resemblance to the old domestic abuser's credo "You made me do it": the very existence of the child or the lover has provoked the painful response. In many cases the violence begins before a child can walk or speak. Beatings are to be administered only in the case of "deliberate disobedience," but often this includes a look, a sigh, a hesitancy, a "defiant arching of the back." The parent is to scrutinize the child and always assume ill intent. For women in particular who are raised in a church culture whose highest ideal for them is submission and obedience to the headship of a husband, the pressure to react to abuse with further submission and obedience is both internal and external. Abuse breeds abuse; captivity feeds off captivity. In *Unholy Charade: Unmasking the Domestic Abuser in the Church*, the pastor Jeff Crippen explained and countered a series of theological justifications for abuse. In particular, he singled out the idea of total and unquestioning submission to authority, as conveyed in the teachings of the wildly popular Christian homeschooling guru Bill Gothard, as a means to quell "rebellion" in women who are being abused.[21]

Gothard, as it turned out, was allegedly serially sexually abusing his young female parishioners even as he built an empire based on obedience and chastity. While creating curricula, lectures, and youth institutions for young Christians that emphasized corporal punishment and rigid discipline, Gothard himself, as scores of women alleged, indulged his sexual fantasies with the young female staffers he kept as his "personal secretaries," inappropriately touching them at every opportunity—and in 2014 resigned from the titanic Christian educational empire he had built due to the scandal caused by the victims of his long history of alleged sexual harassment coming forward. (He has not been convicted of any crime.) The titan of purity and encourager of discipline to keep women obedient was, it appeared, a personally abusive man—and his teachings were abusive on a broader scale. "Teachings like this, which strike fear into the heart of an obedient Christian," Crippen wrote, "can work to keep a victim in a domestically abusive situation far past the time when the situation has become intolerable for her and her children."[22]

The very need for Crippen to write a book-length refutation of teachings about obedience, purity, chastity, and physical discipline indicates their popularity. It's difficult to overstate the profile of figures such as Dobson, Gothard, Tomczak, and others within the evangelical community: these charismatic figures embodied political and social forces that made corporal punishment of children not just permissible but nearly mandatory within church communities. Their relentless pursuit of obedience in children created a culture across evangelical denominations that made the beating of children with rods and hands a daily ritual; the theological framework they provided made it seem like a mortal sin to refrain from doing so; and they preached to congregations that took sin very seriously indeed. The generations that were molded by those brutal teachings are grown now, running congregations of their own.

Child abuse happens in the big denominations, the famous sects, the rich and well-furnished churches. But not just there. By now there are practically as many flavors of Christianity in America as there are people, as schisms and more schisms turn churches into slivers and prophetic inspiration reaches hitherto untroubled minds. Some sects never get names and never surface in the public. They merely consume a few lives and are consumed in turn—all of that wild faith here in a land that seems inhospitable to gods. Maybe that's why it so often turns to violence.

One such sect is something of a case study: not any major headline-making group, just a small, fanatical cult that dissolved after poisoning a generation or so and whose philosophy had a strong, if small, online footprint as well. The group sprang up in suburban Detroit in the 1990s, and its center of gravity was St. Clair Shores, Michigan, settled in the sixteenth century as "L'Anse Creuse," the Hollow Cove. The founder of the tiny and nameless cult first sold accordions and then became a real estate agent.

His name was Joseph LaQuiere, and his 2014 obituary identified him as a "spiritual father" and "true leader."[23] His son John, whom I called at the family real estate office, told me that families had heard word of his father's wisdom, and he had offered them a way to live: as Christians who observed Sabbath laws and followed certain Old Testament practices in the name of Christ. There are other Christian sects that appropriate elements of Jewish practice, although these are generally condemned as "legalistic" by mainstream Christians—a term of great scorn for the Jewish rules of observance cast off by the early church. LaQuiere also instructed his flock on how to raise their children. In this, he appears not to have swerved much from the breathtaking current of violence toward children that runs through a number of fundamentalist evangelical denominations; I have interviewed survivors of these child-rearing practices from all over the country, and all describe internal wounds that can't be readily healed.

According to the testimony of an ex–cult member I spoke to, an instruction manual emerged from the small confines of the LaQuiere group that enshrined Joseph LaQuiere's child-rearing advice for the whole world to read. There's also a rather bare-bones website associated with the tome and a cheerful, sunny gardening metaphor that enfolds it all; it's called Raising Godly Tomatoes. Tomatoes are a fruit of the Americas that were never mentioned in the Bible, a product of the same land as the author and her spiritual mentor.

Raising Godly Tomatoes: Loving Parenting with Only Occasional Trips to the Woodshed is a crude-looking book with a DIY air to it—appropriate, as it was published by Krueger Publishing, a name shared with its author, L. Elizabeth Krueger, in 2007.[24] The cover features a bright, cheerful drawing of a tomato plant, thoroughly staked and flourishing; a stylized sun sits awkwardly in the top-right corner of the cover, its rays dripping down like a Salvador Dalí clock but sharp as blades.

The book is not entirely dissimilar to other evangelical parenting guides, and many of its rhetorical devices are identical: the frequent invocations of Bible verses, the transparently staged "questions" from devotees of the author's practices, and most of all, the staggering cruelty it advocates toward children. Krueger's chief innovation is in her persistent use of gardening metaphors. The "Godly Tomatoes" she describes are children; her method is called "tomato staking," evoking the way tomato plants grow in a profuse, dense tangle, then droop under their own weight unless tied firmly to stakes from the start.

"Think of your child as a tomato plant," Krueger wrote. "Most parents provide too little staking for their growing young tomatoes. They care for them intimately when they are babies, but soon afterwards, begin letting them grow their own way. They feel uncomfortable assuming authority over their children...And just like the sprawling, unattended, unstaked tomato plant, there comes a point when it's simply too late." The philosophy—tethering your children with absolute control, battling their inherent nature into submission—echoes through a book that can be seen as little more than a manual for physical and emotional abuse cloaked in the word of God, a treatment that begins in a child's earliest days. The contest of wills the author describes, in which the parent must absolutely and always achieve domination, echoes so many other guides in this regard; it is a triumph, in Krueger's world, when merely asking your child to fetch the wooden paddle you will use to strike him or her results in complete and cowering submission. Although she does not name LaQuiere specifically, Krueger noted in the introduction her emulation of "a couple whose family impressed us...we began to solicit this couple's parenting advice (much of which appears in this book)."[25]

Krueger is a mother of ten living in the Detroit suburbs less than fifteen minutes from St. Clair Shores. She co-owns an equestrian club with her husband, Gerald, in Grosse Pointe, offering children lessons in dressage riding and proudly declaring on the website that she trained her second horse, Galileo—evincing a passion for training that extended emphatically to her children. Before giving birth to her ten children, she wrote, she felt "generally uncomfortable around children" and "simply avoided them." Perhaps she grew out of that dislike through ten pregnancies and births. Or perhaps this is what suffuses the advice she doles out: to begin training at six months, to "ambush" your child—putting the infant into a situation of temptation, only to leap out, admonish, and strike. She suggests offering no warnings. "If my child does not respond to my initial verbal instruction, I spank," she wrote. "It is quick, simple, and easily understood." It's part of a larger method, though one that is no kinder. "Remember this: **Watch, Ambush, Repeat!**" she wrote, nominally to a mother whose baby had a habit of touching her houseplants.[26]

Maria (not her real name) started the process of leaving her evangelical faith in 2017. At the time, she wrote, "I feel like my beliefs are like a wall or stack of bricks. Each brick represents one doctrine—like one brick represents the doctrine of Heaven and Hell, another brick represents the doctrine of biblical inerrancy, another represents the idea of wives submitting to their husbands, etc....And I worry that God is mad at me for letting the bricks fall or at the very least grieving...but the bricks are falling over and I cannot stop them."

By then she had raised her two sons according to the doctrines of

Raising Godly Tomatoes from preschool onward, taking pains to ascribe fully to its policies of physical violence, shame, and constant surveillance. At the age of eighteen, one of her sons threatened suicide with a loaded gun to his head and cut himself with barbed wire, recalling panic attacks about repentance that had begun at the age of nine. "In my opinion, he likely has PTSD as a result of how I raised him," Maria said. "And it is too late to fix or repair things. The damage is done. I am guilty."

From 2003 onward, Maria not only read Krueger's book but also took part in a then-lively message board on the Raising Godly Tomatoes website. A snapshot of the now-defunct message board in 2007 showed more than three thousand active users, with screen names such as "cheaperbythedzn," "ahappymama," and "twinmom." Maria spent a great deal of time on the board and told me that it had had various sections for crafting, hobbies, and miscellaneous socializing. "The Raising Godly Tomatoes board had all these different subsections on homeschooling curricula, recipes, and there was one on submitting to your husband—but the most popular one was the one about beating your children," she said.

Feeling relatively isolated in Vermont, Maria spent a lot of time on the internet, searching out other Christian homeschooling moms and taking their advice on child rearing. "The Christian conservative fundamentalist homeschooling community, that subset of the homeschooling community, is also very into hitting their kids, largely," she told me.

The Raising Godly Tomatoes board was especially central to her experience—in no small part because Krueger herself often responded to child-rearing queries, an experience that left the asker feeling bathed in her regard. Krueger and Maria began to email back and forth, with Maria writing plaintively about problems with unruly toddlers, attention spans, and how best to homeschool her children. Writing from the email address "momoftensofar" (mom of ten so far) with the display name "The Woodshed," Krueger offered Maria sage pieces of advice with a personal touch, emails Maria provided me for review. Krueger could not be reached for comment, despite repeated attempts.

When Maria complained in a 2007 email that her preschool-age son didn't enjoy chores and sat on his chair for schoolwork with a surly expression, Krueger wrote back a few hours later, "I really think this child is crafty and loves getting away with something—anything. It is almost his source of amusement. I think you really need to make his life miserable whenever he starts this. You really need to correct for the little stuff. Less talk on your part and more paddling."

In another email exchange about the limits on paddling, Maria asked if eighteen "swats" in a row was too much for an eight-year-old. Krueger responded that the user was likely new and thus could not expect "first-time obedience" from her child. "18 swats in a row? Or 18 spaced out?" she asked. "When I first started demanding obedience from my kids, Shane was 6 years old and he got at least 12 separate spankings (with multiple swats each and I was not Mr. Nice Guy) before noon the first day."

In both her online advice and her book, Krueger recommends using a wooden paddle instead of, or in addition to, one's hand for spanking young children, saying that a mother's hand may not suffice for the amount of discipline required. Not knowing where to obtain a spanking paddle, Maria turned to other moms on the board, who directed her to an online shop run by a California man named Steve Haymond. Haymond routinely advertised child-beating implements in homeschooling magazines and other Christian publications, according to several news organizations that reported on community discontent with Haymond's website, biblicalchildtraining.com. Among other implements, Haymond sold what he advertised as "The Rod," a flexible nylon rod for "more control during application" with a "durable" nonslip vinyl handle. The advertisement listed the implements as $5 each, plus shipping and handling, and was accompanied by a poem:

Spoons are for cooking
Belts are for holding up pants

Hands are for loving
☺*RODS are for chastening.*[27]

Haymond sold several child training books, including the Pearls', but his main bread and butter was *Our Chastening Instrument*, described in a letter he mailed to potential customers after public outcry shut down the website: "the blue spanker is 9″ long, 1.5″ wide and ³⁄₁₆″ thick. Made of virtually indestructible polyurethane, it is extremely flexible and quite portable (easily fits in a purse, back pocket or diaper bag)."[28]

"Some of us, including me, bought paddles from him," Maria said.

For Maria, the guilt she feels about her past actions nearly matches the fervor she felt while hitting, chastising, or isolating her children. It was all, according to her, part of a pressure to be "perfect"—to be the perfect wife, the perfect mother, with perfect children and a perfect home. On the playground, her children, schooled by rigorous beatings into silent obedience, were meant to be a testament to the power of a Christian upbringing— and a potential lure for impressed fellow moms to learn about the ways of Christ. Krueger made clear in her book that her philosophy derived from a "godly older" person of her acquaintance—who influenced her as completely as Krueger influenced Maria's parenting, though Maria never met Krueger in person.

After Krueger published her book in 2007, however, one ex-member of the LaQuiere cult made the connection clear online in a ferocious review rejecting the Raising Godly Tomatoes ethos. "Mrs. Krueger's book, and her advice, is really the somewhat-milder face of Joe LaQuiere's teaching: the public face, if you will," the ex-member wrote on a website chronicling homeschooling abuses. "She watched more violent abuse occur, and was taught that it was acceptable: babies having their faces stuffed into couch cushions to teach them not to cry—children being beaten mercilessly with 'The Paddle,' not once, as she writes in her book, but often 20 or 30 times. Children being dragged by their hair, thrown against walls, or dangled in the air by their throats. My own siblings endured all of these abuses, and I was made to watch." The ex–cult member described watching her one-year-old younger brother being subjected to six-hour "training sessions" in which he was spanked every time he did not sit still, amounting to dozens of separate blows; she watched him turn into a "quiet, sullen baby who rarely smiled" and did not speak until the age of four.[29]

I spoke to another brother of the reviewer, Ben Rossol, now in his thirties, who described being "tortured" as a child under the aegis of Joseph LaQuiere. At one point, his family lived with LaQuiere for several months, and LaQuiere, he alleged, was consistently present during the more brutal child-rearing sessions. From age six to thirteen, he said, his treatment had included being "punched, dragged by the hair, forced to be spanked by a very long hard board with holes drilled in it in front of the whole group, private beatings." Worst of all, he said, was the mental torture: being repeatedly called a liar when he had told the truth, forced to stand in the middle of the room all day with no food or water and without talking to anyone, forced to repeat hundreds of times "It is I, and I loathe myself." The treatment stopped, Rossol said, only once his family split with the LaQuiere group; Krueger, he said, was present "here and there"—once a week for a meeting, witnessing some of the behavior described.

The LaQuiere group, such as it was—despite outreach to some of the principals, I found it hard to determine how many of the original cult members remain—constituted some thirty to forty families. According to John LaQuiere, his father's numerous descendants continue to follow his teachings to varying degrees, although he would not discuss how those beliefs pertained to child rearing.

This group, despite the intimate constellations of violence it nurtured for decades, is a minuscule spot on the face of American religion—like the nameless cult run by Lori Vallow that led her to murder her children, and the countless other sects, some named, some not, that seem to grow so thickly from the ground all over this country. Reaching toward God, mediated through unfeeling zealotry, they treat their own children as beasts to be broken to the yoke. The public policy this mindset proffers is violence in the name of God, dictated by people whose lives were formed from their earliest moments by the same violence. It is a mindset visible across the spectrum of the Christian Right that encourages and relishes suffering, particularly of those smaller and weaker than oneself. If this sort of faith is a plant, it's a plant that was restrained too much, choked on itself, and grew in unnatural profusion around the stakes and ropes and twine. The vine runs wild in ground gone soft with decay, and its fruits are poison.

Maria had never really wanted to hit her children, she said. But she had, and she had gone on doing it, afraid that if she didn't, she would be damning them. She later came to penitence. But penitence can't erase pain. It never does.

It's not incidental that the stated goal of this physical violence is to enforce a doctrine of obedience. Children who are well behaved, in the model described by evangelical parenting books, obey orders immediately and without hesitation, with an outward display of good cheer, without expressing doubts or reservations. Questioning—internal or external—is viewed as a sinful expression of selfishness and punished physically until such tendencies are either drummed out entirely or become the root of an eventual departure from the faith. The correspondents who described violent religious childhoods to me are, naturally, in the latter camp—people who have, at great pain and personal cost, broken from their communities of origin, facing the loss of both family and community and navigating a wider world whose assumptions differ greatly from those of the insular evangelical world.

But many people remain; if 24 million people—that is, half of all white evangelicals—are raised in homes that enthusiastically embrace a child-rearing philosophy of physical violence, the vast majority of them remain in the faith community, shaping its values and building its politics. Passing on that root-and-bone combination of faith and fear and pride is an important value: some 70 percent of white evangelicals in one Pew Research Center poll said that it was "very important" for their children to embrace the same religious beliefs they did. One method of ensuring that continuity of belief is through force, repetition, and repetitive force: it is a self-perpetuating system. And the politics of the Christian Right are a politics of violently enforced obedience.

Just as Alice Miller described the abusive family as a totalitarian state in miniature—with the father as dictator, the submissive mother as an analogue for the state security forces, the children as hapless subjects who cannot control their own fate or protect themselves against violence—the same analogy can apply in reverse: abusive parenting begets abusive policy. As such, it is worth examining the policy goals of the evangelical establishment, those who most loudly proclaim their faith as part of their politics, in the context of violent and authoritarian childhoods. Scrutinizing the speech of public figures who loudly proclaim themselves Christian nationalists—people such as congresswomen Lauren Boebert and Marjorie Taylor Greene; pastors such as Robert Jeffress and John Hagee; and a goodly portion of the January 6 insurrectionists—it's plain that a desire for violent retribution surges through their words and in some cases their deeds as well.

Andrew L. Whitehead and Samuel L. Perry, the authors of *Taking America Back for God: Christian Nationalism in the United States*, estimate that about 20 percent of Americans—some 10 million people—are full-throated "ambassadors" whose identity is inextricable from fundamentalist Christianity, and who are willing to take spiritual warfare to the streets if necessary.[30] Their religiosity and thirst for violence are inextricable—just as a childhood of obedience enforced by divine mandate and wooden paddle alike make love, God, and authority hopelessly tangled in a child's heart. When that child grows up, he or she may become, as Miller postulated, able to empathize only with the aggressor—and thus be perfectly willing, as the culture of the Christian Right evinces, to embrace the most violent excesses of police forces; to advocate for draconian policies to punish pregnant women who seek abortion care and their doctors; to speak of immigrants as a plague and a scourge and act accordingly.

"The political ideology that seeks to merge American and Christian identities is deeply embedded in American society and manifests itself in a number of different ways, some more obviously harmful than others," Amanda Tyler, the executive director of the Baptist Joint Committee for Religious Liberty, told the Center for American Progress in an April 2022 interview. "The most violent expressions, such as what we saw at the January 6 insurrection, get most of the attention. But the more subtle ones—like state legislative efforts to promote the teaching of the Bible in public schools or to require the posting of 'In God We Trust' in public schools and other public places—are also dangerous in that they perpetuate the false narrative that to be a true American one must be Christian—and often a certain type of Christian."[31] That belief is common among evangelicals, very nearly a formal part of their belief system, and certainly so in the case of those who embrace Christian nationalism.

A politics that arises out of a culture steeped in uncompromising punishment, punishment that falls hardest on the most vulnerable, is inclined to carry out a mimicry of private violence in the public sphere. It is not a coincidence that those who most publicly espouse their faith are also advocates of violent sweeps against unhoused individuals, jail sentences for miscarriages, the brutality of incarceration and the death penalty, and the elimination in toto* of the social safety net. While brutality to children may not be the sole root of the cruelty of the Christian Right's policies, it would be a mistake to ignore it—as most mainstream commentators do.

The other small tragedy built up of small tragedies, like the innumerable tiny men who make up a state in the famous illustration of Thomas Hobbes's *Leviathan*, is that sometimes parents don't want to beat their children—until they are told that God wants them to.[32] It's some combination of the voice of God, the voice of a pastor, and the voices of the ladies at church who give you the parenting books that impel the hand holding the paddle, and the impact is no less painful even if the parent holding it is weeping. The true cunning of such a system is the way it makes people into copies of itself, machines to perpetuate cruelty.

---

* Totally or entirely.

If an internal landscape is built on violence—with punishment and control its chief features, the peaks and troughs etched out in dominance and recrimination—the guidance it offers can lead to a similar landscape in adulthood and a desire to remake the world in that image. The compass points toward both pain and love, and they are found in the same direction, an inner north that pulls and pulls the pliant heart into the wastes.

CHAPTER 12

ONE BIG HAPPY FAMILY

According to R. L. Stollar, a child liberation theologian and cofounder of the now-defunct website Homeschoolers Anonymous, the political movement in support of homeschooling began in earnest at much the same time—and for much the same reasons—as the broader mobilization of the Christian Right.[1] When the federal government began to enforce school desegregation in earnest in the 1960s, legions of southern white Christians began to pull their children out of public schools, leaving school systems across the South bereft of the majority of their students. A patchwork of parochial segregated academies sprang up and began to be supplemented by home education.[2] Compulsory education laws requiring all children over the age of seven to be educated had blanketed the country by the early twentieth century. The legal status of homeschooling—instruction outside of public or recognized private schools—was precarious and uncertain. But from 1950 onward, a trickle of court cases in different states began to grant exemptions from truancy laws to religious parents, allowing them to instruct their children via correspondence courses and independent Christian curricula. At the same time, within the more extreme sectors of the Christian Right, a growing foment against government-run schools, whose purported indoctrination of children was presented as an obstacle to true religious liberty, began to encourage the Christian faithful to remove their children from the system. Still, homeschooling was rare and perpetually in conflict with state laws against truancy and educational deprivation.

In 1982, an evangelical titan, the preacher Francis A. Schaeffer, gave a thundering denunciation of public schools in a speech at a Fort Lauderdale church made famous under the title *A Christian Manifesto*.[3]

> **By law**, you are no more allowed to teach religious values and religious views in our public schools than you are in the schools of Russia tonight…
>
> It's illegal, in many places, for youngsters to merely meet and pray on the geographical location of the public schools…
>
> We must absolutely set out to smash the lie of the new and novel concept of the separation of religion from the state.[4]

Schaeffer encouraged a "cobelligerency" among the various strata of the Christian Right—Catholics, Protestants, Mormons, and other sects—with mixed success.[5]

It was in the Reagan eighties, the full effulgence of the Christian Right's power, that the institution that would provide the legal armature for the homeschooling movement was born. Michael Farris, a blue-eyed, sharp-jawed Christian lawyer whose status as a colossus in the movement for "parental rights" would grow to mythic status over the ensuing decades, decided, after withdrawing his own children from the school system, to use his legal acumen to enable other parents to do the same. While working as an attorney for Concerned Women for America, an organization that fought tooth and nail against the Equal Rights Amendment, Farris cofounded the Home School Legal Defense Association (HSLDA), an institution that would come to exercise influence over the lives of millions of children, all without being known to most people—which is just how the Christian Right likes it.[6]

By the mid-1980s, the HSLDA had a Washington, DC–area office and full-time employees and began to hammer at the network of laws that kept schooling in schools. Over the course of the 1980s and 1990s, laws about truancy and mandatory education fell in the face of determined opposition by the nascent homeschooling movement. As the historian Milton Gaither put it in *Homeschool: An American History*, the story of changing educational legislation to permit homeschooling is really fifty separate stories, as truancy laws as well as approaches to domestic and private education differed in each state.[7] By and large, before the 1980s home education had been confined to a small number of parents with idiosyncratic and passionate approaches to their children's education, friendly relations with local school authorities, and relatively little contact with court enforcement and the attendant legal battles. The influx, as Gaither put it, of "thousands of angry Protestants who were that convinced public schools were 'Satanic hothouses'" changed everything.[8]

The rhetoric of the HSLDA about a parent's right to educate their children as they wished as a constitutional right to privacy found a home with Republican state legislators, who were willing partners in overturning largely antiquated truancy laws that had been set into place between 1850 and 1929. Deftly navigating a complex web of laws that neglected to mention home instruction, required strict state oversight, or even, in the case of six states, required home educators to have academic credentials equivalent to those of accredited teachers, the Christian Right steamrolled from coast to coast. By 1992, homeschooling was legalized in every state in a series of triumphs that quietly overturned the fundamental nature of American education. The homeschool movement transformed education into a province of the domestic sphere—a matter of parental influence alone, whose ultimate arbiters were parents who had been divinely appointed to train up their children.

Born out of the crucible of Christian anger, HSLDA is unabashed about its faith-based origins. It may support parents of every sect or none, but its true constituency is clear. According to Harvard Law School professor Elizabeth Bartholet, conservative Christians still make up the majority of homeschoolers in the United States, with estimates of the number of children homeschooled for primarily religious reasons ranging up to 90 percent of all homeschooled children in the country.[9]

In 1995, testifying before Congress about the spread of homeschooling, Farris said that his work had been to change the laws for a higher purpose. Parental rights, he said, were as fundamental as the freedom to worship, and as sacred.[10]

According to a 2019 report from the US Department of Education's Institute of Education Sciences, 3.7 percent of students ages five to seventeen were educated at home. White children are homeschooled at more than double the rates of their Black and Hispanic counterparts. The rhetoric of homeschooling parents indicates that this is part of a strongly activist agenda: 75 percent of parents reported they chose homeschooling because they wanted "to provide moral instruction."[11] Since the covid-19 pandemic, these numbers have increased significantly, as a war against public schools commingles with an activist movement to get Christian parents to embrace homeschooling. Nearly 3 million children get their only education at home, scattered across a country whose laws about home instruction are slipshod and bare, not so much cracks as abysses for children to fall through.

The laws are intentional; they were systematically defanged into laxity. They are nearly universally staggeringly laissez-faire. They have been pushed into place over decades by a small, determined, largely Christian lobby, whose watchword is "parental rights" and whose actions are as deliberate and unmistakable as shackles on a child's wrists.[12]

The Coalition for Responsible Home Education is a small nonprofit founded in 2013 by home school alumni, with a mission to address the use of homeschooling to abuse and isolate children. CRHE keeps a grim little ledger tucked away in a corner of its matter-of-fact website. It's a list of children who have died while being homeschooled. It is incomplete and focused primarily on cases that occurred after 2000, when internet usage became more commonplace and cases easier to find. Nonetheless, from 2000 to the present, 211 fatalities have been logged onto that little spreadsheet. Where available, a tiny portrait of the child adorns his or her ledger entry.[13] Some are infamous cases, such as that of Raymond Wood of Warrensburg, Missouri, who in 2000 shot his wife and four of his children—all homeschooled at his direction—under the delusion that he was God. He had appealed to ministers at his church for help but had refused to take his medication. The children, isolated from mandatory reporters to whom they might have confided their father's increasingly erratic behavior, died at ages ten, eight, seven, and five. Two more, ages three and eighteen months, were wounded but survived. When he fled from the police, Ray believed that he was invisible.

Other cases are less notorious and less bloody but no less instructive about the harms of isolation. Away from teachers, school counselors and nurses, and the scrutiny of outsiders, it is easier to harm a child, even to kill him by inches. Abuse has its own logic, the hot clockwork of cruelty, and it runs best undisturbed. Without external intervention, an abusive home can run on that logic all the way to the end. Such was the case of Stephen Hill, whose parents, Jay and Linda Hill of the aptly named White Settlement, Texas, took him out of school at age nine.[14] Four years later, the boy was found by emergency responders unconscious and in shackles. At age thirteen, he weighed only fifty-five pounds. According to an appeals court judge, "The first impressions of the three EMTs that attended to Stephen were vivid ones. They each believed he was in the final stages of a long-term illness or terminal disease such as cancer or AIDS. None of the EMTs recognized Stephen's physical appearance as that of a thirteen-year-old boy. They each believed him to be only six to eight years old. Stephen was taken to the hospital where he remained comatose until his death."[15]

His mother said she'd shackled him for eighteen months prior to his death to keep him from getting at the food, that she'd resorted to starving him because hitting didn't seem to work anymore. In her 911 call, when she said the boy wasn't breathing right, she said she was afraid she wasn't a very good parent. By the time he died thirteen days later, on November 16, 1991, she had recanted her confession. In any case, it was too late for Stephen Hill.

Of course, not all homeschooling stories are stories of torture, of chains and starvation or whipping with hosepipes, burns and scalds and shattered skulls. Some are. Too many—one would be too many. Not every child dies, of course, their small lives neat entries in the terrible ledger. Some children escape. There were the Turpin Thirteen, who became the subjects of lurid tabloid coverage and overheated books when one of the thirteen children—Jordan, who was seventeen but looked eleven, malnourished and deprived of daylight—escaped and called the cops on a smuggled-out, deactivated cell phone. Their parents were Pentecostal Christians and had shuffled their growing brood around Texas and then to California; in their prior residences, neighbors had found feces, mounds of garbage, and beds with ropes tied to them for restraining the children. By the end, they were tied up almost all the time, reduced to eating mustard and ice when they could get it and almost never allowed to go outside. The oldest of the Turpin children was twenty-nine when authorities descended on the home in 2018; all thirteen children spent two months in the hospital, suffering from cognitive delays, heart damage, and other symptoms of severe malnutrition. Their parents, David and Louise Turpin, were sentenced to life imprisonment in 2019 on fourteen felony counts, including torture, cruelty to dependent adults, child endangerment, and false imprisonment. It had all started when Christ had called on David and Louise to have as many children as they could. It had continued because under the lax regulations governing homeschooling in the United States, no one had looked into a house where shackles and starvation were the only means of instruction.[16]

There have been other escapees, other near deaths, other dire situations of extremity that can develop in isolation, isolating victims being the keystone and chief sign of abuse. In a 2014 study of child abuse so severe that she described it with the term *child torture*, researcher Barbara L. Knox of the University of Wisconsin found that 47 percent of the school-age victims she studied had been removed from school to be homeschooled.[17] The abuse, she found, had typically intensified after homeschooling had begun. In a similar and more recent piece of data, Connecticut's child advocate published a 2018 study of six school districts that found that 36 percent of students withdrawn from public schools came from families that had already experienced one documented instance of neglect reported to the state's Department of Children and Families.[18]

There are also other, quieter stories of deep neglect. There are children who cannot read because they were homeschooled. There are children trained not to believe in evolution and children whose knowledge of history is as abbreviated and propagandistic as a KKK pamphlet. There are children left to do workbooks on their own by busy parents with many other children to care for, to fast-forward educational DVDs as they will, children for whom schooling is an occasional treat, children who by dint of never having a benchmark of comparison don't know what they don't know until they move into a world for which they were never prepared.

Over the years, the HSLDA, prompted by high-profile child abuse cases, moved beyond its original mandate into a broader societal project: utilizing its legal resources to insulate parents against child abuse charges and weakening state child-welfare agencies.[19] By the mid-1990s, the HSLDA was routinely providing legal support to homeschooling families accused of child abuse. In the 2000s, the organization announced to its members that it would fight against new or expanded child welfare laws, which, in the organization's conception, infringed on the absolute nature of parental rights. In 2005, the HSLDA took on the case of Michael and Sharen Gravelle, an Ohio couple who had adopted eleven children, some with disabilities, and kept them at home to be schooled. In September 2005, sheriff's deputies found nine homemade cages of wood and chicken wire that reeked of urine, some with wired-in alarms, in the home. The children told authorities that they were made to sleep in the cages at night; they talked about being hit with boards and having their heads held under freezing water as punishment.[20]

HSLDA attorney Scott Somerville told the *Akron Beacon-Journal*, "[Michael Gravelle] told me why they adopted these children and told me the problems they were trying to solve. I think he is a hero."[21] On its website, the HSLDA states that its mandate "extends to helping families whose decision to homeschool subjects them to suspicions of abuse or neglect," although it officially condemns physical abuse.[22]

The organization has nonetheless continued to push for yet more deregulation in education and for the weakening of child welfare laws in all

states. In 2018 alone, the HSLDA spent nearly $2.4 million on legal advo-
cacy, education, and protection for homeschooling parents.[23] Within the
world of municipal and state legislation—and with the aid of a network of
churches and statehouses across the country—a few million dollars can go
a very long way when judiciously applied and multiplied year upon year.
Cases in which judges reach publicized judicial decisions represent a frac-
tion of the parents represented by the organization; in a 2020 report, the
HSLDA claimed to have participated in 797 cases that year on behalf of
homeschooling parents.

The HSLDA has consistently used its legal influence to weigh in on
child abuse cases and legislation, well beyond the specific provenance of
homeschooling. In 2008, it went to the mat against a proposed revision
in California legislation. Elaborating on an established law that made the
causation of "unjustifiable physical pain or mental suffering" on a child
illegal, the amended bill would have added specifics, allowing juries to
consider whether a defendant had used implements ("including, but not
limited to, a stick, a rod, a switch, an electrical cord, an extension cord, a
belt, a broom, or a shoe"), in addition to throwing, kicking, burning, or
cutting a child or interfering with their breathing.[24]

In a fiery op-ed for the *Washington Times*, HSLDA's then copresident,
Michael Smith, wrote a passionate screed in opposition to the law's amendment and for the right of parents to strike their child with implements. "If
this law passes, it will have a chilling effect on parents who reasonably
exercise discipline through the use of spanking with an implement," he
wrote. "Although this is not a home-school issue, it is a parental rights
issue. One of the foundations for the right to home-school is based upon
the fundamental right of parents to direct the upbringing and education
of their children."[25]

The amendment failed.

Only four states in the entire country—New York, Pennsylvania, Massachusetts, and Rhode Island—are "high regulation," according to the
HSLDA, twelve are "moderate regulation," and the rest are either "low regulation" or unknown. As CRHE notes, "Only Pennsylvania and Arkansas

prevent convicted child abusers or sex offenders from homeschooling. In every other state in the country, parents may homeschool their children regardless of what crimes they may have committed and irrespective of past evidence of instability or abuse."[26]

In low-regulation states, such as Ohio and Nevada, no teaching qualifications are required for those who teach children at home, no external educational assessments are required, and no immunization requirements are in place.[27] The Ohio requirements are laughably simple: parents must notify the state of how many students are enrolled in their homeschool each fall and state that they will provide instruction in English language arts, mathematics, science, history, government, and social studies. One form, once a year, with no assessments, inspections, or other government involvement. In other states it is not even required for parents to notify local schools that they have withdrawn their children from school. It is a system designed for children to tidily disappear into. And whenever state legislatures, prompted by activists, many of whom are former home-schooled students, attempt to impose stricter regulations, the HSLDA is there to marshal a team of high-priced attorneys and a groundswell of support from the faithful.

Public education has many virtues, the chief one being providing the tools of learning at no cost to families. But another of its traits is the way it breaks down homogeny, forcing children to be in a community with others unlike them, of different races and different creeds. For a movement determined to exist in splendid isolation, creating a parallel and parasitic Christian Right culture that apes broader, secular Americana while maintaining an arm's-length distance from its corrupting influence, this element of public education is a profound threat. For decades, the Christian Right has developed a thriving material culture: in pursuit of separation from worldly corruption, it has created a parallel and parasitic subculture with its own novels (supernatural thrillers that inevitably owe debts to John Grisham and Stephen King); thrillers (*Die Hard* but with angels!); bands (DC Talk, the Christian version of Nirvana; Ark of the Covenant, a Christian metalcore alternative to Metallica); cartoons (*Veggie Tales*;

the Spandex-clad, Truth-bearing Bibleman from *Pure Flix*); schools, universities, TV shows, and radio programs. Exposure to the real stuff would shatter the carefully constructed carapace; Christian grunge pales in comparison to Kurt Cobain, and former evangelicals have told me about the wonder—and the anger—of finally experiencing elements of a wider culture long denied them. The Christian Right's emphasis on homeschooling is also an emphasis on isolation from the world at large, a protective measure to preserve zealotry while telling the general public a story of parents robbed of control of their own children.

The quality of public school teaching varies by district and by classroom; that of homeschooling varies by the individual home. Each parent has their own parenting style, their own number of children, their own inclination to dole out the rod of punishment as an academic tool, their own level of teaching ability, their own amount of money or time, their own struggles with substance abuse and dependence, their own family systems of support or lack thereof. As Elizabeth Bartholet pointed out in a 2020 article for *Arizona Law Review*, many homeschooling parents do not have the academic qualifications to teach their children complex topics; 15 percent of homeschooling parents surveyed had a high school degree or less. Some parents, she pointed out, are not interested in educating their children or remove their children from school simply because they have been accused of truancy or to avoid scrutiny over child protection laws.[28]

Public school isn't perfect, but it's public; it ensures that children can't be hidden away and deprived of an education. Public school teachers, counselors, and nurses are mandatory reporters of child abuse. Moreover, public schools exist within a system, however flawed, that has accountability built in, in the form of broader statewide and national bureaucracies. Homeschooling, under the lax laws of the United States, is designed to erase that accountability—and render children invisible.

What do homeschooled children learn under the aegis of Christianity? How do they learn to see the world and react to it once they leave the bounds of home? Within the world of Christian homeschool education, there are a variety of curricula, each held to as tightly as any church or denomination. There are the books churned out by Bob Jones University Press, the Abeka courses, the wisdom booklets of the Institute in Basic Life Principles, the Young Earth Creationism–infused materials of Answers in Genesis, the "Christ-centered, family-oriented" materials of Sonlight Curriculum, the "classical Christian education" of Tapestry of Grace. Each purports to cover the areas required by state law, with mixed results; all are grounded in a Christian, patriarchal worldview, which grounds worldly knowledge in the framework of godly values. They instruct children to be separate from the world even as they lay out the perfunctory requirements of being part of it.

Homeschooling is not all horror, not all cruelty and neglect—although absolute deregulation and a ready set of hard-right curricula render such horror stories infinitely more possible. There are plainly cases of homeschooling success when parents' inclinations suit the needs of children who require plentiful attention and grow into happy, lively kids. Many parents find a happy match of ability, facility, and desire for their children's betterment; other children thrive in the comparative freedom and privacy of home education.

But in the Christian realm, success in the homeschool environment entails a different goal than simple happiness or even intellectual success: Christian homeschoolers who distinguish themselves are drafted as child soldiers in the broader spiritual war. Those who excel in Christian homeschool may find themselves elevated within the insular institutions that cater to religious home education. It is these elites that Michael Farris calls the "Joshua Generation" of young homeschoolers, whose role is to "engage wholeheartedly in the battle to take the land" for the Christian faith.[29] There are some in every elite law school who wind up as clerks for Supreme Court justices; who are groomed for office on every level of government; who are the instruments of power. One vivid example is Alex Harris, the son of two passionate advocates for homeschooling who educated him and his six siblings at home. Harris wound up attending Harvard Law School and becoming a law clerk for Supreme Court justices Neil Gorsuch and Anthony Kennedy. "The Joshua Generation is an influential concept—one

I embraced most of my life," he wrote for the Gospel Coalition, "that my generation would rise up and attain positions of power and influence in government, law, and beyond, and in so doing help restore the United States as a Christian nation."[30]

The youth-targeted political program makes for a potent force of spiritual and political warriors. And there are plenty of organizations designed to help. The National Christian Forensics and Communications Association (NCFCA), for example, is a nationwide speech and debate organization founded in 1997 "with the goal of training up Christian home school students to learn the skills necessary to reach their world with God's truth."[31] Nowadays, NCFCA runs programs that reach thousands of students per year, training them to be polished, conservative "ambassadors for Christ." Nationally, the organization TeenPact offers seminars, tours of the Capitol, political communication workshops, and political leadership training for students ages eight to nineteen, attracting a large audience particularly among Christian homeschoolers.[32] PursueGod.org, an evangelical youth education resource, encourages Christian teens to read John 15:18 ("If the world hates you, remember that it hated me first" [NLT]) and speak out against abortion with ardency.[33] Each year, the Texas Youth Summit, routinely attended by conservative politicians and pundits such as Ted Cruz, Matt Gaetz, and Candace Owens, offers free admission to those twelve to twenty-six years old and provides both religious and political education explicitly rooted in Christian values to thousands of participants. Its slogan: "Empowering youth to be catalysts to win the Culture War." It is both a promise and a threat.[34]

Certainly, the right-wing establishment has sat up and taken notice of the rapid expansion of the homeschool lobby and its growing power as generations of alumni come into their own as adults. Donald Trump, a careful arbiter of fair winds and cultivator of allies, paid special attention to homeschooling parents in a statement in September 2023. "As President, it was my honor to support America's homeschool families—and to protect the God-given right of every parent to be the steward of their children's education," he said in a video. "To every homeschool family, I will be your champion!"[35]

The power brokers of the right wing and the homeschool lobby know that kids who don't die grow up. An army can't march without soldiers, and soldiers are best instructed in a totalistic environment, one that isolates them from outside influence, keeps them within homes that are shaped by authoritarian faith. Some children die, forming part of that terrible list of casualties. Most of them live to be the future of the faith militant.

SUSANNA WESLEY, THE MOTHER OF JOHN AND CHARLES WESLEY, THE founders of Methodism, was a kitchen table lay preacher in her time and the wife of an eccentric who squandered the family's scant funds on writing a quixotic exegesis of the trials of Job. She bore nineteen children.

Though enough of her writings survive to fill a sturdy volume, it is primarily one piece of correspondence that is quoted in Protestant circles of various denominations. The letter discusses her methods of child rearing, which she outlined in a letter to her son John in 1732:

When turned a year old (and some before) they were taught to fear the rod and to cry softly; by which means they escaped abundance of correction they might otherwise have had; and that most odious noise of the crying of children was rarely heard in the house, but the family usually lived in as much quietness as if there had not been a child among them...

...Drinking or eating between meals was never allowed, unless in case of sickness, which seldom happened. Nor were they suffered to go into the kitchen to ask anything of the servants, when they were at meat: if it was known they did, they were certainly beaten...

...Whenever a child is corrected it must be conquered. This will not be hard to do if he is not grown headstrong by too much indulgence. When the will of a child is totally subdued, and it is brought to revere and stand in awe of the parents, then a great many childish follies, and faults may be past over. Some should be overlooked and taken no notice of, and others mildly reproved. No willful transgression ought ever to be forgiven children, without chastisement, less or more, as the nature and circumstances of the offense require.[36]

The evangelical parenting industrial complex has a number of devoted Susanna Wesley fans, notably James Dobson and Larry Tomczak, though her influence is not limited to Reagan-era evangelicals. She lived to be seventy-three years old, long enough to witness the death of eleven of her children. Nine died before the age of two, one accidentally smothered by a nurse. Susanna was nearly continuously pregnant from 1690 to 1709. It is this bonneted, severe-looking woman whom twentieth- and twenty-first-century evangelicals have turned to in crafting their parenting advice. It's worth mentioning that her most famous son, John Wesley, was rather more temperate in his admonition to utilize the rod of correction than his mother. In his sermon "On Family Religion," published in 1762, he noted that corporal punishment, while ultimately commanded by God, should be used last, after all other means are exhausted. "Whatever is done should be done with mildness; nay, indeed, with kindness too," he wrote. "Otherwise your own spirit will suffer loss, and the child will reap little advantage."[37]

What exactly the spirit suffers—or suffering in the name of the Spirit—is ultimately the subject of Part 2 of this book; it is a chronicle, in fits and starts, by an outsider (or "infidel," as one Christian I interviewed dubbed me) of pain inflicted on children. Those who wrote to me—and those who confessed later that they couldn't, that they had wanted to, that they had feared to—had been beaten with an astounding array of household objects in the name of Christ the Savior. Some parents had been eager to perform the duty of punishment, others less so but influenced by the social milieus of their churches and the doctrines of popular preachers to believe that there was no other way to ensure their children's salvation. For some children, the physical brutality of corporal punishment served as a primary source of trauma. For many others, the prescribed multistep ritual—the waiting for the "neutral object" (a paddle, an oar, a hanger, a fishing rod, a dowel, a peach-tree switch), the coerced confession, the arrival at a state of brokenness indicated by a specific tenor of weeping, the subsequent coerced reunion with its embraces and declarations of love—was a source of enduring confusion and emotional pain. The books I have read span from 1970 to 2018: forty-eight years of the doctrine of absolute obedience and generations of children raised in its shadow.

The stated reason for all of this pain is that children do not remain children. They grow up into morally culpable subjects of God and the world; in order to prosper, they must be taught to obey authority at all times; they will someday instruct children of their own. And they have, millions of them. Many have stayed within the bounds of the church, passing on, with each percussive blow, the doctrine of the rod of correction. Elisabeth Elliot, the daughter of two missionaries, wrote in her 1992 memoir, *The Shaping of a Christian Family: How My Parents Nurtured My Faith*, about being struck with switches and hairbrushes beginning long before she could talk, having her mouth washed out with "a great bar of yellow soap," and how her refusal to cry caused greater punishment. Her reaction was gratitude for her parents' "vigilance"; those practices, she wrote, do not seem oppressive to her looking back, and though she is sure there must have been "nervousness and anxiety at times," she cannot remember those feelings clearly.[38]

Most people raised this way remain in contact with their parents, perhaps even, in a country bereft of affordable child care, offering up new young bodies to their tender mercies. But others have left—for other churches or for no church at all. Even bonds of blood, tested with sufficient force, can fray. Some families are the families you choose. And the children you raise do not have to be raised as you were.

"I do not have a relationship with my parents," Lois, thirty-five, wrote to me. "While it's probably for the best that we don't have a relationship, it's very painful just the same. They live 10 minutes away and I have nightmares that I see them out and about with my children."

It is difficult and sometimes even frightening to acknowledge both that you love your parents and that they have deeply wronged you. The sense of fractured authority, the internalization of endured experiences, can create a dissonance in the self. Those who have been taught to submit their will may have difficulty seeing the gravity of injustice that has been done to them. There is a peculiar loneliness to pain inflicted by your parents, who serve, in the earliest years of life, as one's chief sources of love, nurturing, and guidance, particularly in the social context of a close-knit religious community that prides itself on its morality. Such isolation is intentional. The teaching during fifty years of evangelical parenting books has been remarkably firm on this front: spanking is "an event," and it should be done in private. (Benny and Sheree Phillips, in their 1981 book *Raising Kids Who Hunger for God*, confess that with their large family, it feels as if "much of the day is spent in the bathroom spanking the children.")[39] The bell jar of private pain can descend even in public if the community approves of such punishment. (Sheree Phillips, regarding her three-year-old son's tantrum after she gave a parenting class in a church: "I carried my screaming child to the restroom...I spent quite some time calming Jesse down, disciplining him for his wrong attitude, re-disciplining for refusing to receive his spanking willingly, and completing the restoration process.")[40]

Not every relationship between parent and child survives, and the very institutions that manufacture child abuse on an industrial scale offer up solutions for bereft parents, bewildered by abandonment when the children they struck cut ties with them. Among Focus on the Family's enormous body of readily available wisdom is a growing body of work on parental estrangement and how to cope when your children don't talk to you anymore. Pray daily for your adult child, the writers advise.[41] "Over the past several years, I've listened as many parents of teens or young adults have openly grieved about a **prodigal child**. They often have no idea what caused a son or daughter to cut them out of their lives," wrote Joannie Debrito on Focus on the Family's website in a post entitled "Hope for Parents of Prodigal Children." "They wonder when or if they will see them again. Some feel the loss of a grandchild they have not yet met and the sting of one more special event without any contact. There is a great sense of loss."[42] In the gospel of Luke, the prodigal son is one who misspends his inheritance on debauchery and is forced to return in humility to his parent; he is celebrated as one who was dead but now is alive again. In Focus on the Family's worldview, there may not have been any debauchery that led to parental estrangement—but certainly there must have been outside influence for children to declare their parents "toxic" and, of course, the "entitlement and narcissism" to demand that their needs "must be met." Her advice is to lean in to God's Word. Below the post there is an advertisement for Focus on Parenting, the ministry's parenting podcast, which offers "biblical truths." It's a handy trick to teach parents how to drive their children away, then counsel them in their grief; it gets you coming and going, all for the low price of books and tapes and newsletter subscriptions, and the higher price, which is everything.

"My mother died seven years ago, alone and miserable after having alienated virtually everyone she ever knew," said Naomi, fifty, who was struck, sat on, and pinned down while her mother prayed for demons to depart from her. "I have never shed a tear, never mourned her passing."

The voices of people abused as children under the aegis of godly parenting are a sussurus of pain beneath the words of the child-rearing manuals: an echoing litany still felt years into adulthood, a melody of estrangement.

"I remember being yelled at to stop crying after being spanked, and feeling this burning resentment towards my parents over it, because they were the reason I was crying," wrote Miriam, thirty-five. "My relationship with them is limited to a handful of phone calls a year."

"I have almost no relationship with my parents or siblings beyond the occasional happy birthday text and a twenty-five-dollar gift for the Christmas name drawing," said Mara, thirty-five, who was beaten with hoses, drumsticks, and spoons starting at six months of age. "My parents and eight siblings are all caught in various cultlike churches that emphasize obedience as a primary virtue."

Darlene, who is in her late forties, experienced eighteen months of homelessness after leaving the church and being cut off by her parents. "If I ever make enough money to have a pet project, I plan to open transitional housing for single moms leaving evangelical families," she said. "We nearly always lose our families, and providing a place for women to start over where they don't have to struggle like my daughter and I have had to is a dream of mine: Darlene's Home for Inconvenient Women."

Paradoxically, it is the violent efforts to bind children to the church that often force an estrangement from it on the part of people who were formerly abused under the doctrine of the rod and the sinful child. Many former evangelicals describe the process of leaving the church as "deconstruction," a term that came to Christianity by way of the Algerian French philosopher Jacques Derrida and a handful of ambitious, academically minded theologians. Like so many terms relating to this isolated world, it is widely known and feared in fundamentalist circles; tentatively embraced by those in the process of leaving; and entirely unknown by most outside the evangelical community.

Deconstruction, as many progressive Christians understand it, is the effort to unravel all the myriad threaded-together assumptions that make up life in a stringent faith community—corporal punishment, Republican politics, submission to God, love of one's parents, abnegation of the self, and so on—to understand how they are interconnected, and, thus armed, choose among them, clear-eyed.[43]

Those who have written to me have complex relationships with faith: some have embraced gentler forms of Christianity; others violently oppose religion of any kind.

"I will not set foot in a church again ever for any reason," said Johnny H., forty, who recalled a childhood filled with horrific pain and whose parents are not allowed in his home. "I am extremely hesitant to allow my kids to be alone with any adult who attends church regularly."

"I am a Christian. My primary act of worship is in caring for others as a nurse and as a professor," said Dinah, fifty. "I believe that every human is created in the image of God and that to care for them is a privilege."

The attempt to raise children as warriors of God sometimes brings a family line to an end and sometimes begins a new era of alienation from a faith experienced as cruelty from the earliest days of life. Some of the people who wrote to me have chosen never to have children, so as not to inflict the cycle of abuse on a new generation. Others chose to have children and to break that cycle by other means—often by deliberately and painfully overriding the lifetime of violent instinct that had been ground into their bodies. One man recounted to me a bemused dialogue he had with his lively son, explaining to him that he didn't know how to do this—how to parent without violence; that they would have to figure it out together.

For Johnny, having children was an opportunity to sever himself permanently from the practices with which he had been raised, a decision he has never since questioned. "If there was a difficulty in finding an alternative," he said, "it was because I had to learn to see parenting as being about something other than domination over a child."

"My children were not raised with violence. But it was really hard for me to learn to inhibit and not use violence and corporal punishment, since I was raised in a family with it," said Hannah, sixty. "I slapped my daughter once, not hard, when she was a really mouthy adolescent; big mistake. I totally was wrong and apologized profusely, and she *still* talks about it."

Other parents' deconstruction began after they had raised their children violently. One woman wrote to me, simply, "I can't believe I used to hit my children with a stick."

For some parents, the act of having a child was in and of itself the beginning of the dissolution of their faith. Their instincts—their very bodies—rebelled against striking and beating their offspring; watching their sons and daughters grow up without the shadow of punishment, they mourned their own lost childhoods and the children they could have been.

"Not a day goes by that I don't wish things had been different for me and my siblings as children. Not a single day," said Lois. "I'm starting to feel more comfortable parenting myself along with my kids—silently in my own mind, but acknowledging little Lois just the same and showing up for her in the ways I needed most."

Susanna Wesley's grave lies in Bunhill Fields Burial Ground in London, its white marble tombstone spackled with lichen. "She was the Mother of nineteen Children of whom the most eminent were the Revs. JOHN and CHARLES WESLEY," reads part of the inscription. Her husband, Samuel, is buried nearly two hundred miles away at St Andrew's Churchyard in Epworth, North Lincolnshire. Of her children who died before the age they would have been taught, with the rod, to cry softly—Annesley and Jedediah, Susanna, John, Benjamin, and four who never had names at all—scant record is to be found. They are likely buried where they were born, in Epworth and South Ormesby, under the small infant tombstones that are more numerous the older the graveyard and whose scant details are nearly always worn away. Despite what Susanna asserted in her famous letter, only in such a grave is the will of a child totally subdued.

What struck me most in the testimony provided to me, which I regard as a form of sacred trust, was how isolated each incidence of suffering was. Each child, despite the industrial-scale child abuse provided by the evangelical parenting template, despite the sweeping social changes proposed by the Christian Right, experienced his or her own suffering in solitude, within the unbreachable walls of the family unit or the church.

I have spent my life, as a New York Jew, living with a sense of precarity—when my post-Holocaust grandparents settled here in 1948, the trauma they endured permeated my own family in complex and sometimes violent ways, down through the subsequent generations. Part of it is a perpetually defensive mindset, the lifelong and acute knowledge that I am not a "real American" and can never be one: real Americans are white Christians who celebrate Christmas, go to church, are interviewed in diners by the press as a kind of gestural realpolitik.* Real Americans never

---

* A term used mainly to describe realist foreign policy; when applied to politics in general, it refers to political realism or a practical approach to politics, basing policy on power relations instead of set ideals.

had family members gassed, nor were they the products of fear and flight; real Americans were planted here solidly under the cross, unobjectionable in their triumphant faith. My own life is in a real sense the product of violence, of refugees who fled annihilation to create a new life in a golden land, yet found themselves outside the true boundaries of Americanness. The exaltation of pious Christians as the essential "soul" of America had as much to do with the mythmaking of the Moral Majority and the Reagan eighties as it did with centuries of hostility toward immigrants and ethnic and religious minorities—the very politics embraced and furthered by the Christian Right. Yet the central wound of my own sense of precarity, of the falseness and contingency of my American identity, led me to explore Christian Right ideology in the way that a tongue explores a wound in the mouth. And it was belied in every respect by the ex-evangelicals who entrusted me with their pain.

White Protestant Christianity did not immure my interlocutors from pain; on the contrary, brutal doctrines had led them to live lives of isolated suffering, the confiding of which, in anyone, was impossible. Though planted under the cross, secure and American as corn, they had endured immeasurable pain without being able to speak its name. Moving away from the faith that had hurt them so badly had led them to be spurned by their families or to spurn their families in turn. They had experienced intergenerational trauma as the doctrine of the rod passed from parent to child; they had felt precarity and contingency in the sense that every wounded child lives a precarious life contingent on the whims of his or her abusers. Compassion had been absent in their lives or meted out more stingily than lashes; they had experienced a sense that their true selves were false, riven in two by crises of faith; they had experienced banishment.

They had also experienced voicelessness, since very little attention had been and is paid to the crisis of child abuse that daily harms millions of American children under the aegis of faith—or the rising forces of the-ocracy that ex-evangelicals anticipate and warn against to little response. They risked much to speak out and were not heeded except by a stranger, a writer who did her best to transcribe their pain legibly and turn it into part of a larger picture. Still more, informed by their perspectives, I realized I was watching a gathering storm of societal violence built up in generations of homes that had imprisoned children under the rod and the policy doctrine of parental rights—a storm that threatens to upturn the golden land that was the subject of my ancestors' dreams. There was so much pain in their voices, more pain than could be encompassed should I have quoted double or triple the material I quote here, sought out more testimony, and more. It is the pain of those children that has transmuted into a society guided by and suffused with violence.

Still: if you live, you can change, slowly as a root breaking a stone or quickly. To surrender the absolution of faith, to strike out into the unknown, to parent counter to every model you had is an act of courage; to heal from the welts and the stripes and the scars the beatings left in your mind is an act of courage; which is not to say that it is seamless or perfect.

"I will probably be rebuilding for the rest of my life," Susannah told me. "As a child, I had a strong sense of justice and fairness, and that was the beginning of the rift between my childhood and adulthood and between my parents and me. That need to make the world a more just place is still there. I am proud of it."

CHAPTER 13

THE BURNING PATH

As I write these words, a US election is going on in the way that US elections go on (and on and on)—months and years of unfun pageantry as grim-faced candidates and odds-obsessed journalists take stock of a contest for power. It's surreal, in a way, to go on with life—the making and eating of meals, the earning of small money, the doing of everyday deeds—knowing that by the time this book is published, the character of this country will be on the precipice of a dark and permanent alteration.

Americans have a tendency to believe that authoritarianism will arise here in a swirl of drama, obvious malefactors emerging from the ether to work their evil; even more, we have a sense that our democracy, the most powerful in the world, is immune to becoming a dictatorship, and this form of American exceptionalism has a tendency to blind us to what is directly before our eyes.

Such was the case in fall 2023 and the winter of 2024, when cable news duly covered the slate of also-ran Republican candidates, making their overtures toward power before duly making obeisance to the already gilded figure of Trump: the chosen one, God's messenger, the man who would be king. Pat slogans on dull debate stages obscured the fact that compared to Trump, other candidates' polling numbers were minuscule. Coverage of the primaries thus had the disconcerting effect of obscuring the threat of autocracy by rendering it invisible, as, offstage, the end of democracy in the arms of militant angels lurked behind the threadbare curtains.

The fact of the matter is that the Republican Party, in step with and guided by a small and powerful theocratic minority, and with a profoundly vengeful and militant demagogue at its head, is poised to win an election that will render moot the need for any subsequent elections. It is the logical offspring of half a century of the Christian Right's building power, and in the shadow of this contest, the mundanities of life become impossibly small, in the way that people live ordinary lives until a tsunami hits, and then all that's left is the bones of the drowned and their shattered houses.

Watching the dull pageantry unfold on cable news in the fall of 2023, waiting for Donald Trump to seal his candidacy again despite or perhaps because of the indictments that dog him, rendered that cognitive dissonance acute to the point of pain. It's life in the shadow of a rumbling Vesuvius; it's being Cassandra in the streets of Troy; it's being American and terrified, waiting for the reins of the hegemon to be given over to the crooks and ghouls. This election has been profoundly odd because it's haunted by unacknowledged ghosts, ones that aren't in the room, aren't on the debate stage, don't rate a mention in the horse-race coverage about odds and public perceptions.

One of them is vengeance.

The Republican candidate is a man who declared the last presidential contest, which he lost, illegitimate, a claim that has launched a thousand grifts and enticed millions of people into the belief that all electoral contests are fraudulent, rigged. This candidate's first promise is that once in office, he will exact vengeance on his enemies. It's his chief refrain in posts on his custom-built social media site, Truth Social, where he regularly inveighs against the Marxists and the godless and the "vermin" who kept him from his second term and who will suffer his righteous anger should he attain, once again, control of a world power. He talks about a nation with poisoned blood, about the bloodbath that will ensue should he fail to be elected, and despite his worldly griminess, his disciples are washed clean in the blood of the Lord.

The prophets and their flocks that once heralded him haven't left his side; evangelicals are once again primed to form a central bloc in the Republican voting base. And it makes a profound kind of sense that vows of vengeance, talk of enemies everywhere, reverberate with them. After all, their worldview is girded by a spiritual war: they were already armed for battle, and their standard-bearer's words match their own fever pitch. If they thrum to the hymn of vengeance, it's only to be expected; it is the signature mindset of a group that believes themselves to be suffering martyrs of a heathen world who must attain worldly power in order to avenge their grievances and prevent them from ever happening again.

The other silent specter in this electoral contest is that if this candidate is elected, it may signal the end of true elections in this country; a move with historical precedent—democracy undoing itself by rendering power to someone for whom surrendering it is unthinkable.

This, too, is consonant with spiritual warfare, with the Seven Mountain Mandate of attaining worldly power. At the heart of evangelical faith is ecstatic worship of a king and adherence to the word of his earthly representatives. Obeisance and obedience are built into this structure; the scattershot and febrile mess that is free will has no place in it. Authoritarianism harmonizes here like a choir carol; responsiveness to edicts from above has been drilled into this segment of the population from childhood, with attendant violence that makes it impossible to ignore. Childhoods racked with violence have enforced their obedience, have trained authoritarians from before the moment they spoke their first word, molded by blows to be soldiers for the faith.

It would be easier to ignore this unsettling drumbeat—the music of authoritarianism on the march—if its most loyal servants hadn't accrued, over the last half century, so very much power, far disproportionate to their percentage of the population. That power is most concentrated in the judiciary branch of the US government, though it has ancillaries in the legislative branch and seeks to capture the executive branch as well, a tripartite plan of attack to secure God's kingdom.

A judiciary branch linked at its core to a religious authoritarian movement cannot be trusted to preserve such a worldly value as a secular democracy. In particular, the multiracial democracy so dearly won by the fighters of the civil rights movement—the only time in the United States' history that it has been a multiracial democracy is the past half century—that has allowed abortion, gay and interracial marriage, integrated schooling, public education, and social safety net programs. All of these are on the chopping block, and there is a hunger, everywhere, for righteous destruction of it all.

The Heritage Foundation, Paul Weyrich's brainchild and a subsequent hyperactive Christian Right lobbying juggernaut, has laid out a comprehensive vision for a conservative future in its Project 2025. Among the materials it has assembled is a thirty-chapter book, *Mandate for Leadership: The Conservative Promise.*[1] It mentions religion and religious freedom thirty-five times and presents thirty different conservative "solutions" for government institutions that are, in essence, an instruction manual for destroying federal institutions from within. Its partners and contributors include numerous prominent Christian Right organizations from Family Research Council to Susan B. Anthony Pro-Life America to Hillsdale College, and the government it imagines is one whose sole purpose appears to be war and policing, the armature of surveillance and violence. All other functions of the state should be left to private religious institutions, which should be free to discriminate as they wish.

In the first Trump administration, many of the members of his cabinet were heroes of the religious Right—and overt, joyous saboteurs of the institutions they were meant to safeguard. One example was Betsy DeVos, the billionaire heiress to the Edgar Prince fortune and someone who, up to the moment of her appointment as secretary of education, had spent her adult life devoted to undermining public education and promoting private religious education in its stead.[2] During her tenure, she continued that subversion apace in obedience to a devout Christian faith that found public education ungodly.[3]

The recent past is the future laid out in blueprint, and Project 2025 lays out further details for the immediate, burning path forward. The first Trump administration eagerly co-opted Heritage Foundation suggestions, and all indicia point toward a second crowning of MAGA's florid Cyrus becoming an orgy of wish fulfillment for the Christian Right.

Should this not be the case—should Cyrus go uncrowned—a congregation primed on waiting for a messiah's return in blood will not be daunted. An organization that has trained up its children to be dutiful and obedient, patient and sweet until the sword must be taken up will bide its time. It will cultivate its power further, keeping its mobs at a distance from its more respectable iterations, until the time comes again when the reins of power are within its grasp. This is a group that rebounds from unfulfilled prophecies by making further ones; a group that sees the Devil's hand in its failures and the work of angels in its successes. Against a backdrop of celestial warfare, its members do their work; they will continue to do it until they have succeeded in their aims. The chorus of ex-evangelicals, made up of people who have witnessed the rapacity, cruelty, and ambition of the movement, has for years expressed dire warnings as to the imminence of such a takeover of the government. It is time and past time that the rest of us listen.

The desire for America to be a Christian hegemon, a kingdom that crushes infidels within and without, will not wane or abate until the public at large decides that this movement represents a legitimate threat and works to countermand it. This is difficult, painful work and demands a counterzeal that is not easy to muster in the dull, painful, costly, and challenging world. Nonetheless, it is required of us, in this time and for and of our children, to ensure that the momentum of half a century is stopped by a collective heaving against that mass of kinetic energy. A nation bound by Christian authoritarianism whose mandate is cruelty in private and austerity in public—which claims to love you as it burns you alive—is not to be countenanced; not in our schools, our courts, our cops, our corners.

It must be rooted out from the public square and left to rot in ignominy, robbed of its power to hurt and to shame.

What do you hear in the darkness around you? Is it the whirl of devils and angels in battle or silence or rain or the mundane miracle of dawn or the sleep of the one you love at your side? Somewhere in that aural landscape are the war drums marching, the horns of Jericho in full, florid trumpet, ready to shake down the cracked remaining guardrails against autocracy in this country. In response, we must take up a countermarch, thrill to its cacophonic strains, and rise to spurn a faith that has overrun its banks and spilled out into wild and untrammeled hate.

AFTERWORD

This book started, although I didn't know it at the time, when I was watching a documentary called *The Way Down*, which is about a church.[1] The name of the church doesn't matter; it was showy and excessive in its habits, with a charismatic leader, but that is true of many churches in this country. In one episode, former parishioners began to explain the church's attitude toward the discipline of children and the tools they used to do it. There had been a case, some years earlier, when a church parishioner's child had died of maltreatment and the church had defended his parents.

I began to wonder how many children had been disciplined like that but hadn't died and what had happened to them afterward. And so I asked.

I didn't intend for this book to be the story of what theocracy does to the women and children under its care, nor even for it to be a portrait of nascent theocracy. It was supposed to be a big, loud book about terrorism. Instead, it became a big, loud book about quiet and terrible grief, belief, and pain and how they are all connected—and how the ideas that let you beat your child in the name of God may make you think you can beat a country into obedience, too. And perhaps even how, in opposing one form of injustice, you oppose the other kind at the same time.

In some ways I was an unlikely messenger for this book, being the proverbial stranger at the great strange feast of Christianity—unwilling to sup from it, though morsels of it are pressed upon me all the time. Still, sometimes it takes an outsider to see things clearly. I don't have a competing version of Jesus to defend; I just listen to what people tell me they believe and act and write accordingly. I know, though, that when I asked what pain people had been through, they trusted me, and they told me. And I listened.

I hope that I saw some things clearly enough, and I told them to you because I had to.

I know that under my breastbone the grief given me in trust still sits and always will. I know it made me angry. I did what I could to turn that anger into a story. I know there are omissions, but some were necessary, and I hope you may be inspired to fill in the gaps yourself.

From the readers of this book I ask two things: The first is to really and truly acknowledge that the people who say they believe in things—that, for example, the fate of the United States rests on a spiritual war between Jesus and the forces of Hell, which are everywhere manifest, that God is watching and listening and rooting for their side—really and truly believe them. That they really and truly want the United States to become Christ's kingdom and will do everything in their power to make that vision a reality. And your actions in response should be informed by that truth.

The story of zealotry in America is often a story of absurd excess: wild things done in the name of glory, deeds and dioramas of glitter and blood. This book is full of stories of demons and spirits that may feel slightly glassy and unreal to people who feel they do most things for rational reasons and are inclined to condescend to those who believe firmly that they are driven by the realms of the spirit. I do not ask you to unwind your condescension. I ask you to ask yourself what is hidden from you by your own laughter—not only the danger to your country, to democracy, to the rule of law and institutions and other abstractions that mean a very great deal to a great many people; not even the danger to you yourself if you fall outside the narrow prerogatives of a zeal that is ready to erase you in the name of the wild and ungovernable faith it wields. I ask you what your laughter obscures, because it may be the pain of a great many people who cannot speak for themselves because they arc too young, they are too frightened, they believe they deserve it. And no one deserves that kind of pain.

If you get right down to it, having written a book about faith, that's the only thing I really believe.

I believe that evil can come in quiet places; that it is perpetuated by complacency; that complacency might be yours, if you choose, now, not to act on what you know; that no one deserves the kind of pain that makes you perpetuate it from within, that teaches you that you are irredeemable. That kind of pain is passed on, spreads around a country like salt over a crop field, leaving bitter earth.

I do not call myself a patriot; that word was taken from me a long time ago, and it's too easily used by people who use it as a license to smite the unrighteous. I do believe that Earth should not be bitter, not be salted with the tears of the weakest among us, not be gashed by the rage of those who have grown strong on the pain of others. And that the piece of it I'm standing on, beside you, is worth fighting for.

ACKNOWLEDGMENTS

THIS BOOK WOULD NOT HAVE BEEN POSSIBLE WITHOUT THE MANY EX-evangelicals who entrusted their stories to me, and especially Eve Ettinger, who served as a crisp and careful guide to a strange world. My beloved Alex knows how much he gave me. Thanks to my agent, Dan Mandel, whose combination of skilled schmoozing, sagacity, and faith in me has sustained me through two books so far. I want to thank Sam Thielman for his eleventh-hour ride to the rescue and sage, fantastically informed advice along the way. I need to thank Varsha Venkatasubramanian for being the supreme mistress of endnotes, and Erin Biba for counting Gaddhafi's medals—the world's best fact-checker. To David Swanson, editor, friend, consummate archivist, and steady hand at the newsletter helm when my book took me away from the wheel. Iggy's Thursdates and Elie's chevrutas kept the weeks from melting into one another. And thanks as always to the Grotto for keeping an eye on the ever-shifting word count and smoothing out the peaks and troughs of despair. And to the Anti Nazi Friends Collective, who inspired me to get my hands dirty in the first place and who awe me daily. Most of all, I must thank my parents for housing both my body and my soul as I worked on this book.

NOTES

Chapter 1: Devils in the Dining Room

1. Will Sommer, "Devilish Danny DeVito Cartoon Sparks GOP Satanic Panic," Daily Beast, September 8, 2022, https://www.thedailybeast.com/devilish -danny-devito-cartoon-sparks-gop-satanic-panic.

2. Jordan Smith, "Believing the Children," *Austin Chronicle*, March 27, 2009, https:// www.austinchronicle.com/news/2009-03-27/believing-the-children/.

3. Gary Cartwright, "The Innocent and the Damned," in *Turn Out the Lights: Chronicles of Texas During the 80s and 90s* (Austin: University of Texas Press, 2000).

4. Michael Shelton, "A Cautionary Tale: Are the Memories True?" *Psychology Today*, November 6, 2023, https://www.psychologytoday.com/us/blog/sex-life -of-the-american-male/202310/when-therapy-harms#:~:text=Recovered%20 memory%20therapy%2C%20defined%20by%20the%20American%20 Psychological,and%20reached%20its%20apex%20in%20the%20following%20decade.

5. C. A. Ross, *Satanic Ritual Abuse: Principles of Treatment* (Toronto: University of Toronto Press, 1995).

6. Karen Franklin, "Multiple Personality Excluded in Twilight Rapist Insanity Case," *Psychology Today*, October 14, 2011, https://www.psychologytoday.com/us/blog /witness/201110/multiple-personality-excluded-in-twilight-rapist-insanity-case.

7. Robert Wilonsky, "Colin Ross Has an Eyebeam of Energy He'd Like You to Hear," *Dallas Observer*, August 1, 2008, https://www.dallasobserver.com/news/colin -ross-has-an-eyebeam-of-energy-hed-like-you-to-hear-7121325.

8. Denise Gamino and Pamela Ward, "Speaking the Unspeakable: Nightmares of Fran's Day Care Stalk Families," *Austin American-Statesman*, December 13, 1992, on Newspapers.com.

9. Jordan Smith, "Freedom for the Kellers: Fran and Dan Released After 21 Years for 'Satanic Abuse,'" *Austin Chronicle*, December 6, 2013, https://www.austinchronicle.com /news/2013-12-06/freedom-for-the-kellers/.

10. Author's interview with Debbie Nathan, September 2020.

11. Richard Beck, *We Believe the Children: A Moral Panic in the 1980s* (New York: PublicAffairs, 2015), 144.

12. Gigi Griffis, "I Grew Up in the Satanic Panic—and It's Happening Again," *Salon*, June 19, 2003, https://www.salon.com/2023/06/19/i-grew-up-in-the-satanic-panic—and-its-happening-again/.

13. Beck, *We Believe the Children,* 17, 156–59.

14. Mary De Young, *The Day Care Ritual Abuse Moral Panic* (Jefferson, NC: McFarland, 2004).

15. Smith, "Believing the Children."

16. Becky Sullivan, "The Proportion of White Christians in the US Has Stopped Shrinking, Study Finds," NPR, July 8, 2021, https://www.npr.org/2021/07/08/1014047885/americas-white-christian-plurality-has-stopped-shrinking-a-new-study-finds.

17. Sullivan, "Proportion of White Christians in the US Has Stopped Shrinking."

18. Justin Nortey, "Most White Americans Who Regularly Attend Worship Services Voted for Trump in 2020," Pew Research Center, August 30, 2021, https://www.pewresearch.org/short-reads/2021/08/30/most-white-americans-who-regularly-attend-worship-services-voted-for-trump-in-2020/.

19. Eugene Scott, "More Than Half of White Evangelicals Say America's Declining White Population Is a Bad Thing," *Washington Post*, July 18, 2018, https://www.washingtonpost.com/news/the-fix/wp/2018/07/18/more-than-half-of-white-evangelicals-say-americas-declining-white-population-is-a-negative-thing/.

20. Hannah Hartig, "Republicans Turn More Negative Toward Refugees as Number Admitted to the US Plummets," Pew Research Center, May 24, 2018, https://www.pewresearch.org/short-reads/2018/05/24/republicans-turn-more-negative-toward-refugees-as-number-admitted-to-u-s-plummets/.

21. Carol Pipes, "Lifeway to Focus on Digital Retail, Close Brick-and-Mortar Stores," Lifeway, March 20, 2019, https://news.lifeway.com/2019/03/20/lifeway-to-focus-on-digital-retail-close-brick-and-mortar-stores/.

22. Bob Shillingstad, "Frank Peretti, 'Father of Christian Fiction,'" *Coeur d'Alene/Post Falls Press*, July 13, 2019, https://cdapress.com/news/2019/jul/13/frank-peretti-father-of-christian-fiction-5/.

23. Frank Peretti, *This Present Darkness* (Wheaton, IL: Crossway Books, 1986), 139.

24. Katie Jagel, "Poll Results: Exorcism | YouGov." September 17, 2013. https://today.yougov.com/society/articles/7267-poll-results-exorcism.

25. Grant Wacker, *Heaven Below: Early Pentecostals and American Culture* (Cambridge, MA: Harvard University Press, 2003), 91.

26. Kate Burns, "Feucht's Kingdom: How a Singing Hate-Preacher Wants to Push Christian Nationalism on America," Left Coast Right Watch, February 2, 2024, https://leftcoastrightwatch.org/articles/feuchts-kingdom-how-a-singing-hate-preacher-wants-to-push-christian-nationalism-on-america/.

27. Leah Anaya, "Saturday's March in Downtown Portland Culminated with a Band from Sacramento Leading a Worship Concert, Prayer, and Baptisms," Clark County Today, July 10, 2023, https://www.clarkcountytoday.com/people/clark-county-residents-participate-in-jesus-march/.

28. United Revival, "Our Beliefs," accessed January 22, 2024, https://unitedrevival.org/beliefs/.

29. Tonilee Adamson and Bobbye Brooks, *Spiritual Warfare: Truth Cries Out* (Carlsbad, CA: Daily Disciples Publishing, 2015), 9, 11.

30. John Milton, *Paradise Lost*, Poetry Foundation, accessed January 22, 2024, https://www.poetryfoundation.org/poems/45718/paradise-lost-book-1-1674-version.

31. W. Scott Poole, *Satan in America: The Devil We Know* (Lanham, MD: Rowman & Littlefield, 2009), 85.

32. Poole, *Satan in America*, 177.

33. J. Lee Grady, "Six Ways to Identify the Anti Christ Spirit," Faith News Network, June 25, 2020, https://www.faithnews.cc/?p=30397.

34. Margalit Fox, "Ira Levin, of 'Rosemary's Baby,' Dies at 78," *New York Times*, November 14, 2007, https://www.nytimes.com/2007/11/14/books/14levin.html.

35. HiRezTV, "This Is a War," YouTube, October 7, 2021, https://www.youtube.com/watch?v=O9a_P0evO7Y.

36. Clara Martiny, "Various Social Media Platforms Are Enabling Known COVID-19 Misinformers to Promote an Anti-vaccine March in Washington, DC," Media Matters for America, January 1, 2021, https://www.mediamatters.org/facebook/various-social-media-platforms-are-enabling-known-covid-19-misinformers-promote-anti.

37. Author's interview with Amanda Moore and reference photos from same source, January 2022.

38. Katy Waldman, "It's All Connected," Slate, September 16, 2014, https://slate.com/technology/2014/09/apophenia-makes-unrelated-things-seem-connected-metaphors-paranormal-beliefs-conspiracies-delusions.html.

39. Mihir Zaveri and Johnny Diaz, "Paula White Says Video About 'Satanic Pregnancies' Was Taken Out of Context," *New York Times*, January 27, 2020, https://www.nytimes.com/2020/01/27/us/politics/paula-white-miscarriage-video.html.

40. Doris M. Wagner, *How to Cast Out Demons: A Guide to the Basics* (Minneapolis: Chosen Books, 2000), 32–33.

41. Wagner, *How to Cast Out Demons*, 118–39.

42. Mitch Weiss, "AP Exclusive: Ex-congregants Reveal Years of Ungodly Abuse," Associated Press, January 27, 2017, https://apnews.com/article/nc-state-wire-broken-faith-north-carolina-us-news-religion-e9404784f9c6428a8d4382f5ada8f463.

43. Mitch Weiss and Holbrook Mohr, *Broken Faith: Inside the World of Faith Fellowship, One of America's Most Dangerous Cults* (New York: Hanover Square Press, 2020).

44. Joel Gehrke, "CIA Director Mike Pompeo Vows Crackdown on 'Demons' at Wikileaks," *Washington Examiner*, April 13, 2017, https://www.washingtonexaminer.com/news/783327/cia-director-mike-pompeo-vows-crackdown-on-demons-at-wikileaks/.

45. Ed Kilgore, "Christian Right Leaders Suggest Trump Critics Are Possessed by Demons," *New York*, November 26, 2019, https://nymag.com/intelligencer/2019/11/christian-right-leaders-trump-critics-possessed-by-demons.html.

46. Kylee Griswold, "The Demonic Left Will Stop at Nothing—Including Destroying the Supreme Court—to Kill Babies," Federalist, May 3, 2022, https://thefederalist.com/2022/05/03/the-demonic-left-will-stop-at-nothing-including-destroying-the-supreme-court-to-kill-babies/.

47. Katherine Stewart, "The Rise of Spirit Warriors on the Christian Right," *New Republic*, January 23, 2023, https://newrepublic.com/article/170027/rise-spirit-warriors-christian-right-politics.

48. Poole, *Satan in America*, 120.

49. Frank Hammond and Ida Mae Hammond, *Pigs in the Parlor: The Practical Guide to Deliverance* (Kirkwood, MO: Impact Books, 1990).

50. THV11, "Trump Supporters Pray Outside Election Building in Nevada," YouTube, November 6, 2020, https://www.youtube.com/watch?v=C-mSGuYLG6c.

51. Stewart, "Rise of Spirit Warriors on the Christian Right."

52. Ephesians 6:11–18, King James Version, Bible Gateway, accessed January 25, 2024, https://www.biblegateway.com/passage/?search=Ephesians%20 6%3A11-18&version=KJV.

53. Brandy Zadrozny, "Satanic Panic Is Making a Comeback, Fueled by QAnon Believers and GOP Influencers," NBC News, September 14, 2022, https://www .nbcnews.com/tech/internet/satanic-panic-making-comeback-fueled-qanon-believers -gop-influencers-rcna38795.

54. "HB0196," accessed March 19, 2024, https://le.utah.gov/~2024/bills/static /HB0196.html.

55. "The Seven Mountains of Societal Influence," Generals International, accessed January 25, 2024, https://www.generals.org/the-seven-mountains.

56. Lance Wallnau and Bill Johnson, *Invading Babylon: The 7 Mountain Mandate* (Shippensburg, PA: Destiny Image Publishers, July 2013), 63.

57. Elizabeth McAlister, "The Militarization of Prayer in America: White and Native American Spiritual Warfare," *Journal of Religion and Political Practice*, 2, no. 1 (January 2016): 114–30, https://www.tandfonline.com/doi/full/10.1080/20566093.2016 .1085239.

Chapter 2: Filthy Lucre

1. David Weigel, "Why Conservatives Listen to Carson's Pitch of Dietary Supplements," *Washington Post*, November 7, 2015, https://www.washington post.com/politics/why-conservatives-listen-to-carsons-pitch-of-dietary-supplements /2015/11/07/691efb7a-7f0a-11e5-b575-d8dcfedb4ea1_story.html.

2. Mike Adams, "Comet Impacts, Pre-Adamic Civilization, Lost Worlds and the Luciferian WAR Against Humanity—a Conversation with Timothy Alberino," Natural News, December 28, 2022, https://www.naturalnews.com/2022-12-28-comet -impacts-civilization-lost-worlds-luciferian-war.html.

3. News Editors, "The America We Grew Up In Is Already Gone—What Remains Is Some Sick, Perverted Leftist Version of the Twilight Zone Where People Now Identify as Cats and Dogs," Natural News, January 7, 2023, https://www.naturalnews .com/2023-01-07-america-we-grew-up-is-already-gone.html.

4. Ed Kilgore, "White Evangelicals Are Still the Heart of Trump's Base," *New York*, March 18, 2019, https://nymag.com/intelligencer/2019/03/white-evangelicals-are-still -the-heart-of-trumps-base.html.

5. Sam Gringlas, "Trump's Campaign Is Making Millions off His Fulton County Mugshot, but Who Owns the Rights to the Image?," WABE News, November 21, 2023, https://www.wabe.org/trumps-campaign-is-making-millions-off-his-fulton -county-mugshot-but-who-owns-the-rights-to-the-image/.

6. David Klepper, "Choose Your Reality: Trust Wanes, Conspiracy Theories Rise," Associated Press, July 9, 2022, https://apnews.com/article/covid-technology -health-government-and-politics-new-york-cfb56a95aec23dddbabcf3ebbe839f05.

7. Norman Cohn, *Europe's Inner Demons: The Demonization of Christians in Medieval Christendom* (Chicago: University of Chicago Press, 2001).

8. David Gilbert, "QAnon Has a Disturbing Takeover Plot to 'Eliminate' Elected Officials," Vice, June 2, 2021, https://www.vice.com/en/article/dyv3da/qanon-has-a -disturbing-takeover-plot-to-eliminate-elected-officials.

9. Adam Rawnsley and Kelly Weill, "Far-Right Streamers Are Making a Killing on Twitch," Daily Beast, October 9, 2021, https://www.thedailybeast.com /far-right-streamers-are-making-a-killing-on-twitch-hack-terpsichore-maras-lindeman.

10. Sam Thielman, "When the News Becomes Religion," *Columbia Journalism Review*, August 11, 2020, https://www.cjr.org/first_person/qanon-conspiracy-religion -journalism.php.

11. Anna Merlan and Tim Marchman, "Tim Ballard Has 'Stepped Away' from Operation Underground Railroad, Org Says," Vice, July 13, 2023, https://www.vice.com/en/article /k7z74x/tim-ballard-sound-of-freedom-operation-underground-railroad-stepped-away.

12. Jake Traylor, "Trump to Screen Controversial 'Sound of Freedom' Film at His Golf Club," NBC News, July 13, 2023, https://www.nbcnews.com/meet-the-press /meetthepressblog/trump-screen-controversial-sound-freedom-film-golf-club-rcna94207.

13. Meg Conley, "Called by God," Slate, May 11, 2021, https://slate.com/human -interest/2021/05/sex-trafficking-raid-operation-underground-railroad.html; Anna Merlan and Tim Marchman, "Inside a Massive Anti-trafficking Charity's Blundering Overseas Missions," Vice, March 8, 2021, https://www.vice.com/en/article/bvxev5 /inside-a-massive-anti-trafficking-charitys-blundering-overseas-missions.

14. Miles Klee, "They Made 'Sound of Freedom' a Hit—but Were They Deceiving Their Audience?," *Rolling Stone*, December 14, 2023, https://www.rollingstone .com/culture/culture-features/sound-of-freedom-angel-studios-audience-business -practices-1234928374/.

15. Miles Klee, "'Sound of Freedom' Fans and AMC Investors Wage War of Conspiracy Theories," *Rolling Stone*, July 14, 2023, https://www.rollingstone.com/culture /culture-features/sound-of-freedom-amc-conspiracy-theories-1234787961/.

16. Ben Sixsmith, "Fear and Adrenochrome," *Spectator*, May 4, 2020, https://the spectator.com/uncategorized/fear-adrenochrome-conspiracy-theory-drug/.

17. Rachel M. Cohen, "The Republican Push to Weaken Child Labor Laws, Explained," Vox, May 5, 2023, https://www.vox.com/policy/2023/5/3/23702464 /child-labor-laws-youth-migrants-work-shortage.

18. Peter Wade, "Fox Host's Fear-Filled Rant: If Trump Wins, He and Other Conservatives Will Be Murdered," *Rolling Stone*, September 10, 2020, https://www.rollingstone

.com/politics/politics-news/fox-host-rant-if-trump-wins-conservatives-will-be-murdered
-1058056/.

19. Lalee Ibssa and Soo Rin Kim, "Trump, While Addressing Auto Industry, Says There Will Be 'Bloodbath' If He Loses 2024 Election," March 17, 2024, ABC 7 Chicago, https://abc7chicago.com/donald-trump-bloodbath-comment-speech-in-ohio-rally/1453 5948/.

20. Alex Kaplan, "Here Are the QAnon Supporters Running for Congress in 2020," Media Matters for America, September 30, 2022, https://www.mediamatters.org /qanon-conspiracy-theory/here-are-qanon-supporters-running-congress-2020.

21. Jonathan Weisman and Katie Glueck, "Extreme Candidates and Positions Came Back to Bite in Midterms," November 14, 2022, *New York Times*, https://www.nytimes .com/2022/11/14/us/politics/gop-far-right-election-voters.html.

22. Stuart A. Thompson, "QAnon Candidates Aren't Thriving, but Some of Their Ideas Are," *New York Times*, July 25, 2022, https://www.nytimes.com/2022/07/25 /technology/qanon-midterms.html.

23. Timothy Charles Holmseth Reports, https://timothycharlesholmseth.com/author /tholmseth/.

24. "Basic Training for Spiritual Battle," Benny Hinn Ministries, https://www .bennyhinn.org/basic-training-for-spiritual-battle/.

25. E. J. Dickson, "Wellness Influencers Are Calling Out QAnon Conspiracy Theorists for Spreading Lies," *Rolling Stone*, September 15, 2020, https://www.rollingstone .com/culture/culture-news/qanon-wellness-influencers-seane-corn-yoga-1059856/.

26. "Survivor Voices of Human Trafficking," Combatting Trafficking in Persons, U.S. Department of Defense, https://ctip.defense.gov/Survivor-Voices/.

27. "The Dark Truth About Blackwater," Brookings Institution, October 2, 2007, https://www.brookings.edu/articles/the-dark-truth-about-blackwater/.

28. Nick Wing, "Milwaukee Sheriff David Clarke Blames Inmates for Dying at His Jail," HuffPost, December 8, 2016, https://www.huffpost.com/entry /david-clarke-jail-deaths_n_58499ebbe4b04002fa803ec9.

29. Jeremy Schwartz and Paula Trevizo, "They Built the Wall. Problems Remain After Founder's Guilty Plea," ProPublica, May 22, 2022, https://www.propublica.org/articl e/they-built-the-wall-problems-remain-after-founders-guilty-plea.

30. Brandy Zadrozny and Ben Collins, "Behind the Viral #GoFundTheWall Fundraiser, a Rising Conservative Star and a Shadowy Email Harvesting Operation," NBC News, January 11, 2019, https://www.nbcnews.com/tech/tech-news/behind-viral -gofundthewall-fundraiser-rising-conservative-star-shadowy-email-harvesting-n957896.

31. Chris Anderson, "Anderson: Sarasota County Man Faces Prison While Bannon Walks Along and Whistles," *Sarasota Herald-Tribune*, January 23, 2021, https://www .heraldtribune.com/story/opinion/2021/01/23/sarasota-mans-case-grows-complicated -after-trump-pardons-bannon/6685812002/.

32. "Two Sentenced to Prison for 'We Build the Wall' Online Fundraising Fraud Scheme," United States Attorney's Office, Southern District of New York, April 26, 2023, https://www.justice.gov/usao-sdny/pr/two-sentenced-prison-we-build-wall-online -fundraising-fraud-scheme.

33. Colin Moynihan, "Man Sentenced to 5 Years in Scheme Tied to Trump-Inspired Border Wall," *New York Times,* July 25, 2023, https://www.nytimes.com/2023/07/25 /nyregion/shea-trump-border-wall-fraud-sentencing.html.

34. Kathryn Joyce, "Ketchup with Those Fries? Sure—as Long as It's Anti-woke," *New Republic*, September 12, 2023, https://newrepublic.com/article/175370/anti-woke -bud-light-right-wing-culture-wars.

35. Rick Perlstein, "The Long Con," the Baffler, November 14, 2012, https://the baffler.com/salvos/the-long-con.

36. Maria Konnikova, *The Confidence Game* (New York: Penguin Books, 2017), 8.

Chapter 3: Prophets in the Parlor

1. Hemant Mehta, "The 'Watchman Decree' Is a Scary Vision of Christian Nationalism in Action," OnlySky, July 15, 2022, https://onlysky.media/hemant-mehta /the-watchman-decree-is-a-scary-vision-of-christian-nationalism-in-action/.

2. Alan S. Bandy, "Views of the Millennium," Gospel Coalition, accessed January 2024, https://www.thegospelcoalition.org/essay/views-of-the-millennium/.

3. Wayne Jackson, "Cyrus the Great in Biblical Prophecy," *Christian Courier*, accessed January 2024, https://christiancourier.com/articles/cyrus-the-great-in-biblical -prophecy.

4. "Lance Wallnau: Why Trump Is 'God's Chaos Candidate' and 'Wrecking Ball,'" Christian Broadcasting Network, March 21, 2017, https://www2.cbn.com/news/us /lance-wallnau-why-trump-gods-chaos-candidate-and-wrecking-ball.

5. Ed Kilgore, "Perry Says Trump Is the 'Chosen One,'" *New York*, November 25, 2019, https://nymag.com/intelligencer/2019/11/perry-tells-trump-he-is-indeed-the-chosen-one .html.

6. Chris Mitchell, "'I See Us in the Middle of Prophecy!' Mike Evans Has 30M Evangelicals Praying for Jerusalem," Christian Broadcasting Network, December 10, 2017, https://www2.cbn.com/news/news/i-see-us-middle-prophecy-mike-evans-has -30m-evangelicals-praying-jerusalem.

7. Lyn Millner, *The Allure of Immortality: An American Cult, a Florida Swamp, and a Renegade Prophet* (Tallahassee: University Press of Florida, October 2015).

8. Richard Vijgen and Bregtje van der Haak, "Atlas of Pentecostalism: A Dynamic Database of the Fastest-Growing Religion in the World," accessed January 2024, http:// www.atlasofpentecostalism.net/.

9. Terry Gross, "A Leading Figure in the New Apostolic Reformation," *Fresh Air*, NPR, October 3, 2011, https://www.npr.org/2011/10/03/140946482/apostolic-leader-weighs -religions-role-in-politics.

10. *Superspreader: The Rise of #LetUsWorship*, Josh Franer, director, Through the Woods Films, September 2022.

11. Sean Feucht, Twitter, https://x.com/seanfeucht/status/1540333978279809024?s=20.

12. Sean Feucht, Twitter, June 25, 2022, https://x.com/seanfeucht/status/15407321 91910420486?s=20.

13. Sean Feucht, Twitter, May 5, 2023, https://x.com/seanfeucht/status/165459 1900655951873?s=20.

14. Sean Feucht, "Camp Elah," accessed January 2024, https://www.seanfeucht.com/camp-elah.

15. Dutch Sheets, *Giants Will Fall* (Colorado Springs, CO: Dutch Sheets Ministries, 2018).

16. Elle Hardy, "The Right-Wing Christian Sect Plotting a Political Take-over," *New Republic*, August 23, 2022, https://newrepublic.com/article/167499/new-apostolic-reformation-mastriano-christian.

17. Trinity Church Cedar Hill, "Cindy Jacobs | Prophetic Word for 2022 | 9am," You-Tube, January 4, 2022, https://www.youtube.com/watch?v=THiSt3vls34.

18. Bob Smietana, "The 'Prophets' and 'Apostles' Leading the Quiet Revolution in American Religion," *Christianity Today*, August 3, 2017, https://christianitytoday.com/ct/2017/august-web-only/bethel-church-international-house-prayer-prophets-apostles.html.

19. Cindy Jacobs, "Cindy Jacobs Prophesies: The Lord Says, 'I Am Coming with a Wave of Joy,'" Charisma News, June 9, 2022, https://www.charismanews.com/culture/89398-cindy-jacobs-prophesies-the-lord-says-i-am-coming-with-a-wave-of-joy.

20. "Roe v. Wade Is Overturned," Generals International, accessed January 31, 2024, https://www.generals.org/blog/roe-v-wade-is-overturned-06242022.

21. Lance Wallnau, *God's Chaos Candidate: Donald J. Trump and the American Unraveling* (Roanoke, TX: Killer Sheep Media, 2016), 7, 8.

22. JNM, Facebook, July 11, 2022, https://www.facebook.com/permalink.php?story_fbid=pfbid02DDeeJkyx24XcSfmySUNf91SbgSg6EGt1CPT6PjAnBBReoNHyH4ZNRvewm6hdYJuul&id=105330424741106.

23. Elizabeth McAlister, "The Militarization of Prayer in America: White and Native American Spiritual Warfare," *Journal of Religious and Political Practice* 2, no. 1 (January 2016): 114–30, https://doi.org/10.1080/20566093.2016.1085239.

24. Joshua 6:5, 21, King James Version, Bible Gateway, accessed January 31, 2024, https://www.biblegateway.com/passage/?search=Joshua%206&version=KJV.

25. Calling the 7000, https://www.callingthe7000.com/about-the-call.

26. Black Robe Regiment, http://www.blackrobereg.org/.

27. Crawford Gribben, *Survival and Resistance in Evangelical America: Christian Reconstruction in the Pacific Northwest* (New York: Oxford University Press, 2021).

28. "About Us," Maryland Black Robe Regiment, accessed February 1, 2024, https://blackrobemd.org/about-us/.

29. Robert N. Bellah, "Civil Religion in America," *Daedalus* 117, no. 3 (1967): 97–118, https://www.jstor.org/stable/20028013?seq=1.

30. "The Rise of My Trumpet Is About to Be Heard," Julie Green Ministries, accessed February 1, 2024, https://www.jgminternational.org/prophecies/the-rise-of-my-trumpet-is-about-to-be-heard.

31. "A Righteous Rebellion Is Growing All Over This World," Julie Green Ministries, accessed February 1, 2024, https://www.jgminternational.org/prophecies/righteous-rebellion-is-growing-all-over-this-world.

Chapter 4: The Agony and the Ecstasy

1. Ian M. Giatti, "'Fasten Your Seat Belt': Pastor Greg Laurie Talks Potential Fulfillment of Bible Prophecy in Israel-Hamas War," Christian Post, October 10, 2023, https://www.christianpost.com/news/greg-laurie-talks-potential-fulfillment-of-bible-prophecy-israel.html.

2. Wayne J. Edwards, "Israel: God's Timepiece," Heritage Baptist Church, October 11, 2023, https://theheritagechurch.org/sermon/israel-gods-timepiece-matthew-2432-34/.

3. Sean Illing, "This Is Why Evangelicals Love Trump's Israel Policy," Vox, May 14, 2018, https://www.vox.com/2017/12/12/16761540/jerusalem-israel-embassy-palestinians-trump-evangelicals.

4. Lawrence Wright, "Forcing the End," New Yorker, July 12, 1998, https://www.newyorker.com/magazine/1998/07/20/forcing-the-end.

5. Eugene Scott, "A Look at Robert Jeffress, the Controversial Figure Giving the Prayer at the U.S. Embassy in Jerusalem Today," Washington Post, May 14, 2018, https://www.washingtonpost.com/news/the-fix/wp/2018/05/14/a-look-at-robert-jeffress-the-controversial-figure-giving-the-prayer-at-the-u-s-embassy-in-jerusalem-today/.

6. John Hagee, Jerusalem Countdown: A Warning to the World (Lake Mary, FL: Frontline, 2005), 145, 150.

7. "DeSantis, Haley Respond to Use of U.S. Military Force against Iran" (video), NBC News, November 8, 2023, https://www.nbcnews.com/video/desantis-haley-respond-to-use-of-u-s-military-force-against-iran-197431877624.

8. Daniel Benjamin, "Why John McCain Should Reject the Reverend John Hagee," Brookings Institution, May 23, 2008, https://www.brookings.edu/articles/why-john-mccain-should-reject-the-reverend-john-hagee/.

9. "Evangelical Attitudes Toward Israel Research Study," Lifeway Research, December 2017, https://research.lifeway.com/wp-content/uploads/2017/12/Evangelical-Attitudes-Toward-Israel-Research-Study-Report.pdf.

10. Andrew Solender, "'They Want to Put Chips Inside Us': Kanye West Cites Debunked Anti-vaccine Conspiracy Theories," Forbes, July 8, 2020, https://www.forbes.com/sites/andrewsolender/2020/07/08/they-want-to-put-chips-inside-us-kanye-west-cites-debunked-anti-vaccine-conspiracy-theories/?sh=69067e1824b8.

11. Mark Hitchcock, Corona Crisis: Plagues, Pandemics, and the Coming Apocalypse (Nashville, TN: Thomas Nelson, 2020); Mark Hitchcock, 101 Answers to Questions About the Book of Revelation (Eugene, OR: Harvest House, 2012); Mark Hitchcock, The End: A Complete Overview of Bible Prophecy and the End of Days (Carol Stream, IL: Tyndale Momentum, 2012).

12. Carla Hinton, "No, the COVID Vaccine Is Not the 'Mark of the Beast.' Here's What an Oklahoma Bible Prophecy Expert Says," Oklahoman, January 25, 2021, https://www.oklahoman.com/story/news/religion/2021/01/25/the-covid-vaccine-not-the-mark-of-the-beast-here-is-what-an-edmond-bible-prophecy-expert-has-to-say/323205007/.

13. "Jesus Christ's Return to Earth," Pew Research Center, July 14, 2010, https://www.pewresearch.org/short-reads/2010/07/14/jesus-christs-return-to-earth/.

14. David Van Biema, "The End: How It Got That Way," *Time*, July 1, 2002, https://content.time.com/time/subscriber/article/0,33009,1002760-3,00.html.

15. Tim LaHaye and Jerry B. Jenkins, *Left Behind: A Novel of the Earth's Last Days* (Carol Stream, IL: Tyndale House, 2011).

16. Frank Peretti, *This Present Darkness* (Brighton: Kingsway Publishing, 1992).

17. Joshua Rivera, "Vanished from the Earth," Slate, May 2, 2021, https://slate.com/human-interest/2021/05/rapture-fear-evangelical-americans-church-miller.html.

18. "RFID: Sign of the (End) Times?," Wired, June 6, 2006, https://www.wired.com/2006/06/rfid-sign-of-the-end-times/.

19. Matthew Avery Sutton, *American Apocalypse: A History of Modern Evangelicalism* (Cambridge, MA: Harvard University Press, 2017), 244.

20. Lawrence Hurley, "U.S. Supreme Court Rebuffs 'Number of the Beast' Religious Dispute." Reuters, June 28, 2021, https://www.reuters.com/world/us/us-supreme-court-rebuffs-number-beast-religious-dispute-2021-06-28/.

21. Sutton, *American Apocalypse*, ii.

22. Hal Lindsey, *The Late Great Planet Earth* (Grand Rapids, MI: Zondervan, 2016), 82, 128, 129, 210.

23. Hal and Carole C. Carlson, *Satan Is Alive and Well on Planet Earth* (Grand Rapids, MI: Zondervan, 1972); Hal Lindsey, *The Rapture: Truth or Consequences* (New York: Random House, 1983); Hal Lindsey, *There's a New World Coming: An In-Depth Analysis of the Book of Revelation* (Eugene, OR: Harvest House, 1984).

24. Katherine Albrecht and Liz McIntyre, *The Spychips Threat: Why Christians Should Resist RFID and Electronic Surveillance* (Nashville, TN: Thomas Nelson, 2006), 3.

25. Luke Hilton, "Christians, Now Is Your Time to Stand," *The Israel Guys by HaYovel* (blog), November 1, 2023, https://theisraelguys.com/now-is-the-time/.

Chapter 5: Sex and Death

1. Iker Seisdedos, "David Gunn: 30 Years Since the Assassination of a Doctor Sparked the US 'Abortion Wars,'" *EL PAÍS*, March 10, 2023, https://english.elpais.com/usa/2023-03-10/david-gunn-30-years-since-the-assassination-of-a-doctor-sparked-the-us-abortion-wars.html.

2. Carter Sherman, "This Convicted Planned Parenthood Bomber Was at the Capitol 'Fighting' for Trump," Vice, January 14, 2021, https://www.vice.com/en/article/z3vwka/this-convicted-planned-parenthood-bomber-was-at-the-capitol-fighting-for-trump.

3. Randall Balmer, "The Religious Right and the Abortion Myth," Politico, May 10, 2022, https://www.politico.com/news/magazine/2022/05/10/abortion-history-right-white-evangelical-1970s-00031480.

4. Thomas B. Edsall, "Abortion Has Never Been Just About Abortion," *New York Times*, September 15, 2021, https://www.nytimes.com/2021/09/15/opinion/abortion-evangelicals-conservatives.html.

5. Balmer, "Religious Right and the Abortion Myth."

6. Lorraine Boissoneault, "The 1977 Conference on Women's Rights That Split

America in Two," *Smithsonian Magazine*, February 15, 2017, https://www.smithsonian mag.com/history/1977-conference-womens-rights-split-america-two-180962174/.

7. Chloe Foussianes, "How Phyllis Schlafly, an Anti-ERA Conservative Activist, Left an Enduring Mark on the Republican Party," *Town & Country*, April 18, 2020, https://www.townandcountrymag.com/leisure/arts-and-culture/a31944041 /phyllis-schlafly-mrs-america-era-true-story/.

8. Gillian Frank, "Phyllis Schlafly's Legacy of Anti-gay Activism," Slate, September 6, 2016, https://slate.com/human-interest/2016/09/phyllis-schlaflys-legacy-of-anti-gay -activism.html.

9. "Religious Landscape Study," Pew Research Center, accessed February 5, 2024, https://www.pewresearch.org/religion/religious-landscape-study/.

10. "The Clergy on George Wallace," *Christianity Today*, October 25, 1968, https:// www.christianitytoday.com/ct/1968/october-25/clergy-on-george-wallace.html.

11. James Tunstead Burtchaell, *Rachel Weeping: The Case Against Abortion* (San Francisco: HarperCollins, 1984), 271.

12. "Remarks by Susan B. Anthony List President Marjorie Dannenfelser," Susan B. Anthony Pro-Life America, December 1, 2021, https://sbaprolife.org/uncategorized /remarks-by-susan-b-anthony-list-president-marjorie-dannenfelser.

13. *Whatever Happened to the Human Race?*, Vision Video, 1979; Francis A. Schaeffer and Charles Everett Koop, *Whatever Happened to the Human Race?* (London: Marshall, Morgan & Scott, 1980).

14. "*Whatever Happened to the Human Race?*—Revisited," accessed February 6, 2024, http://www.johnling.co.uk/whtthr.htm.

15. "Eric Robert Rudolph to Plead Guilty to Serial Bombing Attacks in Atlanta and Birmingham; Will Receive Life Sentences," Department of Justice, April 8, 2005, https:// www.justice.gov/archive/opa/pr/2005/April/05_crm_176.htm.

16. "A Historic Document, The Army of God Manual," Army of God, accessed February 6, 2024, https://www.armyofgod.com/AOGhistory.html.

17. Gabriel Winant, "O'Reilly's Campaign Against Murdered Doctor," Salon, June 1, 2009, https://www.salon.com/2009/05/31/tiller_2/.

18. Roxana Hegeman, "Man Who Killed Abortion Doctor Gets More Lenient Sentence," AP News, November 24, 2016, https://apnews.com/general-news-domestic-news -domestic-news-24fcd54bbf054d75b3d56aa48e391852.

19. Sirin Kale, "Anti-abortion 'Terrorist' Who Shot George Tiller Is Out of Jail," Vice, November 8, 2018, https://www.vice.com/en/article/59vznb/anti-abortion -terrorist-shelley-shannon-released-prison.

20. William Claiborne, "A Decade Later, Abortion Foes Again Gather in Wichita," *Washington Post*, July 16, 2001, https://www.washingtonpost.com/archive /politics/2001/07/16/a-decade-later-abortion-foes-again-gather-in-wichita/a9a94faf-1c0b -4e77-9395-273d28b1cd05/.

21. Cara C. Heuser and Christina Han, "Antiabortion Heartbeat Bills Are Not Morally, Scientifically or Legally Sound," *Scientific American*, January 23, 2023, https://www.scientificamerican.com/article/antiabortion-heartbeat-bills -are-neither-morally-nor-legally-sound/.

22. "NAF 2022 Violence & Disruption Statistics," National Abortion Federation, accessed February 6, 2024, https://prochoice.org/our-work/provider-security/2022-naf-violence-disruption/.

23. Mark Creech, "Statement on Overturning of Roe v. Wade," Christian Action League of North Carolina, June 24, 2022, https://christianactionleague.org/statement-on-overturning-of-roe-v-wade/.

24. Kathryn Joyce, *Quiverfull: Inside the Christian Patriarchy Movement* (Boston: Beacon Press, 2010), 11.

25. Creech, "Statement on Overturning of Roe v. Wade."

26. Tessa Stuart, "House Speaker Mike Johnson's Long Crusade Against Birth Control," *Rolling Stone*, October 31, 2023, https://www.rollingstone.com/politics/politics-features/mike-johnson-crusade-birth-control-1234865718/.

27. *Estelle T. Griswold et al. v. State of Connecticut*, 381 U.S. 479 (1965).

28. Schuyler Mitchell, "Clinic Fire Deals Blow to Abortion Access on California-Arizona Border," Intercept, August 16, 2023, https://theintercept.com/2023/08/16/abortion-clinic-planned-parenthood-imperial-valley/.

29. Jesus Jiménez, "Man Who Set Fire to Planned Parenthood Clinic Gets 10 Years in Prison," *New York Times*, August 15, 2023, https://www.nytimes.com/2023/08/15/us/tyler-massengill-sentenced-planned-parenthood-fire.html.

30. Mary Tuma, "Testifying Against Texas, Women Denied Abortions Relive the Pregnancies That Almost Killed Them," Intercept, July 21, 2023, https://theintercept.com/2023/07/21/texas-abortion-zurawski-lawsuit/.

31. Jessica Valenti, "Of Course They Want Us Dead," Abortion, Every Day, January 3, 2024, https://jessica.substack.com/p/of-course-they-want-us-dead.

Chapter 6: Let the Fire Make You Pure

1. "Bullard Files Bill Prohibiting Genital Mutilation of Youth Under 26," Oklahoma Senate, January 10, 2023, https://oksenate.gov/press-releases/bullard-files-bill-prohibiting-genital-mutilation-youth-under-26.

2. Andrew L. Seidel, "Christian Nationalist Legislator Introduces Anti-trans 'Millstone Act' Suggesting Biblical Retribution," Religion Dispatches, February 2, 2023, https://religiondispatches.org/christian-nationalist-legislator-introduces-anti-trans-bill-suggesting-biblical-retribution/.

3. Melissa Mayer, "I Kissed Consent Goodbye: Purity Culture and Sexual Violence on Evangelical Christian Campuses," *Bitch Magazine*, April 15, 2019, https://www.bitchmedia.org/article/i-kissed-consent-goodbye/purity-culture-and-sexual-violence-evangelical-christian-campuses.

4. Joshua Harris, *I Kissed Dating Goodbye: A New Attitude Toward Relationships and Romance* (New York: Crown, 2012).

5. Harris, *I Kissed Dating Goodbye*, 103.

6. Mark Oppenheimer, "'Purity Balls' Get Attention, but Might Not Be All They Claim," *New York Times*, July 21, 2012, https://www.nytimes.com/2012/07/21/us/purity-balls-local-tradition-or-national-trend.html.

7. Linda Kay Klein, *Pure: Inside the Evangelical Movement That Shamed a Generation of Young Women and How I Broke Free* (New York: Simon & Schuster, 2018).

8. Klein, *Pure*, 7.

9. Rachel Mipro, "Kansas Democrats Describe Attempt to Ban Transgender Student Athletes as 'Crushing Weight,'" Kansas Reflector, February 14, 2023, https://kansas reflector.com/2023/02/13/kansas-democrats-describe-attempt-to-ban-transgender -student-athletes-as-crushing-weight/.

10. Blake Chastain, "White Christian Nationalists Can Accrue Power in Any Admin-istration," Post-Evangelical Post, November 1, 2023, https://www.postevangelical post.com/p/white-christian-nationalists-can.

11. Ilyse Hogue, "A 'Woodstock' for Right-Wing Legal Activists Kicked Off the 40-Year Plot to Undo Roe v. Wade," Intercept, May 10, 2022, https://theintercept .com/2022/05/10/roe-v-wade-federalist-society-religious-right/.

12. David Grann, "Robespierre of the Right," *New Republic*, October 27, 1997, https:// newrepublic.com/article/61338/robespierre-the-right.

13. Emma Bowman, "As States Ban Abortion, the Texas Bounty Law Offers a Way to Survive Legal Challenges," NPR, July 11, 2022, https://www.npr.org/2022/07 /11/1107741175/texas-abortion-bounty-law.

14. Kim Chandler and Geoff Mulvhill, "What's Next After the Alabama Ruling That Counts IVF Embryos as Children?" AP News, February 22, 2024, https://apnews.com /article/alabama-frozen-embryos-ivf-storage-questions-1adbc349e0f99851973a609e 360c242c.

15. "Criminalized Care: How Louisiana's Abortion Bans Endanger Patients and Clinicians," Lift Louisiana, March 2024, https://static1.squarespace.com /static/64b951a07cb4e21d8a4f0322/t/65f5ad322c31fd00ca010e56/1710599477106 /Criminalized+Care+Report+FINAL.pdf.

16. Natasha Ishak, "Trigger Laws and Abortion Restrictions, Explained," Vox, June 25, 2022, https://www.vox.com/2022/6/25/23182753/roe-overturned-abortion-access -reproductive-rights-trigger-laws.

17. Kimberly A. Hamlin, "Femicide Is Up. American History Says That's Not Surprising," *Washington Post*, February 2, 2023, https://www.washingtonpost.com /made-by-history/2023/02/03/femicide-violence-against-women/.

18. Julie Carr Smyth, "Ohio Voters Just Passed Abortion Protections. When and How They Take Effect Is Before the Courts," AP News, November 24, 2023, https:// apnews.com/article/abortion-ohio-constitutional-amendment-republicans-courts -fb1762537585350caeee589d68fe5a0d.

Chapter 7: Brownshirts v. the Board of Education

1. "Defenders of State Sovereignty and Individual Liberties," Old Dominion Univer-sity Libraries Digital Collections, https://olddomuni.access.preservica.com/uncategorized /IO_4a2a0f31-6de6-4531-b5bf-fb9e0d43aac2/.

2. Brian Lee, "A Matter of National Concern: The Kennedy Administration and Prince Edward County, Virginia," Virginia Commonwealth University VCU Scholars

Compass, 2009, https://scholarscompass.vcu.edu/cgi/viewcontent.cgi?article=2876& context=etd.

3. "Joseph B. Wall Dies," *Washington Post*, October 7, 1985, https://www.washington post.com/archive/local/1985/10/07/joseph-b-wall-dies/d7b37f45-4a5f-426e -be7e-dbcfb74bed22/.

4. Alabama Council on Human Relations et al., *It's Not Over in the South: School Desegregation in Forty-Three Southern Cities Eighteen Years After Brown*, May 1972, Internet Archive, http://archive.org/details/ERIC_ED065646.

5. Defenders' News and Views, October 1958, Old Dominion University Libraries Digital Collections, pp. 2–3, https://olddomuni.access.preservica.com/uncategorized /IO_b7b03451-829a-43fa-88cd-d82871e5127f/.

6. Russell S. Doughten, Jr., "A Thief in the Night Film Series," http://archive.org /details/AThiefInTheNightFilmSeries.

7. Randall Balmer, *Bad Faith: Race and the Rise of the Religious Right* (Grand Rapids, MI: Eerdmans, 2021); *Green v. Kennedy*, 309 F. Supp. 1127 (D.D.C. 1970).

8. Wilfred F. Drake, "Tax Status of Private Segregated Schools: The New Revenue Procedure," *William & Mary Law Review* 20, no. 3 (March 1979), https://scholarship.law .wm.edu/cgi/viewcontent.cgi?article=2368&context=wmlr.

9. *Green v. Kennedy*, 309 F. Supp. 1127 (D.D.C. 1970).

10. Radio Diaries, "'Segregation Forever': A Fiery Pledge Forgiven, but Not Forgotten," NPR, January 10, 2013, https://www.npr.org/2013/01/14/169080969 /segregation-forever-a-fiery-pledge-forgiven-but-not-forgotten.

11. Tyler J. Poff, "Mobilizing the Moral Majority: Paul Weyrich and the Creation of a Conservative Coalition, 1968–1988," Graduate Theses, Dissertations, and Problem Reports, West Virginia University, 2018, https://researchrepository.wvu.edu/etd /6427.

12. "About ALEC," American Legislative Exchange Council, accessed February 5, 2024, https://alec.org/about/.

13. *Obergefell et al. v. Hodges, Director, Ohio Department of Health, et al.*, 576 U.S. 644 (2015).

14. One Hundred Forty-Eight Signatories, "Manhattan Declaration: A Call of Christian Conscience," First Things, November 20, 2009, https://www.firstthings.com /web-exclusives/2009/11/manhattan-declaration-a-call-of-christian-conscience.

15. Jonathan Lange, "10 Years Later, the Manhattan Declaration's Defense of Marriage Is Even More Needed," Federalist, November 20, 2019, https://thefederalist .com/2019/11/20/10-years-later-the-manhattan-declarations-defense-of-marriage-is -even-more-needed/.

16. "About Us," Moms for Liberty, accessed February 5, 2024, https://www.moms forliberty.org/about/.

17. Jennifer D. Jenkins, "I'm a Florida School Board Member. This Is How Protesters Come After Me," *Washington Post*, October 20, 2021, https://www.washingtonpost.com /outlook/2021/10/20/jennifer-jenkins-brevard-school-board-masks-threats/.

18. Anna Gustafson, "Kent Co. Health Director Tells Commissioners After Almost Being Run Off the Road: 'I Need Help,'" *Michigan Advance*, September 20, 2021,

https://michiganadvance.com/2021/09/20/kent-co-health-director-tells-commissioners
-after-almost-being-run-off-the-road-i-need-help/.

19. Julian Mark, "Tennessee Parents Make Threats After School Board Mandates Masks: 'We Will Find You,'" *Washington Post*, August 12, 2021, https://www.washington post.com/nation/2021/08/12/tennessee-parents-masks-school-board/.

20. Mimi Swartz, "The Campaign to Sabotage Texas's Public Schools," *Texas Monthly*, February 13, 2023, https://www.texasmonthly.com/news-politics/campaign -to-sabotage-texas-public-schools/.

21. Christina Pushaw, Twitter, March 4, 2022, https://twitter.com/ChristinaPushaw /status/1499886619259777029.

22. Christina Pushaw, Twitter, March 4, 2022, https://twitter.com/ChristinaPushaw /status/1499890719691051008.

23. Jaclyn Diaz, "Florida's Governor Signs Controversial Law Opponents Dubbed 'Don't Say Gay,'" NPR, March 28, 2022, https://www.npr.org/2022/03/28/1089221657 /dont-say-gay-florida-desantis.

24. "Jack Posobiec," Southern Poverty Law Center, accessed February 10, 2024, https://www.splcenter.org/fighting-hate/extremist-files/individual/jack-posobiec.

25. Tess Owen, "'Anti-Grooming' Rally at Disney Is Latest Stop for Culture War Traveling Circus," Vice, April 8, 2022, https://www.vice.com/en/article/88g3ep /anti-grooming-rally-at-disney-is-latest-stop-for-culture-war-traveling-circus.

26. Alex Cooper, "Ex–GOP Candidate Calls for 'Firing Squads' for Trans Rights Supporters," Advocate, March 29, 2022, https://www.advocate.com/politics/2022/3/29 /ex-gop-candidate-robert-foster-calls-firing-squads-trans-rights-supporters.

27. "Understanding State Statutes on Minimum Marriage Age and Excep-tions," Tahirih Justice Center, November 2023, https://www.tahirih.org/wp-content /uploads/2020/05/2023-State-Statutory-Compilation.pdf.

28. "United States' Child Marriage Problem," Unchained at Last, April 2021, https:// www.unchainedatlast.org/united-states-child-marriage-problem-study-findings-april-2021/.

29. Stephanie Colombini, "New Law Makes Changes to High School Sports and Allows Prayer Before Games," WJCT 89.9 News, May 19, 2023, https:// news.wjct.org/state-news/2023-05-19/new-law-makes-changes-to-high-school -sports-and-allows-prayer-before-games.

30. "DeSantis Signs Bills Targeting Drag Shows, Transgender Kids and the Use of Bathrooms and Pronouns," AP News, May 22, 2023, https://apnews.com/article /desantis-florida-lgbtq-education-health-c68a7e5fe5cf22ab8cca324b00644119.

31. Ana Goñi-Lessan, "AP Psychology 'Effectively Banned' in Florida Because of Gen-der, Sexuality Chapter," *USA Today*, August 3, 2023, https://www.usatoday.com/story /news/education/2023/08/03/ap-psychology-banned-florida/70523459007/.

32. Hi-Rez and Jimmy Levy, "God over Government," 2022, https://genius.com /Hi-rez-and-jimmy-levy-god-over-government-lyrics.

33. Talia Jane, Twitter, August 22, 2023, https://x.com/taliaotg/status/1694 038299717800017?s=20.

34. *Florida's State Academic Standards–Social Studies, 2023*, Florida Department of Education, https://www.fldoe.org/core/fileparse.php/20653/urlt/6-4.pdf, 71.

35. "Nikki Haley Backpedals Civil War Comments in Which She Made No Mention of Slavery," CNBC, December 28, 2023, https://www.cnbc.com/2023/12/28/nikki-haley-makes-no-mention-of-slavery-when-asked-to-name-cause-of-civil-war.html.

36. Hannah Natanson, "An Explosion of Culture War Laws Is Changing Schools," *Washington Post*, October 18, 2022, https://www.washingtonpost.com/education/2022/10/18/education-laws-culture-war/.

37. Scholastic, "A Message from Scholastic on U.S. Book Fairs," October 2023, http://mediaroom.scholastic.com/press-release/message-scholastic-book-fairs.

38. "Educational Intimidation Bills," PEN America, August 23, 2023, https://pen.org/report/educational-intimidation/.

Chapter 8: Good Christian Fathers

1. Author's interview with Eddie K., October 2021.

2. A. J. Willingham, "What Is No-Fault Divorce, and Why Do Some Conservatives Want to Get Rid of It?" CNN, November 27, 2023. https://www.cnn.com/2023/11/27/us/no-fault-divorce-explained-history-wellness-cec/index.html.

3. Republican Party of Texas, "Platform and Resolutions as Amended and Adopted by the 2022 State Convention of the Republican Party of Texas," https://texasgop.org/wp-content/uploads/2022/07/2022-RPT-Platform.pdf.

4. Republican Party of Texas, "Platform and Resolutions as Amended and Adopted by the 2022 State Convention of the Republican Party of Texas."

5. "Family," Nebraska Republican Party, https://ne.gop/family/.

6. Julie O'Donoghue, "Louisiana Republican Party Considers Backing Elimination of No-Fault Divorce," WWNO, January 12, 2023, https://www.wwno.org/news/2023-01-12/louisiana-republican-party-considers-backing-elimination-of-no-fault-divorce.

7. Caroline Shanley, "The Right's Move Against No-Fault Divorce Is an Attack on Women," CNN, May 18, 2023, https://www.cnn.com/2023/05/18/opinions/crowder-right-wing-rhetoric-about-divorce-ignores-history-shanley/index.html.

8. Focus on the Family, *Finding Hope for Your Desperate Marriage—Gary Chapman Part 2*, YouTube, March 27, 2019, https://www.youtube.com/watch?v=cqoKkY-gnOk.

9. Tim Chastain, "Patriarchy, Bill Gothard, and the Umbrella of Protection," Jesus Without Baggage, March 13, 2017, https://jesuswithoutbaggage.wordpress.com/2017/03/13/patriarchy-bill-gothard-and-the-umbrella-of-protection/.

10. "Wisdom Booklets," Institute in Basic Life Principles, accessed February 4, 2024, https://store.iblp.org/wisdom-booklets.

11. *Shiny Happy People: Duggar Family Secrets*, Chick Entertainment, Story Force Entertainment, Cinemart, 2023.

12. Rick Paulas, "The Power Team Was the Bloody, Evangelical Freakshow That Ruled the 80s," Vice, February 4, 2015, https://www.vice.com/en/article/5gkvjn/evangelical-freak-show-the-power-team-were-christian-superstars-of-the-80s-456.

13. "Frequently Asked Questions," Power Team 2.0, https://www.thepowerteam.com/faqs/.

14. "About Promise Keepers," Promise Keepers, https://promisekeepers.org/about-us/.

15. Kristin Kobes Du Mez, *Jesus and John Wayne: How White Evangelicals Corrupted a Faith and Fractured a Nation* (New York: Liveright, 2020).

16. "The Christian Gun Owner," Christian Gun Owner, accessed February 4, 2024, https://www.christiangunowner.com/.

17. Mark Rogers, *Your Guide to Armed Volunteer Church Security: Protecting Your Faith-Bsed Congregation in Today's Threatening World of Violence with Weapons*, Kindle, December 7, 2022.

18. "ALERT Cadet," Institute in Basic Life Principles, March 7, 2018, https://iblp.org/alert-cadet/.

19. Jeri Loftland, "Cult Identity," *Heresy in the Heartland* (blog), June 21, 2023, https://heresyintheheartland.blogspot.com/2023/06/cult-identity.html.

20. Jeri Loftland, "Heresy in the Heartland: A *Real* Investigation into IBLP," *Heresy in the Heartland* (blog), June 22, 2014, https://heresyintheheartland.blogspot.com/2014/06/a-real-investigation-into-iblp.html.

21. David A., "My Life in ATI, Part Two," Recovering Grace, December 5, 2011, https://www.recoveringgrace.org/2011/12/my-life-in-ati-part-two/.

22. Meg Anderson and Domenico Montanaro, "5 Things to Know About Mike Pence Before Tuesday's Debate," NPR, July 14, 2016, https://www.npr.org/2016/07/14/486032078/5-things-to-know-about-mike-pence.

23. Greg Gonsalves and Forrest Crawford, "How Mike Pence Made Indiana's HIV Outbreak Worse," Politico, March 2, 2020, https://www.politico.com/news/magazine/2020/03/02/how-mike-pence-made-indianas-hiv-outbreak-worse-118648.

24. Author's interview with Calvin Bushman, July 2023.

25. Katha Pollitt, "The Right's Latest Target: No-Fault Divorce," *Nation*, June 8, 2023, https://www.thenation.com/?post_type=article&p=447133.

26. Author's interview with Joel Stanley, October 2021.

27. Author's interview with Eddie K., October 2021.

Chapter 9: Gentle, Smiling Mothers

1. *Sex, Lies &...The Truth*, Focus on the Family Films, 1996.

2. Stormie Omartian, *The Power of a Praying Wife* (Eugene, OR: Harvest House, 2014).

3. Jennifer Murtoff, "Enuma Elish," *Encyclopaedia Britannica*, accessed February 4, 2024, https://www.britannica.com/topic/Enuma-Elish.

4. Debi Pearl, *Created to Be His Help Meet: Discover How God Can Make Your Marriage Glorious*, 10th anniversary ed. (Pleasantville, TN: No Greater Joy Ministries, 2014).

5. Michael Pearl, *Created to Need a Help Meet: A Marriage Guide for Men*, 2nd paperback ed. (Pleasantville, TN: No Greater Joy Ministries, 2012).

6. Pearl, *Created to Be His Help Meet*, 33, 58, 119, 120.

7. John and Stasi Eldredge, *Captivating: Unveiling the Mystery of a Woman's Soul*, revised and expanded ed. (Nashville, TN: Thomas Nelson, 2011).

8. Eldredge and Eldredge, *Captivating*, 54.

9. Elisabeth Elliot, *Let Me Be a Woman* (Carol Stream, IL: Tyndale Momentum, 1999).

10. Elliot, *Let Me Be a Woman*, vii, 44.

11. "Our History," Council on Biblical Manhood and Womanhood, accessed February 4, 2024, https://cbmw.org/about/history/.

12. "The Danvers Statement," Council on Biblical Manhood and Womanhood, https://cbmw.org/about/danvers-statement/.

13. "Our History," *Christianity Today*, accessed February 4, 2024, https://www.christianitytoday.org/who-we-are/our-history/.

14. John Piper and Wayne Grudem, eds., *Recovering Biblical Manhood and Womanhood: A Response to Evangelical Feminism* (Wheaton, IL: Crossway Books, 2012).

15. *Lourdes Torres-Manteufel v. Douglas Phillips, Vision Forum, Inc., and Vision Forum Ministries, Inc.*, Bexar County District Court, Texas, case no. 2014-CI-05999, April 15, 2014, https://extras.mysanantonio.com/pdf/2014CI05999.pdf.

16. *Lourdes Torres-Manteufel v. Douglas Phillips, Vision Forum, Inc., and Vision Forum Ministries, Inc.*, 2014-CI-05999, 438th Judicial District, Bexar County, Texas, filed 4/15/2014, https://extras.mysanantonio.com/pdf/2014CI05999.pdf.

17. Julie Anne, "Fathers and Daughters: Who Owns a Daughter's Heart?," Spiritual Sounding Board, November 6, 2012, https://spiritualsoundingboard.com/2012/11/06/fathers-and-daughters-who-owns-a-daughters-heart/.

18. Anna Sofia Botkin and Elizabeth Botkin, *The Return of the Daughters: A Vision of Victory for the Single Women of the 21st Century*, First Pacific Media, 2007.

19. Botkin Sisters: Thoughts on Womanhood, Christianity & Culture, accessed February 4, 2024, https://botkinsisters.com.

20. Anna Sofia and Elizabeth Botkin. "Spiritual Self-Defense, Part 1: Acknowledge the Power of Your Actions," *Botkin Sisters* (blog), May 1, 2018, https://botkinsisters.com/article/spiritual-self-defense-part-1-acknowledge-the-power-of-your-actions.

21. Anna Sofia and Elizabeth Botkin, "Spiritual Self-Defense, Part 2: Know What God Requires," *Botkin Sisters* (blog), May 1, 2018, https://botkinsisters.com/article/spiritual-self-defense-part-2-know-what-god-requires.

22. Edward Tripp. *The Meridian Handbook of Classical Mythology*, New American Library, 197, 495, http://archive.org/details/meridianhandbook00trip.

23. Valerie Richardson, "South Dakota Gov. Kristi Noem Signs Bill Banning Gender-Transition Treatments for Minors," *Washington Times*, February 13, 2023, https://www.washingtontimes.com/news/2023/feb/13/kristi-noem-south-dakota-governor-signs-bill-banni/.

24. Austin Goss, "SD State Lawmakers Want Ban on Gender Surgery, Puberty Blockers," Dakota News Now, January 17, 2023, https://www.dakotanewsnow.com/2023/01/17/sd-lawmakers-announce-bill-prohibiting-transitional-care-minors/.

25. Homepage, Family Voice, accessed February 4, 2024, https://www.familyheritagealliance.org//.

26. Goss, "SD State Lawmakers Want Ban on Gender Surgery, Puberty Blockers."

27. Stanley G. Payne, *A History of Fascism, 1914–1945* (Madison: University of Wisconsin Press, 1995), 13.

28. Omartian, *Power of a Praying Wife*, 10.

29. Omartian, *Power of a Praying Wife*, 13, 14.

30. Omartian, *Power of a Praying Wife*, 13.

31. Omartian, *Power of a Praying Wife*, 15.

Chapter 10: Train Up a Child in the Way He Should Go

1. Alice Miller, *For Your Own Good: Hidden Cruelty in Child-Rearing and the Roots of Violence*, 3rd ed., trans. Hildegarde Hannum and Hunter Hannum (New York: Farrar, Straus and Giroux, 1990).

2. Miller, *For Your Own Good*, 81.

3. W. H. Auden, "September 1, 1939," Poets.org, https://poets.org/poem/september-1-1939.

4. Miller, *For Your Own Good*, 14.

5. Miller, *For Your Own Good*, 115.

6. Author's interview, October 2021.

7. Author's interview, October 2021.

8. María Luisa Paúl, "Okla. Lawmaker Says Bible Endorses Corporal Punishment of Disabled Children," *Washington Post*, March 15, 2023, https://www.washingtonpost.com/nation/2023/03/15/oklahoma-corporal-punishment-disabled-students/.

9. James C. Dobson, *Dare to Discipline* (Wheaton, IL: Tyndale House, 1970).

10. Dobson, *Dare to Discipline*, 61, 245.

11. Author's interview with Kristin Kobes Du Mez, October 2021.

12. Author's interview with Kristin Kobes Du Mez, October 2021.

13. James C. Dobson, *The Strong-Willed Child: Birth Through Adolescence*, 14th ed. (Wheaton, IL: Tyndale House, 1985).

14. Janet Heimlich, *Breaking Their Will: Shedding Light on Religious Child Maltreatment* (Amherst, NY: Prometheus, 2011).

15. Luisa Blanchfield, "The United Nations Convention on the Rights of the Child," Congressional Research Service, July 27, 2015, https://crsreports.congress.gov/product/pdf/R/R40484/25.

16. Michael and Debi Pearl, *To Train Up a Child: Child Training for the 21st Century* (Pleasantville, TN: No Greater Joy Ministries, 2015).

17. Tedd Tripp, *Shepherding a Child's Heart* (Wapwallopen, PA: Shepherd Press, 1995).

18. Karis Kimmel Murray, *Grace Based Discipline: How to Be at Your Best When Your Kids Are at Their Worst* (Family Matters Press, 2017), 198.

19. Author's interview, October 2021.

20. Dobson, *Strong-Willed Child*, 63.

21. Sandee Lamotte, "Spanking Has Declined in America, Study Finds, but Pediatricians Worry About Impact of Pandemic," CNN, July 27, 2020, https://www.cnn.com/2020/07/27/health/spanking-decline-us-wellness/index.html.

22. Becky Sullivan, "The Proportion of White Christians in the US Has Stopped Shrinking, Study Finds," NPR, July 8, 2021, https://www.npr.org/2021/07/08/1014047885/americas-white-christian-plurality-has-stopped-shrinking-a-new-study-finds.

23. Peter Hoekstra, "Text—H.J.Res.97—110th Congress (2007–2008): Proposing an Amendment to the Constitution of the United States Relating to Parental Rights,"

Legislation, July 28, 2008. 2008-06-26. https://www.congress.gov/bill/110th-congress/house-joint-resolution/97/text.

24. Dan Kois, "An Interview with the School Board Chair Who Forced Out a Principal after Michelangelo's David Was Shown in Class," Slate, March 23, 2023, https://slate.com/human-interest/2023/03/florida-principal-fired-michelangelo-david-statue.html.

25. Rick Santorum, "Children Belong to Parents, Not Government," Townhall, April 16, 2013, https://townhall.com/columnists/ricksantorum/2013/04/16/children-belong-to-parents-not-government-n1568098.

26. "About Us," Salt & Light Global, https://www.saltlightglobal.org/about-us/.

27. Sheila Roberts, "The Convention on the Rights of the Child Is Back in Congress," ParentalRights.org, March 4, 2020, https://parentalrights.org/convention-on-the-rights-back/.

28. Dobson, Dare to Discipline, 23.

Chapter 11: And When He Is Old He Will Not Depart from It

1. Interviews in this chapter were conducted by the author.

2. Jillian Keenan, Sex with Shakespeare: Here's Much to Do with Pain, but More with Love (New York: William Morrow, 2017).

3. Keenan, Sex with Shakespeare, 238, 239.

4. Patrick Carnes and Bonnie Phillips, The Betrayal Bond: Breaking Free of Exploitive Relationships, rev. ed. (Deerfield Beach, FL: Health Communications, 2019).

5. Carnes, Betrayal Bond, 67, 69.

6. Bessel van der Kolk, The Body Keeps the Score: Brain, Mind, and Body in the Healing of Trauma (New York: Penguin Books, 2015), 124.

7. J. Richard Fugate, What the Bible Says About.........Child Training: Parenting with Confidence, 2nd ed. (Apache Junction, AZ: Foundation for Biblical Research, 2013).

8. Ginger Hubbard, Don't Make Me Count to Three! A Mom's Look at Heart-Oriented Discipline (Wapwallopen, PA: Shepherd Press, 2004), 72.

9. Roy Lessin, Spanking: A Loving Discipline: Helpful and Practical Answers for Today's Parents, updated ed. (Minneapolis: Bethany House, 2002); Roy Lessin, Spanking: Why, When, How (Minneapolis: Bethany House, 1979).

10. Fugate, What the Bible Says About.........Child Training, 139.

11. Larry Tomczak, God, the Rod, and Your Child's Bod: The Art of Loving Correction for Christian Parents (Old Tappan, NJ: Power Books, 1982).

12. Jane Doe et al v. Sovereign Grace Ministries, Inc., Charles Joseph Mahaney, Lawrence Tomczak et al., Montgomery County Circuit Court, Maryland Civil Division, Case No. 369721, January 11 2013, https://static1.1.sqspcdn.com/static/f/970485/27984345/1536456535893/First+Amended+Complaint+Jan+11+2013.pdf?token=upFFXi8KHCXn0RBRF1pAdCQsuOA%3D.

13. Tomczak, God, the Rod, and Your Child's Bod, 118.

14. "Churches," Sovereign Grace Churches, https://www.sovereigngrace.com/churches.

15. Bob Allen, "Blogger: SBC Leaders Ignoring Abuse Decree," ABP News,

October 11, 2013, https://web.archive.org/web/20131014185553/http:/www.abpnews.com /ministry/organizations/item/8923-blogger-sbc-leaders-ignoring-abuse-decree# .UlnS1lCkrBE.

16. "C. J. Mahaney Supporters Struggle to Find a Sympathetic Following," SBC Tomorrow, May 31, 2013, https://web.archive.org/web/20131028180938/http:/peter lumpkins.typepad.com/peter_lumpkins/2013/05/cj-mahaney-supporters-struggle -to-find-a-sympathetic-following-.html; Bob Allen, "Seminary Cuts Ties with Embattled SGM," July 7, 2014, https://web.archive.org/web/20140707034447/http:/www.abpnews .com:80/ministry/organizations/item/28894-seminary-cuts-ties-with-embattled-sgm.

17. Bob Allen, "Lawsuit Reveals Details About Paige Patterson's 'Break Her Down' Meeting with Woman Alleging Campus Rape," *Baptist News Global*, June 24 2019, https://baptistnews.com/article/lawsuit-reveals-details-about-paige-pattersons-break-her -down-meeting-with-woman-alleging-campus-rape/.

18. Liam Adams, "Southern Baptist Convention Settles in Abuse Case Against Paul Pressler, Case Dismissed," *Tennessean*, December 29, 2023, https://www .tennessean.com/story/news/religion/2023/12/29/southern-baptist-convention -sbc-settles-abuse-case-against-paul-pressler/71133589007/#:~:text=Southern%20 Baptist%20Convention%20settles%20in%20abuse%20case%20against%20Paul%20 Pressler%2C%20case%20dismissed&text=Paul%20Pressler%2C%20who%20is%20 best,case%20for%20alleged%20sexual%20abuse.

19. Kate Shellnutt, "Southern Baptists Refused to Act on Abuse, Despite Secret List of Pastors," *Christianity Today*, May 22, 2022, https://www.christianitytoday.com /news/2022/may/southern-baptist-abuse-investigation-sbc-ec-legal-survivors.html.

20. Kate Shellnutt, "Sovereign Grace Calls Outside Investigation 'Impossible,'" *Christianity Today*, April 18, 2019, https://www.christianitytoday.com/news/2019/april /sovereign-grace-churches-sgc-sgm-independent-investigation-.html.

21. Jeff Crippen with Rebecca Davis, *Unholy Charade: Unmasking the Domestic Abuser in the Church* (Tillamook, OR: Justice Keepers Publishing, 2015).

22. Crippen, *Unholy Charade*, 115.

23. "Obituary: Joseph Gerard LaQuiere," Dignity Memorial, https://www.dignity memorial.com/obituaries/grosse-pointe-woods-mi/joseph-laquiere-10101610.

24. L. Elizabeth Krueger, *Raising Godly Tomatoes: Loving Parenting with Only Occasional Trips to the Woodshed* (Detroit, MI: Krueger Publishing, 2007).

25. Krueger, *Raising Godly Tomatoes*, 4, 87.

26. Krueger, *Raising Godly Tomatoes*, 48, 63.

27. Anna Badkhen, "Christian Crusaders Go to Battle over Spanking/Tools of Discipline Horrify Some of Faithful," SFGATE, February 6, 2005, https://www.sfgate.com /news/article/Christian-crusaders-go-to-battle-over-spanking-2733062.php.

28. Hemant Mehta, "The Christian Who Was Secretly Selling Child-Beating Sticks Has Shut His Business Down," Friendly Atheist, May 21, 2016, https:// friendlyatheist.patheos.com/2016/05/21/the-christian-who-was-secretly-selling -child-beating-sticks-has-shut-his-business-down/.

29. Sarah Dutko, "Raising Godly Tomatoes: Book Review by Sarah Dutko," *Homeschoolers Anonymous* (blog), September 9, 2014, https://homeschoolers

anonymous.net/2014/09/09/review-of-infant-spankingchild-abuse-manual
-raising-godly-tomatoes-by-l-elizabeth-krueger/.

30. Andrew L. Whitehead and Samuel L. Perry, *Taking America Back for God: Christian Nationalism in the United States* (New York: Oxford University Press, 2020).

31. "Christian Nationalism Is 'Single Biggest Threat' to America's Religious Freedom," Center for American Progress, April 13, 2022, https://www.americanprogress.org/article/christian-nationalism-is-single-biggest-threat-to-americas-religious-freedom/.

32. Thomas Hobbes, *Leviathan* (New York: Oxford University Press, 1996).

Chapter 12: One Big Happy Family

1. R. L. Stollar, "Communicators for Christ: How Homeschool Debate Leagues Shaped the Rising Stars of the Christian Right," Religion Dispatches, March 22, 2023, https://religiondispatches.org/communicators-for-christ-how-homeschool-debate-leagues-shaped-the-rising-stars-of-the-christian-right/.

2. R. L. Stollar, "The History of Homeschooling, 1904–Present," Homeschoolers Anonymous, May 4, 2015, https://homeschoolersanonymous.wordpress.com/2015/05/04/the-history-of-homeschooling-1904-present/.

3. Francis A. Schaeffer, *A Christian Manifesto* (Wheaton, IL: Crossway Books, 1981).

4. Francis A. Schaeffer, "A Christian Manifesto," 1982, People for Life, https://peopleforlife.org/francis.html.

5. Kathryn Joyce, "Wifely Submission and Christian Warfare," Religion Dispatches, March 25, 2009, https://religiondispatches.org/irdbooki-wifely-submission-and-christian-warfare/. Schaeffer stated in *A Christian Manifesto*: "It is time for Christians and others who do not accept the narrow and bigoted humanist views rightfully to use the appropriate forms of protest." See also Seth Dowland, "'Family Values' and the Formation of a Christian Right Agenda," *Church History* 78, no. 3 (2009): 606–31.

6. Sarah Pulliam Bailey, "How Christian Home-Schoolers Laid the Groundwork for 'Parental Rights,'" *Washington Post*, June 14, 2022, https://www.washingtonpost.com/religion/2022/06/11/parent-rights-home-schooling/.

7. Milton Gaither, *Homeschool: An American History* (New York: Palgrave Macmillan, 2008).

8. Gaither, *Homeschool*, 183.

9. Elizabeth Bartholet, "Homeschooling: Parent Rights Absolutism vs. Child Rights to Education & Protection," *Arizona Law Review* 62, no. 1 (2020), https://dash.harvard.edu/handle/1/40108859.

10. Parental Rights and Responsibilities Act of 1995, 104th Cong., sess. 1 (1995) (testimony of Michael Farris); Proposing an Amendment to the Constitution of the United States Relating to Parental Rights, 112th Cong., sess. 2 (2012) (testimony of Michael Farris).

11. Institute of Education Sciences, "2019 Homeschooling and Full-Time Virtual Education Rates," Stats in Brief, September 2023, https://nces.ed.gov/pubs2023/2023101.pdf.

12. Sarah Jones, "Children Are Not Property," *New York*, April 8, 2023, https://nymag.com/intelligencer/2023/04/children-are-not-property.html.

13. "Child Abuse and Neglect Fatalities," Coalition for Responsible Home Education,

https://www.hsinvisiblechildren.org/fatalities/; "*Some Preliminary Data on Homeschool Child Fatalities,*" Coalition for Responsible Home Education, https://www.hsinvisible children.org/commentary/some-preliminary-data-on-homeschool-child-fatalities/.

14. "Stephen Hill and 1 Sibling," Coalition for Responsible Home Education, https://www.hsinvisiblechildren.org/2013/06/04/stephen-hill-and-1-sibling/.

15. *Hill v. State*, 881 S.W.2d 897, 899 (Tex. App. 1994).

16. John Glatt, *The Family Next Door: The Heartbreaking Imprisonment of the Thirteen Turpin Siblings and Their Extraordinary Rescue* (New York: St. Martin's Press, 2019).

17. Barbara L. Knox et al., "Child Torture as a Form of Child Abuse," *Journal of Child & Adolescent Trauma* 7, no. 1 (March 2014): 37–49, https://doi.org/10.1007/s40653-014-0009-9.

18. "Examining Connecticut's Safety Net for Children Withdrawn from School for the Purpose of Homeschooling—Supplemental Investigation to OCA's December 12 2017 Report Regarding the Death of Matthew Tirado," Office of the Child Advocate, State of Connecticut, April 26, 2018, https://www.cga.ct.gov/kid/related/20180426_Informational%20Forum%20on%20Homeschooling%20and%20Communication/OCA.Memo.Homeschooling.4.25.2018.pdf.

19. Libby Anne, "HSLDA and Child Abuse: An Introduction," Love, Joy, Feminism, April 17, 2013, https://www.patheos.com/blogs/lovejoyfeminism/2013/04/hslda-child-abuse-and-educational-neglect-an-introduction.html; Libby Anne, "HSLDA's Defense of Child Abuse," Love, Joy, Feminism, April 22, 2013, https://www.patheos.com/blogs/lovejoyfeminism/2013/04/hsldas-defense-of-child-abuse.html.

20. Libby Anne, "HSLDA: Man Who Kept Children in Cages 'a Hero,'" Love, Joy, Feminism, May 6, 2013, https://www.patheos.com/blogs/lovejoyfeminism/2013/05/hslda-man-who-kept-children-in-cages-a-her.html.

21. Dennis J. Willard, Doug Oplinger, and Carl Chancellor, "Adoption Agencies Will Face Scrutiny: Groups Put 11 Children in Huron County Home with Homemade Cages," *Akron Beacon-Journal*, September 15, 2005, https://www.newspapers.com/image/170452017/.

22. HSLDA, "Legal FAQs," accessed March 23, 2024, https://hslda.org/about/faqs/legal.

23. Griffin S. Kelly, "HSLDA Concerned with More Than Just Homeschool," CUNY New York: Craig Newmark Graduate School of Journalism Capstones, no. 559, December 13, 2021, https://academicworks.cuny.edu/gj_etds/559.

24. An Act to Amend Section 273a of the Penal Code, Relating to Corporal Punishment, AB 755, February 22, 2007, http://www.leginfo.ca.gov/pub/07-08/bill/asm/ab_0751-0800/ab_755_bill_20070222_introduced.html.

25. Michael Smith, "California May Ban Spanking," *Washington Times*, April 28, 2008, https://www.washingtontimes.com/news/2008/apr/28/california-may-ban-spanking/.

26. Coalition for Responsible Home Education, "Concealing Abuse by Homeschooling," accessed March 23, 2024, https://responsiblehomeschooling.org/advocacy/policy/homeschooling-abuse-concealing-abuse/.

27. See "Wisconsin Laws," HSLDA, https://hslda.org/legal/wisconsin; "Colorado Laws," HSLDA, https://hslda.org/legal/colorado.

28. Bartholet, "Homeschooling."

29. Emma Brown and Peter Johnson, "The Christian Home-Schooler Who Made 'Parental Rights' a GOP Rallying Cry," *Washington Post*, August 29, 2023, https://www .washingtonpost.com/education/2023/08/29/michael-farris-homeschoolers -parents-rights-ziklag/.

30. Alex Harris, "Amazon's 'Shiny Happy People' Has Lessons to Teach, If We're Willing to Listen," Gospel Coalition, June 2, 2023, https://www.thegospelcoalition.org /article/shiny-happy-people/.

31. "About NCFCA," Christian Speech and Debate League, https://ncfca.org /about/.

32. TeenPact, https://teenpact.com/.

33. "About Us," PursueGOD, https://www.pursuegod.org/about/.

34. "About Texas Youth Summit," Texas Youth Summit, shttps://www.texas youthsummit.com/about.

35. "Agenda47: President Trump's Pledge to Homeschool Families," Donald J. Trump for President, https://www.donaldjtrump.com/agenda47/agenda47-president -trumps-pledge-to-homeschool-families.

36. "How the Wesleys Were Brought Up by John Wesley," *Women of Christianity* (blog), posted April 1, 2011, https://womenofchristianity.com/how-the -wesleys-were-brought-up-by-john-wesley/.

37. John Wesley, "Sermon 94—On Family Religion," 1762, ResourceUMC, accessed February 1, 2024, https://www.resourceumc.org/en/content/sermon-94 -on-family-religion.

38. Elisabeth Elliot, *The Shaping of a Christian Family: How My Parents Nurtured My Faith* (Grand Rapids, MI: Revell, 2005), 167–69.

39. Benny and Sheree Phillips, *Raising Kids Who Hunger for God* (Grand Rapids, MI: Fleming H. Revell, 2001), 143.

40. Phillips and Phillips, *Raising Kids Who Hunger for God*, 146.

41. Rhonda Robinson, "What Do You Do When Your Child Loses Faith in God?," Focus on the Family, April 26, 2023, https://www.focusonthefamily.com/parenting /the-deconstruction-of-christianity-how-christian-parents-can-help-their-adult-children -rediscover-the-beauty-of-the-gospel/.

42. Joannie Debrito, "Hope for Parents of Prodigal Children," Focus on the Family, July 5, 2022, https://www.focusonthefamily.com/parenting/hope-for-parents -of-prodigal-children/.

43. Alisa Childers, "Why We Should Not Redeem 'Deconstruction,'" Gospel Coalition, February 18, 2022, https://www.thegospelcoalition.org/article/redeem -reconstruction/.

Chapter 13: The Burning Path

1. Kevin Roberts and Steven Groves, eds., *Mandate for Leadership: The Conservative Promise* (Washington, DC: Heritage Foundation, 2023).

2. Jack Schneider and Jennifer C. Berkshire, *A Wolf at the Schoolhouse Door: The Dismantling of Public Education and the Future of School* (New York: New Press, 2020).

3. Katie Reilly, "The Biggest Controversies from Betsy DeVos' First Year," *Time*, December 14, 2017, https://time.com/5053007/betsy-devos-education-secretary -2017-controversies/; "How Education Secretary Betsy DeVos Will Be Remembered," *Morning Edition*, NPR, November 19, 2020, https://www.npr.org/2020/11/19/9362 25974/the-legacy-of-education-secretary-betsy-devos.

Afterword

1. *The Way Down: God, Greed and the Cult of Gwen Shamblin*, documentary, Campfire, Huntley Productions, 2021.

ALSO AVAILABLE

"One of the marvels of this furious book is how insolent and funny Lavin is." —*NEW YORK TIMES BOOK REVIEW*

"Wide-ranging, angry, and sadly relevant."
—*THE BOSTON GLOBE*

"Lavin is an entertaining Virgil for this neo-Nazi hell."
—CAROLYN KELLOGG for *THE NEW YORK TIMES*

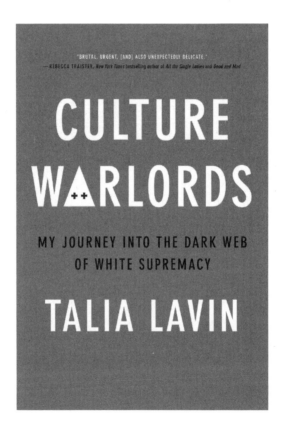

LEGACY
LIT